Managing Partner I

Strategies for Transforming
Underperforming Partners

CONSULTING EDITORS:
NICK JARRETT-KERR AND
JONATHAN MIDDLEBURGH

Commissioning editor
Alex Davies

Managing director
Sian O'Neill

Managing Partner Performance: Strategies for Transforming Underperforming Partners
is published by

Globe Law and Business Ltd
3 Mylor Close
Horsell
Woking
Surrey GU21 4DD
United Kingdom
Tel: +44 20 3745 4770
www.globelawandbusiness.com

Managing Partner Performance: Strategies for Transforming Underperforming Partners

ISBN 978-1-83723-025-9
EPUB ISBN 978-1-83723-026-6
Adobe PDF ISBN 978-1-83723-027-3

Contents

Executive summary

It is a strategic imperative for firms to remain competitive, adaptive, and capable of delivering high-quality legal services in today's complex business environment. Partner performance is a critical issue and will become more so in the coming years as AI threatens to replace or reposition underperforming employees. The dynamic and evolving nature of the legal profession, coupled with external factors such as technology, globalization, and economic changes, underscores the importance of performance management for law firms.

Managing Partner Performance: Strategies for Transforming Underperforming Partners takes a comprehensive look at how to improve underperforming partners within the legal profession. It provides insight and practical solutions for law firm leaders committed to revitalizing their teams and optimizing organizational success. Structured into four parts, the book systematically diagnoses underperformance, its cause and effect, how to deal with underperforming partners, and how to proactively performance manage over the long-term.

Our opening chapter by consulting editor Nick Jarrett-Kerr examines performance in law firms, including post-pandemic trends and the effect of these on performance. The chapter proposes that all firms have a performance curve, resulting in the firm being segmented into high performing A partners, B partners who form the engine room of the firm, and C partners who in relative terms perform less well than their peers. It establishes what motivates partners to perform and the importance of setting and communicating clear and measurable standards. Nick provides a definition of underperformance, including its financial implications, and how firms can manage performance for success. The chapter covers the steps that firms need to take to clarify what they expect of their partners, including agreeing the critical areas of performance or "balanced scorecard" according to which partners need to contribute. It explains how to define specific roles and responsibilities to play to strengths and how to link performance with the firm's values.

In chapter two, Patrick McKenna has the reader imagine themselves as a firm leader with an underperforming partner in their team. They know this particular partner has been underperforming but have been content to let the situation drift without resolution, rather than confront the ugly reality of the circumstances. But today they have the facts thrust before them and something must be done. Before one does anything, it is essential to identify where the problems lie and whether there is any rational way to fix things. This raises two important questions – How are we defining underperformance? Are there legitimate reasons why the lawyer is behaving the way they are? When faced with this challenge, there are numerous reasons why intelligent and highly capable leaders will go to great lengths to avoid taking action. Patrick explains why they should not allow themselves to fall into this trap.

In chapter three, Dr Heidi K. Gardner and Ivan Matviak dive into an increasingly crucial aspect of managing partner performance – hiring laterals. Lateral hiring has skyrocketed in recent years, as firms expand into new geographies, bolster practice groups and disciplinary expertise, and seek ready-made books of business. Many firms see an offensive approach to filling in gaps and obtaining star talent as a crucial part of their growth strategy in today's ultra-competitive legal environment. While firms fiercely compete to recruit and hire the industry's best and brightest, accumulating big names without a strategic plan and simply hoping for the best does not work. Through empirical data and research, the chapter explores the critical role of early, two-way collaboration in newcomers' success – and in turn firm and client performance. The authors then offer a three-stage roadmap, full of proven advice and comprehensive accountability measures, to maximize the likelihood that laterals thrive.

The legal environment in which law firm partners operates continues to evolve – rapidly – and all signs are that, if anything, the pace of change will increase. Chapter four, by Joel Barolsky, managing director of Barolsky Advisors, looks at the continuing tendency of the market to consolidate, focusing on the threats – and opportunities – due to legal tech. AI is likely to be a disruptor. While machines are unlikely to displace lawyers, the role of lawyers will continue to change and law firm partners will need to be highly flexible and adaptable and constantly renew their skills sets. Traditional leverage models are also increasingly under threat and the trend seems to be towards clients wanting partner / senior lawyer input rather than accepting senior lawyers fronting transactions or other matters. Globalization continues to be an important factor, argues Joel, and partners need to navigate not just their own jurisdiction but increasingly operate across others and collaborate with colleagues globally. With this consistently changing landscape, performance can suffer if partners cannot keep abreast of the changes. This chapter addresses these issues.

Part II of the book looks at the effects of underperformance.

Chapter five looks at the role of wellbeing in promoting performance and what law firms can do to prevent and address behavioral health issues, a proven driver of low performance and heightened risk. Bree Buchanan, JD, a global leader in lawyer wellbeing, discusses evidence-based strategies and best practices that managing partners and other firm leaders can utilize to improve the wellbeing of personnel. This chapter includes practical guidance on creating a culture that supports engagement, productivity, and loyalty. Topics covered include the creation of a wellbeing program, an assessment of firm strengths and weaknesses in this area, and an overview of policies that synergistically work to lift the wellbeing of personnel and performance of the firm.

Chapter six, by Jim Lawrence, looks at the issue of substance abuse disorder (SUD) in the legal profession and how this impacts on both the individual and the business. SUD is a critical issue that can significantly impact partner performance. As key decision-makers and leaders, senior partners are integral to the firm's success. When affected by SUD, their ability to perform optimally, maintain client relationships, and uphold ethical standards can be compromised, posing risks to the firm's reputation and financial stability, not to mention the partner's wellbeing. This chapter delves into the author's lived experience with SUD, the prevalence of SUD among lawyers, the signs of SUD in senior partners, appropriate responses, and the importance of destigmatizing SUD within law firms.

In chapter seven, Paula Davis discusses her experiences of burning out at the end of her law practice. Paula outlines the three dimensions of burnout (not to be conflated with stress), warning signs for self and others, and the spectrum of burnout. Paula discusses how elements of burnout and engagement can co-exist, and why this is a huge reason partners consider leaving their firms. The chapter looks at the root cause drivers of burnout – unmanageable workload (the #1 driver of stress), lack of recognition, lack of community (lawyers are among the loneliest professionals), lack of autonomy, values disconnect, and unfairness. Drawing on her recent ALM Psychological Safety & Burnout Survey for the Legal Profession, as well as examples from her own consulting practice, Paula discusses ways in which burnout can be managed.

In chapter eight, Graham Browning looks at the wider costs of poor performance to the legal profession. The chapter considers the costs of typical day-to-day partner underperformance and focuses on the behaviors and decisions of four partners from a different perspective. Each is considered by way of a short "day in the life" case study, including active and passive underperformance. The costs are then drawn out, covering different levels of impact, vis-à-vis the individual (distraction, disengagement, performance, non-collaboration, wellbeing); the team (contagion, conflict, performance, reputation, turnover); the firm (systems, controls, performance, innovation, resources, reputation, talent, retention, regulatory, strategy, ESG); and the profession (standing, purpose, social contract). Graham then includes action points on what to do about it.

Part III then turns to how to deal with partner performance issues.

Chapter nine, by Krystal Champlin-Gerage, looks at performance management issues. Dealing with underperforming partners in the legal industry requires a multifaceted approach that incorporates continuous feedback, identification of key performance indicators (KPIs) and benchmarks, and the utilization of coaching techniques. Continuous feedback serves as a cornerstone, providing regular communication about areas of improvement and recognition of progress. By fostering an open dialogue, both parties gain clarity on expectations and opportunities for growth. Identifying KPIs and benchmarks is essential for setting clear performance standards. These metrics should align with the partner's role and the firm's objectives, serving as tangible markers of success.

Jonathan Middleburgh then expands on this theme in chapter ten, looking at how coaching plays a pivotal role in supporting underperforming partners. Through personalized guidance and development plans, coaches help partners identify strengths, address weaknesses, and cultivate necessary skills. Coaching sessions foster self-awareness, goalsetting, and accountability, empowering partners to drive their own improvement. Effective coaching involves active listening, empathy, and constructive feedback. By building trust and rapport, coaches create a supportive environment conducive to growth and success. Overall, addressing underperformance requires a proactive and holistic approach that integrates continuous feedback, KPIs, and coaching. Through collaborative efforts, underperforming partners can develop the skills and confidence needed to excel in their roles, benefiting both the individual and the firm.

Chapter 11, by Ray D'Cruz, examines the purpose and focus of partner performance reviews and explores the debate about formal reviews versus informal feedback. The chapter provides guidance on how to design an effective review process, assessment criteria, and how to prepare for and facilitate an effective review conversation.

Chapter 12 then explores remuneration models. Michael Roch outlines the different models – EWYK, lockstep, performance-based, merit based, origination, and ownership – and how performance can be managed under each. The chapter discusses how each model can be used to motivate the desired performance and determines what might be the best strategy under different circumstances.

Knowing when to cut your losses is an important part of managing partner performance. In chapter 13, Jonathan Middleburgh returns to examine the main approaches and choices that firms can consider. These could be reinvigorating moderate performers or introducing incremental performance improvement across teams and the entire firm. Firms can also address weak areas using development, training and re-training, by rehabilitating temporary strugglers, de-equitization or by facilitating partner moves, and voluntary and negotiated departure. Expulsion should be a last resort – the chapter seeks to define when this option should be used.

Issues like those detailed above need to be handled carefully and sensitively, and chapter 14, by Stephan Lucks, looks at how to avoid conflict and potential claims of unlawful discrimination. Stephan's focus and approach to this chapter is very much from the perspective of effective leadership = inclusive leadership. Whilst there is clearly legislation to comply with to avoid discrimination, the effective leader will avoid discrimination if they are inclusive in their approach. The chapter covers what we mean by inclusion, the psychology of exclusion and its impact on individuals and firms, and the core components of inclusion and its associated leadership behaviors.

In part IV, we look at proactive performance management.

Nick Jarrett-Kerr returns in chapter 15 to look at the importance of clear purpose and strategy. Communications in law firms is key and never more so than in connection with underperformers. Maintaining honesty and openness on a one-to-one basis, listening and asking questions, and leveraging past accomplishments to link to necessary changes can all aid good communication. Nick provides ten practical suggestions for internal communications and addresses coping with client succession issues as well as ways to communicate and address common obstacles to internal projects. It is important to set clear performance criteria and standards. It is then vital to ensure all partners understand both the consequences of failure to meet standards and the processes that will be brought into effect to deal with underperformance issues.

In chapter 16, Jonathan Middleburgh looks at conflict resolution and team dynamics and explores how interpersonal conflicts within a team can negatively impact partner performance. A highly functioning team supports optimal partner performance. But what does a high functioning team look like? The chapter explores how good law firm leaders can develop and sustain healthy teams, and how to implement conflict resolution strategies for improved teamwork.

Chapter 17, by Martin Hill, helps leadership teams explain the "why, what, and how" of partner development and identify the building blocks needed to develop a thorough curriculum to support partners through their careers. He explores why partners should focus on their career and personal development, and why firms should invest. Individual partner needs and ambitions change over their careers, as does what the business requires from them. Martin outlines partner-led and organization-led approaches to development, as well as making suggestions to identify and address these needs.

He also covers some key areas in professional development, including identifying requirements for effective partner development, a range of formal and informal learning methodologies, and working with different types of external provider. By the end of the chapter, practitioners will identify how to go about developing and delivering a training strategy that will support partner development.

In chapter 18, Jonathan Watmough looks at accountability and consequences. It is essential to establish clear expectations and consequences for underperformance, whilst communicating the impact of underperformance on the firm. This chapter looks at how to balance accountability with support and development opportunities.

Technology is a key part of the partner performance management toolkit. Its role is to drive efficiencies, produce evidenced-based insights, track progress against objectives, and facilitate better quality performance management conversations and ongoing feedback. For most large firms, technology is an indispensable factor in improving the efficiency, effectiveness, and fairness of the partner performance management process. For many others, the use of technology in partner performance management and the move to a real-time feedback culture remain ambitions. Chapter 19, by Ray D'Cruz, looks at how technology can be utilized for partner performance management.

Our final chapter looks at the results of some original research carried out by the consulting editors of this title, into how to improve and maintain partner performance. The consulting editors share details of conversations they have had with senior law firm leaders about how they approach the management of partner performance and conclude by offering thoughts and observations about the continuing evolution and refinement of the management of partner performance.

About the editors

Nick Jarrett-Kerr LLB is a specialist adviser to law firms and professional services firms worldwide on issues of strategy, governance, and leadership development, as well as all important business issues facing firms as they compete in difficult market conditions. Nick is a principal of Edge International, a leading global consultancy to law firms. Over more than two decades, he has established himself as one of the leading UK and international advisers to law firms. Since 2002, he has consulted to firms in more than 25 countries on four different continents on issues relating to strategy, governance, mergers, equity/ownership structures, partner performance, succession issues, profit sharing, and other business-critical matters.

He is a regular writer and speaker on management and leadership topics with an emphasis on strategic and business planning, as well as issues of governance and structure, partner compensation, and strategy execution. Prior to becoming a consultant, Nick (who is a UK solicitor by training) was for eight years the chief executive partner of Bevan Ashford, a leading regional firm in Great Britain, during a period of enormous growth starting in the depths of the 1989-1992 recession. His involvement in professional service firm management, both as a partner in law firm and as a consultant, stretches over more than 30 years.

Nick is the author of *Law Firm Strategy – After the Legal Services Act* published in November 2009 (Law Society Publishing) and of the two editions (2011 and 2019) of the bestselling *Tackling Partner Underperformance in Law Firms* (Globe Law and Business). Nick has been visiting professor at Nottingham Trent University where he has led the strategy modules for the Nottingham Law School MBA strategy modules. Nick is also a Fellow of the College of Law Practice Management in the US.

Jonathan Middleburgh is a specialized and highly experienced consultant to law firms, in-house legal departments, and senior leaders in the legal sector. He advises and consults primarily on issues relating to people, management, and leadership within the legal services sector. He is a principal of Edge International, a leading global consultancy to law firms.

Since around 2003, Jonathan has consulted to law firms and in-house legal departments in the UK, Europe, and internationally, with a focus on developing senior legal leadership, helping senior leaders to interact more effectively, guiding and coaching senior leaders through behavioral change, and steering senior leaders towards the adoption of more effective managerial and leadership behaviors. He has also helped law firms with the development, refinement, and practical implementation of succession strategies and in particular the working through of complex succession transitions, including in founder firms. He has collaborated with colleagues in helping law firms to refine their strategies and to reevaluate and where appropriate overhaul their remuneration structures.

Having studied Law as an undergraduate at Oxford University (where he graduated in the top five of his cohort), Jonathan taught for a year at the University of Chicago and for short stints at Oxford and King's College, London. He then practiced as a barrister for around 12 years. Prior to leaving the Bar, Jonathan obtained undergraduate equivalence in psychology and subsequently Masters' equivalence in occupational psychology. A deep understanding of psychological processes and dynamics underpins the work he does with senior legal leaders.

In recent years, Jonathan has consulted to, and advised, senior lawyers on every continent save for Antarctica. He continues to relish having a broad international practice and advising across a wide range of cultures, as well as spending time with his family in London.

About the authors

Joel Barolsky is a principal of Edge International, managing director of Barolsky Advisors, a senior fellow of the University of Melbourne Law School, and co-author of the Thomson Reuters State of the Australia Legal Market Report. He writes for the *Australian Financial Review* Legal Affairs section and the Law Management Hub. Previously, Joel was head of the strategy practice of Beaton Research & Consulting. Joel is internationally recognized as an outstanding advisor, facilitator, and educator to law, accounting, and business advisory firms. He is a noted expert in the fields of strategy, market positioning, client focus, culture, governance, organization design, succession, and capability development. He is renowned for big-picture thinking and creative problem-solving. His facilitation style is often described as engaging, passionate, sensitive, and outcome-focused. Joel has advised over 100 of Australia and New Zealand's leading law, accounting, and business advisory firms. Over 70 percent of his clients are repeat clients or come directly from referrals from existing clients.

Graham Browning is the director of Arrisan, a consultancy that builds great work culture through training and individual support. Arrisan specializes in practical tools that help people rise to the challenge at work. Clients include Big Tech, management consultancy, and financial services. After a law degree, Graham embarked on a diverse professional journey. He taught at the University of Cambridge, trained at Clifford Chance, and qualified as an employment solicitor at Freshfields Bruckhaus Deringer. For 20 years he held dual roles that combined legal and people responsibilities. He has an MSc in Organizational Behavior and is an executive coach. Beginning his transition into HR, Graham lowered employment claims against Freshfields by a third while reducing settlement and exit costs. As global head of people performance and employee relations he led *Being Freshfields*, a landmark program to transform the firm's culture. While guiding his team through difficulty as they were under threat of redundancy for six years, Graham implemented a new operating model for the firm. He was a founding member of a Stephen

Lawrence Foundation diversity initiative before joining an inclusion consultancy at director level. During COVID-19, Graham trained organizations and built an investigation business that became the company's largest revenue generator. He founded Arrisan to equip clients to navigate workplace trials and tribulations with confidence.

Bree Buchanan, JD, MS is senior advisor for Krill Strategies, a legal consulting firm providing support to AmLaw100 firms seeking to enhance wellbeing among their personnel. In 2020, she worked with a small team to create the Institute for Well-Being in Law and served as its first executive director and board president. In January 2024, Bree was recipient of the Reed Smith Award for Excellence in Well-being in Law in recognition of her pioneering work in the field. Prior to this, she served as director of the Texas Lawyers Assistance Program and Chair of the ABA Commission on Lawyers Assistance Programs. Currently, she serves as a commissioner for the International Bar Association's Professional Wellbeing Commission. Bree's work in lawyer well-being follows a twenty-five-year career spent working on issues related to domestic violence, during which she worked as a litigator, lobbyist, and law school professor.

Krystal Champlin-Gerage is a consultant and business advisor with RJH Consulting and Maverick Coaching Solutions. In her roles, she brings over a decade of experience and expertise to law firms and small businesses across the nation. When working with clients, she empowers them to develop a growth mindset that enables them to take control of their professional careers. Her methodology leads clients to build profitable and sustainable businesses based on their core values and definition of success. When working with law firms as the owner and CEO of RJH Consulting, her core focus is the strategic planning process for law firms, increasing operational efficiency and profitability through systems and reporting, and building solid teams through leadership and organizational development. She has taken the same methodology and tactics to other professional service industries through her coaching business, Maverick Coaching Solutions. Krystal holds several certifications that she applies to her client work. She is a certified executive coach, certified emotional intelligence practitioner, certified DiSC trainer, and holds a Six Sigma Lean certification. She has used her experience and knowledge to help her clients envision the next level of growth while providing the support and guidance they need during the process.

Paula Davis JD, MAPP is the founder and CEO of the Stress & Resilience Institute, a training and consulting firm that partners with law firms, corporate legal departments, and organizations to help them reduce burnout and build more resilient and engaged teams. Paula has been working closely with organizations to create thriving workplaces for more than a decade, and since 2020 alone has delivered nearly 400 workshops, trainings, keynotes, and programs on wellbeing and leadership topics. Paula left her law practice after seven years and earned a master's degree in applied positive psychology from the University of Pennsylvania. As part of her postgraduate training, Paula was selected to be part of the University of Pennsylvania faculty, teaching and training resilience skills to soldiers as part of the Army's Comprehensive Soldier and Family Fitness program.

Ray D'Cruz is CEO and co-founder of Performance Leader, a software firm that designs and implements partner and employee performance management systems. Ray advises firms on setting contribution expectations, objectives, and metrics, measuring and assessing performance, and recognition and reward. Over 25 years, he has worked with over 150 professional firms internationally. Ray is co-author of *The Partner Remuneration Handbook*, a comprehensive guide to partner contribution and compensation management, published by Globe Law & Business. Ray is a former lawyer and has held senior HR roles in law firms.

Dr Heidi K. Gardner is a sought-after advisor, keynote speaker, and facilitator for organizations across a wide range of industries globally. Named by Thinkers50 as both a Next Generation Business Guru and one of the world's foremost leadership experts, she is a distinguished fellow at Harvard Law School and former professor at Harvard Business School. She is currently the faculty chair and instructor in multiple executive education programs at both institutions. Dr Gardner works extensively with her team at Gardner & Co., partnering with boards, executive teams, and other senior leaders to boost performance by embedding the principles and practices of smarter, agile, cross-silo collaboration within those groups and across the broader organization and ecosystem. This results in concrete, quantifiable performance improvements. Altogether, Dr Gardner has authored (or co-authored) more than 100 books, chapters, case studies, and articles. This includes best-selling books *Smarter Collaboration: A New Approach to Breaking Down Barriers and Transforming Work* (2022) and *Smart Collaboration: How*

Professionals and Their Firms Succeed by Breaking Down Silos (2017). Her research received the Academy of Management's prize for Outstanding Practical Implications for Management, and has been selected five times for *Harvard Business Review*'s "best of" collections.

Martin Hill is an experienced learning and organizational development consultant with over 25 years' experience, working primarily with law and other professional services firms. He focuses on leadership development and culture change, and in addition to training and facilitation is an executive coach, working with partners and teams. He has a background in psychology and HR, started his career in the UK, and has been based in Hong Kong for over a decade. Martin now operates as Okano Consulting and partners with a number of other consultancies in Asia and the UK. Prior to setting up Okano, Martin was the global head of learning and development for Freshfields Bruckhaus Deringer and enjoyed a short period as a strategy consultant to law firms.

Jim Lawrence is a partner with the international law firm BCLP. He is a trial lawyer and leads the firm's Kansas City commercial disputes team. He handles a wide range of disputes arising in the US and abroad, representing some of the largest financial institutions, insurance companies, and other national and multinational corporations in complex litigation. He has successfully represented clients in disputes with more than six hundred million dollars at issue. Jim has leveraged his successful law practice to bring attention to legal professionals' wellbeing. Jim chairs BCLP's Global Wellbeing Board and has provided presentations about his own journey with substance abuse disorder among other wellbeing related topics.

Stephan Lucks is a chartered occupational psychologist at Pearn Kandola where he works in the area of diversity and inclusion. He holds degrees in Psychology and Applied Psychology and is a member of the Division of Occupational Psychology of the BPS as well as a registered practicing psychologist with the HCPC. Stephan's work focuses on helping both individuals as well as organizations to become more inclusive in their management and leadership of people. He frequently coaches individuals on the topic of inclusion and advises and designs processes in the areas of assessment and development with fairness and inclusion at their heart. He has led on the design and implementation of a talent program in the legal sector with the explicit intention to achieve a more gender balanced talent pipeline approaching partnership. He also frequently provides advice and training on inclusive recruitment for trainees in the legal sector.

Ivan Matviak has more than 25 years of experience transforming complex global businesses through disciplined strategy, product innovation, operations optimization, and cross-silo collaboration. Currently, Ivan is the CEO of Smarter Collaboration Int'l, a technology company focused on delivering tools to enhance organizational collaboration. Previously, he was executive vice president at Clearwater Analytics, a software-as-a-service fintech company, and an EVP at State Street Corporation.

Patrick J. McKenna is an internationally recognized author, lecturer, strategist, and seasoned advisor to leaders of premier law firms, having the honor of working with one of the largest firms in over a dozen countries. Patrick is author/co-author of 12 books. His three decades of experience led to his being the subject of a Harvard Law School Case Study entitled Innovations In Legal Consulting. One example of that innovation was launching the first instructional program designed to address the issues that new firm leaders face in their first 100 days – graduating over 80 participants, many from AmLaw 100 and 200-sized firms. Patrick is the recipient of an Honorary Fellowship from Leaders Excellence of Harvard Square and was voted by readers of *Legal Business World* as one of only seven international thought leaders.

Michael Roch is the partnerships advisor and founder of MHPR Advisors. He guides partnership boards, managing partners, and senior leaders globally on architecting strong partnerships and on leveraging partnerships for sustainable growth. Michael has advised dozens of organizations on becoming market leaders in relation to their partner profit-sharing systems, partnership governance, and global partnering strategy. His clients range from multinational partnerships and alliances to mid-sized firms to start-ups across the globe; most operate in the professional services, technology, life sciences and related sectors. Michael is co-author of *The Partner Remuneration Handbook*.

Jonathan Watmough qualified as a solicitor in The City of London at Reynolds Porter Chamberlain in 1993. Practicing in corporate, he became a partner at 30, managing partner at 38, and spent the next ten years helping to transform RPC from a London insurance firm into an international, multi-disciplinary professional services business. The firm won Law Firm of the Year three times. Jonathan was also twice-named within The Lawyer's Hot 100 lawyers in the UK. After ten years as managing partner, he retired from the firm in 2016 to help law firms cut through to what matters and emulate the simple things successful firms do differently in private practice. This distils down to practical common sense guidance on what matters most in the real world of commercial law, why, and how to do it to get ahead.

Chapter 1:
What constitutes acceptable performance?

By Nick Jarrett-Kerr, principal, Edge International

Introduction and trends

Law firms are primarily people businesses and rely on the brain power, acumen, and performance of their lawyers to gain results. Correspondingly, law firms and professional service firms place less importance on tangible assets such as plant, machinery, and inventory. The maximization of a law firm's productive capacity is therefore a key element in profitable and sustainable long-term performance.

For many years it has been perceived that, in any people business, a version of the Pareto Principle – the 80/20 rule – applies, with ten to 20 percent of the firm's people making by far the largest contribution to the firm's success. Managers such as Jack Welch, the famous former leader of General Electric, used to apply this principle in segmenting employees into three bands in terms of their performance – the top 20 percent, the middle 70 percent, and the bottom ten percent. The top 20 percent are the firm's stars. The middle 70 percent are enormously valuable to any organization, providing the backbone of skills, energy, and commitment without which the organization could not survive. In the case of some corporations such as Microsoft, and in the world in which Welch used to work, the bottom ten percent have to go. As Welch says:

> *"It's awful to fire people – I even hate that word. But if you have a candid organization with clear performance expectations and a performance evaluation process – a big if, obviously, but that should be everyone's goal – then people in the bottom ten percent generally know who they are. When you tell them, they usually leave before you ask them to. No one wants to be in an organization where they aren't wanted."*[1]

Partners of law firms used to think that they formed the premier cadre in the firm's hierarchy, automatically forming Jack Welch's top 20 percent. It is now accepted that the 20-70-10 rule applies as much in the partnership layer as in the rest of the firm. This was reflected when, more than 25 years ago, David Maister[2] coined the expressions "Dynamos", "Cruisers", and "Losers" to describe the three categories of partner in professional service firms. The term "Cruiser", however, may be unnecessarily pejorative as it implies a bunch of partners who are working in comfort zones, when in reality they form the backbone of the firm. It may therefore be better to think of partners as A partners, B partners, and C partners. In most firms, B partners form the heart and soul of the organization. As Delong, Gabarro, and Lees[3] point out, "The bulk of any firm's talent is its B players – the 70 percent who are neither stars nor failures but consistently solid performers. They are the firm, and the firm is only as good as they are."

In most firms, it is rare to find more than 20 percent of the partners falling into the A or Dynamo category and it is clear also that, in some firms, at least ten percent of partners are underperforming against the firm's agreed standards.

In the early part of the 21st century, research[4] started to show that forced ranking approaches can result in lower productivity, skepticism, reduced collaboration, damaged morale, and mistrust in leadership. This does not mean that an approach that contains elements of forced ranking is in any way invalid. Nor does it mean that all partners have to be equally treated. There should be status tiers in every firm where it is clear who deserves to be at the top and the bottom of the pecking order. But, in any approach where partners are comparatively graded, great care has to be taken to ensure that the perception does not grow in the firm that there are a very few stars at the top and everyone else is somehow inferior. Indeed, there is an implicit forced ranking that takes place in every firm as it develops. The disappearance of some underperforming partners automatically results in other partners falling into the bottom performance tier. As Ed Wesemann explains:

"In part, this is because law firms are grading their partners on the curve. The act of removing significant numbers of 'underproductive' partners from a law firm's equity ranks has the effect of raising the average for the remaining partners. Lawyers who used to be viewed as solid service partners find themselves slipping toward being considered underproductive."[5]

By 2006, even General Electric had abandoned formal, forced ranking and by 2015, it was reported that the company had started to abandon "formal annual reviews and its legacy performance management system for its 300,000-strong workforce over the next couple of years, instead opting for a less regimented system of more frequent feedback via an app".[6]

It is, or should be, a golden rule of any partner performance management system that it should not be just a tool for managing underperformance. Equally, the partner remuneration and compensation system should not be used as a tool to punish under-achievement. However, partners who are working hard and making real contributions to the development of the business find it difficult if the problems of consistent underperformance are not addressed. This issue has become harder for the older partner. In former times, partners would tend to ease off as they approached retirement, and, with the disappearance of goodwill, a gentle decline towards retirement whilst maintaining a full profit share was often felt to be a fair trade-off for years of hard work and loss of goodwill payments. With shrinking margins and increasing competition, however, most modern law firms realize that they simply cannot afford to carry any passengers, and the older partner finds himself or herself in the position of having to work harder in later years than in earlier times in order to justify their profit shares. Sadly, some find this difficult, not least because their client base tends to be made up of individuals and professionals of similar age and can often shrink as their clients reach retirement age and no longer have a need for legal services.

Even if not underachieving, one can find partners at most law firms who are just doing enough to escape scrutiny. Whilst this can be the case at every level, it can particularly be true of the more mature partner. Some senior partners retain huge amounts of energy, but some also may be in decline, with waning productivity and fading appetites for work. Some partners even appear happy to settle for a lower tier of compensation on the basis that lower tiers of compensation or profit share will expect a lower level of hard work and contribution and hence will put them under less pressure to perform. The problem can be exacerbated by the reward system if it fails to have mechanisms in place to achieve a fair but sensitive approach.

Defining underperformance

Underperformance used to be thought of as synonymous with under-productiveness but it is clear that any definition has to go much further than adherence to billing and financial targets.

Underperformance can therefore be defined as the consistent failure of a partner to meet the firm's reasonable expectations or standards for productivity, profitability, quality, technical proficiency, client service, or interpersonal relationships. Underperformance includes poor managerial competence and behaviors (such as bullying, emotional abuse, discrimination, and uncontrollable anger), which are inimical to the firm's values and agreed cultural norms.

How to set standards and manage performance

It is crucial from the outset to clarify the minimum expectations that a firm demands of its partners and then to define what roles and responsibilities it requires them to perform in order to make a sustained and valuable contribution to the firm. Hence, before deciding how to deal with underperforming or underproductive partners, it is important to be clear about what the firm expects of its partners and what roles and responsibilities it needs them to perform. Partners equally need to be clear how they are to discharge their various roles as owners, managers, and producers. The current trend away from the more revenue-based and formulaic systems of partner compensation is no accident. Firms are increasingly responding to the growing realization that such revenue-driven systems reward only a very restrictive set of behaviors and at times actually serve to penalize longer term entrepreneurial activities.

To recognize the wider contributions and expectations of partners, firms usually identify and define four, five, or six specific areas in which they expect partners to perform well. These come with different names from firm to firm but generally cover areas such as financial and business performance, people management and team development, business development and rainmaking, client relationship management, contributions to the firm as an institution, and self-development and professional expertise. Several steps are needed to build the right model. First, and most obviously, the firm needs to agree the performance areas that are important for them. The trick here is not to have too many – four seems to be a minimum and more than six usually leads to duplication and unneeded complexity. Second, it is important for every partner to know how to succeed in the firm and a useful start is to define the parameters for star partners on the highest possible tier or grade and for newly appointed equity partners just starting on their equity careers. Then the intervening levels can be created so that partners are clear as to what they have to achieve to stay on their existing grade or level or to move up to the next level.

These critical areas of performance can then be built into the firm's written system and processes for managing partner performance. The trend towards a written and explicit set of partner performance management guidelines is a relatively recent one, but firms have found that – whether they prefer to be lightly managed or are heavily centrally controlled – that some degree of oversight and performance management is useful and necessary. The framework for a successful performance management system should meet a number of objectives that go far wider than issues of underperformance or partner discipline. The main thrust of any performance management system should be to encourage and support behavior and performance, which contributes towards the profitable development of the firm towards its strategic goals.

In summary, there are seven essential elements that are necessary for a successful partner performance management system. First, it must identify the criteria – the critical areas of performance or "balanced scorecard" against which partners will be evaluated. Second, it must lay out in some detail the processes and systems for partner review and appraisals. It must thirdly clarify the evidence, metrics, and data that the firm will employ to inform the firm's evaluation procedures. It should fourthly contain the firm's requirements for each partner to compile some form of personal business or contribution plan, containing goals and objectives that are directly related to the firm's overall strategic objectives. As a fifth element, the expectations of partners and the firm's leaders should be firmly set in identifying the methodology and frequency by and with which the partners and their teams will be actively managed on a day-to-day basis. Sixth, it must set out the firm's processes for dealing with underperformers. Finally, the performance management system should contain the firm's methodology for partner promotion, progression, and development.

How underperformance can affect others at the firm

It is clear that continuing issues of poor performance or below-standard productivity by one or more partners has a morale-sapping effect on the rest of the partnership group, particularly if it is felt that the situation is not being dealt with in a timely fashion. Underperforming partners may be performing poorly because of periods of depression; equally, partners who are brutally aware that they are not meeting standards may become depressed and feel isolated. Underperformance can often be part of a vicious cycle of depression, isolation, bitterness, and bad behavior. In addition, instances of underperformance can also trigger – albeit accidentally and with the best of intentions – a dynamic in which partners "perceived to be mediocre or weak performers live down to the low expectations their managers have for them".[7] This dynamic has become known as the set-up-to-fail syndrome:

"The process is self-fulfilling because the boss' actions contribute to the very behavior that is expected from weak performers. It is self-reinforcing because the boss' low expectations, in being fulfilled by his subordinates, trigger more of the same behavior on his part, which in turn triggers more of the same behavior on the part of subordinates. And on and on, unintentionally, the relationship spirals downward."[8]

As one firm told the author in confidence, "partner underperformance is not only a financial drag and impediment, but it is bad for the morale of those working hard".

Table 1 shows the tangible and intangible costs of underperformance.

Table 1: Features (and consequences) of underperformance.

	Firm	Underperforming partner
Financial	Adverse effect on bottom line	Penalized through compensation system
Emotional	Morale affected within firm	Depression and loss of confidence
Cultural	Undermining of firm values and internal ecology	Can become isolated, bitter, and mean-spirited
Manipulative	Widespread abuse of the firm's processes leads to loss of trust	Poor performing partners avoid trouble by "gaming the system"
Behavioral	Poor example shown by underperformers can spread like a disease	Dysfunctional behavior such as anger and bitterness
Latent	Toxicity in partner relations	Negativity

Values and culture

Underperformance is not therefore just a question of poor productivity, nor is it necessarily only an issue of hard work versus laziness. Of equal importance are failures to meet standards relating to quality of lawyering, client service, and office behavior. Most firms have a set of values and accepted norms of behaviors and conduct. Table 2 shows how the fine words of the firms in respect of their values are often not reflected in partner behaviors. If even a few partners are exhibiting the behaviors shown in the second column of the table, there will be a detrimental effect on the whole firm in at least three ways.

Table 2: Where the words and music fail to match.

High values	Poor behavior
We maintain high standards	Transgressions are widely tolerated
We are open and honest	We talk about people behind their backs
We believe in empowering our people	We continue to operate hierarchically
We have an open-door policy	Doors are kept firmly closed
We encourage a hard-work ethic	Some partners are lazy and complacent
We believe in cooperation and teamwork	We build walls around our clients
We encourage training and teamwork	We are reluctant to allow staff to attend training sessions

continued on next page

7

High values	Poor behavior
We encourage our staff	We are good at criticizing people when mistakes are made
We believe in proper delegation	We hog work to enhance personal billings
We believe in giving appreciative feedback	We fail to schedule/attend appraisals and review meetings
We believe in satisfying our clients and meeting expectations	We fail to attend to our agreed client relationship management protocols
We believe in giving exceptional value to our clients	We pad our time sheets when we can
We are dedicated to giving high quality, leading edge advice	We fail to keep up to date with our reading and technical/professional development

First, if partners fail to maintain agreed values, or exhibit behaviors that run counter to the firm's espoused culture, this can quickly undermine the firm's internal ecology. Second, the existence of poor partner behavior can have a hugely detrimental effect on staff and partner morale. Third, what is also clear is that people in any organization will take their cues from what they see or feel is going on, more than what they hear. The fine rhetoric of the firm is often not matched by the actions of partners. The words (what is said) often do not fit the music (what is done) and the rhythm (the organizational pulse and atmosphere) can beat out of time as well. For those with management responsibilities, the problem can be acute. Whilst the firm's statements, messages, speeches, and slogans can all be carefully and strategically orchestrated, it is less easy to control what is done by the partners in practice. Fitting the music to the words can be a huge task.

Managing for success
How firms manage issues of underperformance also helps to define how well

the firm is perceived to be run by its partners. One firm with whom we have spoken thought, for example, that the issues have an impact on the credibility of the management team. It is certainly true that high performing partners at most firms can be quick to criticize any softness or slowness on the part of the management team in tackling performance issues. Hence, dealing with underproductive partners often continues to find itself at the top of the "to do" list for a lot of management committees.

It is also clear that these issues provide a constant management concern that does not look likely to disappear.

Whatever shift is made towards some element of partner performance management – including the management of underperformance – it is a huge challenge to figure out and then implement a fair and just system of assessing or judging partner performance, particularly in so-called "subjective" or "soft" areas of performance and behavior. It is clear that firms are trying to take particular care to clarify the evidence and data that is to be examined in any assessment. There are also a number of "best practice" principles at play. First, the firm should be certain to connect the dots between the firm's vision and strategy and the day-to-day expectations for partner performance. There should, in other words, be a clear "line of sight" between a partner's personal objectives and the overall objectives of the firm.

Second, the decision-making process should be carefully formulated and the assessment process and forum for assessment and decision-making should all be accepted as fair and reasonable by all partners. Third, the system must be able to retain sufficient flexibility so that decisions can take into account overall intangible contributions as well as market factors, so as to ensure that high-flyers are treated in such a manner as to minimize the risk of head-hunting, and low-flyers are treated fairly.

In order to manage underperformance, it is vital to set a minimum performance baseline. The philosophy is that sustained underperformance below the baseline will ultimately result in the underperforming partner leaving the firm.

The starting problem is that partners are not always clear how they are to discharge their various roles as owners, managers, and producers – they are more or less aware of what is expected in conceptual terms, but find it difficult to put the concepts into action. Over the last few years, partners have become increasingly and sometimes brutally aware of their production targets – hours clocked, revenues earned, and business generated. But it is common to hear partners complaining that they have no time for management duties because of their hectic client-facing workloads and the expectation of their firms that they should maintain high chargeable hours and revenues. The difficulties encountered by partners in balancing their roles as owners, managers, and producers is covered at length by Joel Barolsky in chapter four.

Over a period of some years, we have asked many firms similar questions about the standards with which they expect partners to comply; we consistently receive similar answers. Indeed, we have now carried out three surveys of the profession, details of the last of which are summarized in chapter 20. We have long noted that some firms have a full set of partner competencies and others have invested in sophisticated performance management systems with partner appraisals, objectives, and key performance indicators that vary according to role and seniority. It is generally felt the partner performance criteria are somewhat dominated by client and financial issues but that firms should strive to include "softer" issues and behaviors such as teamwork. Balanced scorecards seem to be very much in favor although most firms rightly insist on partners hitting financial targets over the medium-term. One firm commented:

> *"We cover the full range of a partner's contribution (to include technical, profile, business development, maintaining and developing clients, running and motivating teams, the team's financial performance in gross profit levels, and demonstrating a one firm ethos)."*

Financial and economic criteria have accordingly always ranked as the most important, followed closely by team and people management, business development, and client relationship management. For some firms, technical knowledge is taken as granted whilst other firms place emphasis on the improvement of specialist skills. A few firms focus on partners' contribution to the management of the firm as a business.

Whilst it is clear that firms are considering and valuing outcomes and results more than effort, work ethic remains an important element amongst a firm's values. One possible starting point, therefore, is for the partners to agree what time commitment is expected of them as partners. Expectations often differ between firms in the major cities of the world – with traditional very long hours and hard-working conditions – and those in regional firms, both in Europe and North America. A common (though not universal) standard is that partners in a regional western law firm should be expected to devote roughly ten hours of the day – not necessarily in the office – to the business. Such an expectation would amount over the course of the year to a time commitment of 2,300 hours (46 weeks × five days × ten hours) or in some cases more.

This can be broken down for partners as:

- Chargeable time: 1,300-1,900 hours.
- Marketing and business development time: commonly 300-500 hours.
- Other non-chargeable time depends on size of team, type of client etc., but is often in the range of 200-300 hours per year, spread across:
  - Client relationship management;
  - Team and human capital management; and
  - Contribution to the firm as an institution.

Within these time frames, it should be possible for the nonchargeable activities to be carried out, even within the context of a large client portfolio.

Whilst it is good to establish the amount of time spent on the firm's business, effort must be matched by efficiency and effectiveness. Accordingly, law firms have largely accepted the importance of developing management and leadership skills in their partners. This recognition is somewhat patchy and inconsistent and there is often a mismatch between what law firms say they value in their partners (in terms of the competencies and characteristics) and what they actually reward (often by recognizing and rewarding billing efforts mainly or exclusively). In addition, there is a growing appreciation that skills and competencies can be developed across the management/leadership spectrum, from a base level through an intermediate level to an advanced state of leadership.

Understanding the "critical areas of performance" in which partners need to contribute

Best practice therefore indicates some typical "critical areas of performance" in which partners need to build capability and competence in order to fulfil their partner role. These have different names in different law firms but often boil down to four, five, or six key areas. It is important not just to label the headline area of performance but to define carefully what each area involves and means in terms of competences and behavioral indicators.

These areas often roughly correspond both with the concepts of intellectual capital and the balanced scorecard (suggested by Balanced Scorecard authors, Kaplan and Norton).[9] The balanced scorecard is a methodology to align an organization's everyday operations to its long-term strategy. Its purpose is to translate vision and strategy into all the actions that the organization undertakes. This is done by looking at desired results from certain perspectives. Law firms often change the basic model in a number of ways. First, the model can be aligned to reflect the concept that the main constituent assets of law firms are elements of human and intellectual capital, rather than tangible assets. Second, the balanced scorecard methodology has to be adapted to fit the environment in which lawyers develop their careers by serving their clients, processing their work, and making profits. Third, the scorecard is often restated in terms that fit in with both the background and strategic imperatives of most law firms.

In the box below we set out a sample set of competencies and behavioral indicators for an entry level partner that are organized into what I have found to be typical "critical areas of performance". There are no particular rights and wrongs about how these areas are labelled and defined – it is important where possible to use the language and context of the particular law firm.

Typical critical areas of performance

Financial and business performance
This includes the manner in which each partner discharges his or her responsibility for managing the business and financial aspects of the team/ department/division for which he or she is responsible:
- Achieving superior financial performance and excellence in cash collections.
- Maintaining good financial discipline.
- Working hard and demonstrating long-term engagement and commitment.

People management, leadership, and team/skills development
- Setting the right leadership example both to his or her own department and to other members of the firm by:
- Achieving cooperation from team members out of respect rather than fear.
- Setting the right example throughout the firm in term of work ethic, personal conduct, and crisis management.
- Developing the profile of the firm's people, their skills, abilities, and strengths/weaknesses in depth and skills.

- Understanding the necessity of getting things done through others.
- Constantly working at communicating, delegating, negotiating, resolving conflict, persuading, and using/responding to authority/ power.
- Understanding the obligation to use power appropriately and the danger of the inappropriate use of power.
- Harnessing the power of the firm by creating, organizing, and energizing powerful teams, including the extent to which individuals within teams are encouraged to push the boundaries of their own team roles.
- Developing and assisting people by coaching, mentoring, counselling, and developing them in any of the following disciplines – law, marketing, sales, finances, career, work–life balance, and networking.

Business development

- Contributions in general to build for the firm's future by targeting better clients and better work.
- Achieving sustained value by originating (or playing a key part in originating) new clients of the firm and by increasing the value of work from established clients.
- Developing the firm's client base to become and remain highly competitive.
- Cross-selling and introducing clients and referrers to others in the firm.
- Building marketing visions and strategies that are long-term, compelling, and market-focused.
- Building the firm's brand, reputation, and profile.
- Performing an ambassadorial role to assist in the building of networks and profile.

Client relationship management

- Nurturing the client base.
- Fulfilling the ongoing requirement to deliver excellent service to clients in the context of their particular needs.
- Working to produce new solutions that create value to the clients.
- Consistently providing streamlined cost-effective services.
- Effectively building, developing, and maintaining strong client relationships.

Contribution to the firm as an institution

Knowledge management and solutions including:

- Taking responsibility in an effective manner for the management of the firm, its various management functions (e.g. marketing, IT, compliance), its departments and its sub-groups.
- Contributing creatively to the strategic planning of the firm and its implementation.
- Contributing to the building of the firm's intellectual property, including precedents, templates, case management, and workflows.
- Assisting in the development of leading-edge knowledge management and high-level technical know-how.
- Demonstrating though own actions and the actions of the team compliance with the firm's policies and procedures, including regulatory compliance and good practice in relation to the firm's own policies on disbursements, bad debts, and client care.
- Actively helping build the firm's processes and systems that contribute to the firm's ability to grow its business, including quality control/improvement, governance, and management structure.
- Contributing to the development of a homogeneous culture and esprit de corps.
- Demonstrating the visions and values of the firm by example rather than in words alone.

Self-development and self-leadership

- Evidencing continued development and commitment to developing competence and skills and challenging oneself to expand personal comfort zones.
- Acquiring new expertise and skills valuable to the firm.
- As a role model, demonstrating confidence and self-belief, consistently acting with integrity, and being naturally trusted by others.
- Providing an example of being self-initiating, self-starting, self-learning, committed, and engaged.
- Displaying the ability to pursue goals with a deep sense of purpose and direction.
- Innovating with a combination of innovative legal approaches, workflow innovations, and networking innovations in order to become more efficient and productive and to improve the client experience.

Changes in performance expectations post-COVID

Post-COVID, law firms all over the world have been struggling to maintain a sense of balance in two different areas of lawyer performance. The first balance is between the benefits of working from home (WFH) and the second is the balance between supply and demand, which was hit hard by the pandemic.

The benefits of WFH balanced with in-office collaboration

Hybrid working was introduced to take advantage of higher levels of productivity and fewer commutes from WFH balanced against the benefits of office attendance. The hybrid arrangement now common to many firms requires lawyers to spend a rolling average of 50 percent or (in some firms) at least three full days per week (or the pro rata equivalent) in the office, or at a client, or in court. As the managing partner of Slaughter and May recently expressed in an email to staff, "While we have all experienced benefits from having some flexibility in our working week, this has to be balanced against the very clear benefits in terms of culture, collaboration, and wellbeing of working together in the office".[10]

The balance between supply and demand

Businesses of every type need to maintain sufficient staff to cope with expected levels of work. Given that it takes considerable time to get lawyers up to speed in any firm, most leadership teams opt to maintain staff ranks at a sufficient level to enable the firm to cope with the high peaks of work that they expect. This is particularly the case in transactional work. The problem is that the market has now been quieter than expected since the start of the pandemic, and this has resulted in firms languishing in the unenviable position of footing large wage and compensation bills for teams of lawyers that are not especially busy, but which managers are reluctant to reduce in the hope and expectation of a market upswing. Some firms have concluded that the gamble is no longer worth the cost and there are regular reports of lay-offs and redundancies at leading firms, some of which involve partners.

In the face of these two changes, an even greater focus has now been brought to bear on utilization rates as a preliminary step to identify and address lawyers who are less than fully utilized. As highlighted earlier in this chapter, utilization rates on their own form a blunt and sometimes misleading indicator. I have often seen work-hogging partners who starve their associates and assistants of work to maintain their own unitization rates. Equally, there are partners who delegate properly and responsibly to their assistants, even at the expense of their own utilization, thereby running the risk of coming under the spotlight for possible action.

References

1   Welch, J., *Winning* (2005) Harper Collins, p.42.
2   Maister, D.H., *True Professionalism*, (1997) Free Press, chapter four.
3   Delong, J., Gabarro, J.J., and Lees, R.J., *When Professionals Have to Lead* (2007) Harvard Business School Press, chapter eight.
4   Novations Group, "Uncovering the Growing Disenchantment with Forced Ranking Performance Management Systems". White paper (Boston, MA: Novations Group, August 2004).
5   Wesemann, H.E., *Looking Tall by Standing Next to Short People* (2007) Authorhouse, p.14.
6   Nisen, Max, 13 August 2015, https://qz.com/428813/ge-performance-review-strategy-shift
7   Manzoni, J.F. and Barsoux, J.L., The Set-Up-To-Fail Syndrome; *HBR*, March-April 2008.
8   *Ibid*
9   Kaplan, Robert S. and Norton, David P., *The Balanced Scorecard* (1996) HBS Press.
10 Quoted on 12 January 2024 in www.rollonfriday.com/news-content/exclusive-slaughter-and-may-clamps-down-office-dodging-solicitors

Chapter 2:
Recognizing common causes of underperformance

By Patrick McKenna, author, lecturer, strategist, and advisor to the leaders of premier law firms

Imagine this: as firm leader, a colleague draws your attention to the fact that one of your partners is misbehaving or underperforming – perhaps bullying some junior, or not achieving their billable goals, or not following through on promises made to perform critical tasks.

Now you knew that this particular partner was misbehaving. It didn't come as a shock. But you were content to let the situation drift without resolution, rather than have to confront the ugly reality of the circumstances. But today you have the facts thrust before you and now something must be done.

In the UK, the Solicitors Regulation Authority[1] holds firm leadership accountable for addressing bullying and other behavioral problems within their firms. The move came in response to the fact that law firms had been known to turn a blind eye to bad behavior, especially from high-billing partners. It has been applauded by many firm leaders, including one firm leader who commented to the legal press[2] that "it is important that everyone at the firm clearly understands the behavior expected of them".

Many firm leaders seem to lose sight of the fact that it is their job to dispense tough love! They have to constantly challenge partners to set an example for others and stretch people toward pursuing higher goals. For any firm leader, there can be no more difficult duty than having to confront and possibly even remove someone from the firm, perhaps a long-time colleague, a friend, or even some partner known to have fed you in your earlier days.

The first decision-making challenge is to identify both how and when to take corrective action.

Before one does anything drastic, it is essential to identify where the problem lies and whether there is any rational way to fix things. Assuming that your strong preference is to provide the ineffective individual with coaching and remediation to help them succeed, then diagnosis is definitely your best place to start.

There are two important questions you need to answer in order to begin your diagnosis.

1. How are we defining underperformance?

Every firm has a different name for this – "problem personality", "performance impaired", or "he who went into retirement without telling us".

In far too many instances we only think of underperformance as a billable production issue and largely because, in many firms, we have not really defined what the total performance obligations of being a partner might include. At its most basic, there are four roles that every lawyer must play, namely to:

1. Be a working member of the firm;
2. Originate some business;
3. Provide some non-billable contributions to support your firm and its people; and
4. Make yourself valuable to clients.

Taking that a step further, I explored with one firm leader how one might define and then measure ideal lawyer behavior. We settled on ten different performance measures, the metrics for which would be slightly different for an equity partner vs a salaried partner, or of counsel vs an associate.

The measures consisted of:

1. Billable hours or collections – and contribution to profitability.
2. Client origination, *i.e.* must generate minimum of $x in business.
3. Personal marketing and branding initiatives, such as papers and blogs published, speeches given, social media presence, etc. For example:
   a. *Equity partner*: minimum of three published articles, blogs, or newsletter contributions, and/or two talks, speeches, webinars per year.
   b. *Salaried partner*: minimum of two published articles, blogs, or newsletter contributions, and/or one talk, speech, webinar per year.
4. Client satisfaction and published testimonials, including major projects managed, client visits made, major projects or deals consummated, etc.
5. New client development efforts, i.e. potential new client calls, pitches made, proposals prepared, RFP responses completed.
6. Coaching, mentoring, and training, i.e. creation of shared tools, templates, technological programs.
7. Teamwork and collaboration.
8. Internal firm management, i.e. committee involvement, significant

firm or group projects or internal tasks, contributions to knowledge management and legal process improvements, etc.

9. Professional skills building, *i.e.* entirely new skill enhancement courses attended, professional development completed.

10. Industry focus, *i.e.* active involvement or committee membership in at least one industry or trade group – not including ABA or IBA.

The point here is that as firm leader you may want to ensure that there exist some clear, specific, written, non-negotiable standards of performance that define "what should we be able to expect of one another – especially as partners in this firm".

2. Are there legitimate reasons why some lawyer is behaving the way they are?

At one roundtable session I attended, a group of firm leaders were asked to brainstorm from their experience a list of reasons why some colleagues were underperforming.

Here was the list they generated:

- Trouble at home or other personal problems.
- Burnout.
- Fear of failure in trying something new or reaching for career progress.
- Quality of life choices – lack of desire to contribute more energy or time to the practice.
- Externally driven reasons, such as the loss of a recent major client or downturn in their chosen area of expertise.
- Failure to keep up in their field; being less in demand.
- Poor time management or other inefficiencies.
- Lack of knowledge about what they should be doing to succeed.
- Being poorly led, managed, coached, or personally challenged.
- Insecurity due to issues like firm merger discussions or unresolved firm issues.

As you consider this list, you can add any other possible causes that you think are missing, but then ask yourself, "Which of these reasons are the most common in your world?"

This particular gathering of leaders selected personal or family issues, burnout, externally driven market changes, loss of enthusiasm, and quality-of-life choices as the major reasons for underperformance in their firms.

The important point to keep in mind here is that the reason some colleague is acting out or not performing is not necessarily because they don't know what is expected of them. Nor is it that they don't want to do it. The incentives to do it are usually already there. If they aren't behaving as they should, it could very well be due to something deeply personal in their lives. The only way to find out what it is, and to meaningfully deal with it, is to talk about it. In other words, in many instances one can view these as temporary setbacks – a correctable glitch. Given some time, coaching, and hands-on assistance, these professionals may get back on track.

Your diagnosis may point to areas where coaching might indeed be highly productive. Other times, the diagnosis may reveal a more pervasive problem. Sometimes the choice, however painful, is clear. No amount of coaching will improve the individual's fundamental performance. At the end of the day, you can coach technique and you can coach certain behavioral patterns, with triggering mechanisms to change how people deal with each other, or how they operate within teams. However, you cannot coach character, ambition, or a fundamental change in personality.

These two initial critical questions therefore follow on from one another:

1. Does your diagnosis indicate that this individual's bad behavior or underperformance lies in a coachable area?
2. What results can be expected from coaching this individual and over what period of time? Even if there is a likelihood of improvement through coaching, is the result worth the expenditure of time and effort to get there?

Tough questions, to be sure. Over the years, I have counseled a number of firm leaders on how they might deal with the challenge of either coaching or removing some team member. I certainly don't want to underestimate the complexity or the intense emotional investment involved in making a decision to take action. But I do make sure that firm leaders realize how relatively few limitations there are on their capacity to remove ineffective and uncoachable individuals.

Indeed, any constraints on taking action are usually self-imposed and will ultimately have – and perhaps are already having – adverse firm-wide effects.

Some common traps that allow the problem to continue
When you are faced with this challenge – and you definitely will be at some point in your tenure as firm leader – you will need to understand that the

consequences of decisive action are rarely as dire as they seem at first glance. Even so, there are typically numerous reasons why intelligent and highly capable leaders will go to great lengths to avoid removing an underproductive or troublesome colleague.

You need to recognize all of these as traps and you need to know what must be done about each of them.

Trap #1: Giving the situation more time and hoping the issue will self-correct

Situations in which sufficient data demonstrates that a particular professional is acting out or no longer doing the job are not always easy to accept. Some leaders are inclined to hold back, waiting for even more information that a colleague is not performing properly.

Yet other leaders have a high need to be loved, admired, and respected by everyone within their group. This is an important part of their personal makeup and what attracted them to take on the position of being a leader in the first place. This need makes it particularly hard for them to deal with conflict of any kind and the thought of having to confront a colleague and peer is an especially painful situation.

Trap #2: The underperformer is rescued by a large project and becomes productive for a while

The excuse I often hear is that, *"This person really is a good lawyer, it's just that they aren't busy enough"*. I observed a managing partner of one firm who put off dealing with an underperforming senior partner for years, continually rationalizing how the partner was slowly coming around.

With any partner who is misbehaving or underperforming, you have to ask yourself: "What are you seeing that makes you think that things are really going to get any better without some intervention? What are the specific signs that this individual is making any significant progress?"

Trap #3: Your concern for how the professional involved may be adversely impacted

If you are like some leaders I've counselled, you will find it natural to be concerned about the impact of some fellow colleague being told that "they are a bully". You are well aware that you are dealing with a professional where this may be seen as the first major failure they have experienced in their career. The shock of confronting that reality, combined with any possible peer embarrassment, may be a crushing blow. It is quite natural to experience internal tension and huge reluctance to confront these people.

Yet at some point you do have to ask yourself how long you, and the teammates afflicted, can reasonably be expected to continue to tolerate underperformance or troublesome behavior. In many cases, we are talking about situations where decisions taken or avoided can have measurable economic consequences on everybody involved.

Trap #4: Concern for how confronting a problem partner will be viewed by others

There is also a profound fear that having to confront some partner is not only likely to provoke embarrassment on the part of the professional involved, but it could also potentially stimulate others to be concerned about their own professional standing and personal security.

You need to realize that even if the situation ultimately results in the departure of a partner, or even a couple of departures within a relatively short period of time, it is not going to destabilize your entire partnership. As you put in place a carefully developed remedial plan for addressing the situation, your fellow partners will soon realize that you are transmitting a powerful signal about how the firm values appropriate behavior, is enforcing standards, and about the level of performance required of all lawyers.

Trap #5: You may have to confront a sense of personal failure as a leader

It is not unusual for an experienced leader to entertain some feeling of having personally failed at preventing the situation from happening. It may be very natural for you to harbor remorse at not knowing how to turn this individual around or fix the situation. You believe that if you had only given this lawyer more guidance, clearer direction, perhaps provided some form of external professional counselling, or spent more time personally in providing coaching, that none of this would have happened.

Your self-imposed guilt ignores a couple of considerations. In most every case I've observed, your partner knows they are not performing in accordance with the standards or with the level that they had performed in the past. The truth is that you can only do so much. For you to personally think that you can help make every professional a "star" is simply not realistic.

Trap #6: You cannot delegate the responsibility to take action

One of the benefits of being a leader is that you can delegate some of the more mundane or distasteful tasks to others. Unfortunately, this is not one of them. The unavoidable fact is that some responsibilities cannot be delegated. Dealing with these kinds of performance issues is one of the key requirements of any effective leader.

In reality, not acting is the same as announcing to everyone in your firm that you will continue to accept unacceptable behavior.

Conclusion

As a young pup in my early 20s, I spent some time in the retail industry and was a "junior executive" (a fancy title for someone in training) at a major national department store. In that capacity I had responsibility for supervising a significant-sized department. I will never forget what happened to me one day. As I was sauntering around the floor, the divisional manager came up behind me, tapped me on the shoulder and said, "McKenna, do you see those two staff people over there, chatting it up with one another rather than serving our customers?" I looked over and rather sheepishly had to say, "Yes". He responded, "Well, if I see that again, you're fired!".

That was one of the most valuable leadership lessons I ever learned and one that I convey to firm and practice leaders whenever I have the chance. Quite simply, you get the behavior you tolerate.

I remember hearing one firm leader ask his colleagues a simple question: "What behaviors do we expect from our fellow partners?". He followed that up by then asking, "And what specific behaviors that do not meet those expectations do we tolerate from them?" He then drew two squares saying, "What we tolerate is what we will get and that then becomes our firm's culture – is that really what any of us wants?"

While there may be those situations where some lawyer's problematic behavior or performance can become troublesome almost overnight, it's a relatively rare occurrence. Typically, these issues are more often gradual and happen over a prolonged period of time. We have to stop allowing one of our professionals to get themselves into a position of becoming a chronic bully or underproductive. Identifying problem behavior and providing one-on-one coaching needs to be one of the primary job responsibilities of every firm, practice, and industry group leader.

References
1   SRA: Workplace environment: risks of failing to protect and support colleagues.
    4 May 2023 www.sra.org.uk/solicitors/guidance/workplace-environment/
2   www.law.com/international-edition/2023/02/27/law-firm-leaders-must-stand-up-to-bullying-partners-following-rule-change/

Chapter 3:
Causes of underperformance – the challenges of lateral hires and how to address them

By Dr Heidi K. Gardner, distinguished fellow, Harvard Law School and CEO, Gardner & Co., and Ivan Matviak, CEO, Smarter Collaboration Int'l and co-founder, Gardner & Co.

The reality of lateral hiring

Lateral hiring has skyrocketed in recent years, as firms expand into new geographies, bolster practice groups and disciplinary expertise, and seek ready-made books of business. Many firms see an offensive approach to filling in gaps and obtaining star talent as a crucial part of their growth strategy in today's ultra-competitive legal environment.

While firms fiercely compete to recruit and hire the industry's best and brightest, accumulating big names without a strategic plan and simply hoping for the best does not work. In reality, firms' success rate with laterals is fairly dismal – only 28 percent of laterally hired partners actually hit their expected client billings in their first year, 20 percent were no longer with the firm one year after joining, and 50 percent had left within five years.[1]

Research into labor economics suggests that the cost of each failed lateral partner is more than double the individual's annual compensation – 213 percent, to be precise.[2] So, for example, the typical cost of replacing an equity partner in the UK will be at least £1 million; for equity partners in top firms, however, that cost rises to a staggering £6.6 million.[3] When considering the cost of failed hires, firms may calculate the direct costs (e.g., recruiter fees, bonus guarantees), but many fail to appreciate indirect costs such as the opportunity costs of partners' time spent interviewing and the reputational damage (and subsequent lost fees) with clients.

Given that two to three years of strong performance are needed to recoup recruiting costs and compensation during the transition period, the attrition of lateral partners at five years is a loss-making proposition for most law firms today.

Lateral partner hiring can also cause internal strife about the compensation system among long-term partners because firms generally need to pay much more for outsiders in order to compensate them for the risk of changing firms. In US law firms, for example, the pressures associated with lateral partner hiring can lead to significant disparities in compensation between partners within the same firm. Although the median spread between the highest- and lowest-paid partners inside a US firm is ten to one (already quite a gap), that ratio swells as high as a staggering 23 to one in one firm where lateral hiring is rampant. As the *New York Times* has reported, eight-figure pay packages – rare in the mid-2010s – are increasingly common for top corporate lawyers.[4]

Overview of costs for sub-par lateral hiring
- Financial: £1-£6.6 million+
- Underperformers who stay and fail to become productive
- Weakened or damaged organizational culture
- Stress on internal resources (such as marketing budgets).
- Internal friction related to unequal compensation
- Weakened client confidence

Another major risk associated with hiring lateral talent might be the dilution – or worse – of a firm's culture. Sometimes, adding employees with different perspectives can benefit firms by introducing new ways of thinking. But unless you are deliberately seeking and hiring candidates with a specific, diverse set of characteristics, you are leaving the evolution of your culture to chance by hiring people who come from firms with cultures that are radically different from your own.

A final cost to mention, which is difficult to quantify but nevertheless significant, is client confidence. Once a client has confidence that a trusted lawyer is invested in its particular business matter, that partner's departure can be devastating to the trust between firm and client. An ever-changing roster conjures unfavorable questions in the client's mind: "If this firm can't handle its personnel, how can it effectively solve my high-stakes problem?"

Why laterals tend to fail – the role of collaboration
Our empirical research, spanning over a decade at Harvard University and across more than 100 law and other professional firms around the globe, conclusively shows that a major reason that laterals fail is that they are not sufficiently integrated into the core work of the firm.[5] They need two-way

collaboration within a relatively short time after joining the firm, and if either direction is missing, they are at a massively higher risk of failure.

By "two-way collaboration," we mean that laterals are being brought into incumbent partners' client work (at least pitches, but ideally billable work), and they are drawing colleagues into work that they generate (see Figure 1).

Figure 1: Collaboration and lateral hires – two paths

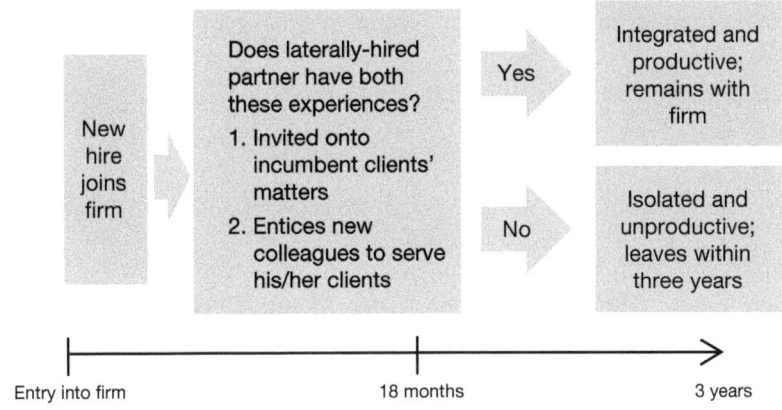

Source: Gardner & Co.

The lack of collaboration stems from two issues:
- *Poor candidate selection.* When laterals are hired solely for their portable book of business, firms fail to appreciate that a "lone wolf" approach to client service in their prior firm is the main reason they can move clients.
- *A lack of tools, processes, and accountability.* Firms generally lack a systemic approach to make sure laterals are collaborating, fully integrated, and successful.

On the first issue, we estimate that at least 75 percent of top law firms have "collaboration" as a central tenet of their overall strategy (and for good reason).[6] But by using a "portable book of business" as the main partner hiring criterion, they are actually undermining collaboration. That's because if somebody has portable clients, it often means they've been poor collaborators in their prior firm.

Our data backs up the assertion that client portability is linked to lone wolf behavior.[7] As shown in Figure 2, clients that are served by a sole relationship partner are overwhelmingly (72 percent) likely to switch providers if that partner departs (e.g., moves to a competitor, or retires). Only 28 percent of those clients would remain with the firm if the solo partner left. In contrast, clients served by two or more partners are sticky – 90 percent would stay with the firm and just ten percent would go elsewhere if one of the relationship partners departed. So, if a lateral candidate claims to be able to bring along their clients, it should be a red flag about how willing and able they had been to open those client relationships to colleagues in their prior firm.

Figure 2: Link between client portability and solo- versus multi-threaded relationships

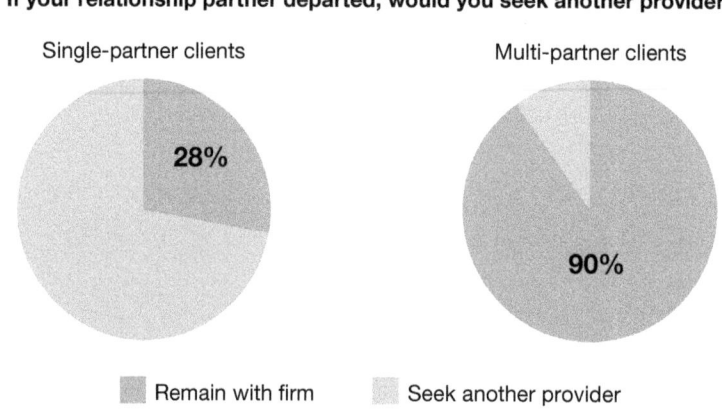

"If your relationship partner departed, would you seek another provider?"

Single-partner clients · Multi-partner clients

28% · 90%

Remain with firm · Seek another provider

Source: Gardner & Co.

The irony is that firms want lawyers who will build the business, which requires smarter collaboration, but they actively seek out and select highly individualistic rainmakers. And then they end up with the kind of situation a partner recently shared with us:

> *"Collaboration should be a two-way street, one that builds mutual trust, but I have seen little or no attempt to introduce me to any clients; I will continue to try to make introductions, but it would be easier if it were more bilateral."*

The second reason that lateral hires fail is that firms generally lack an institutional infrastructure – including tools, processes, and accountability – to make sure they are fully collaborating and well-integrated.

Busy partners don't make time for helping newcomers. Without the proper tools and processes to do this work easily and seamlessly, integration and collaboration never rises to the top of their priority list.[8]

Exacerbating this problem, too many firms take a "sink or swim" approach that places integration accountability solely on the shoulders of the new joiners. Incumbent partners, who might be resentful of a lateral's package, may want the new joiner to "prove their worth". At worst, they might even see the lateral as a competitor.

This was the case in one law firm we advised, where the cut-throat culture and leadership made client service feel like a "zero sum game" where helping others – or asking for help – was not even a consideration. It was shocking to hear a partner in this prestigious firm ask, "Why should I help my competitor?" when asked to introduce a recently-hired lateral partner to a client he served.

A partner in another law firm told us:

"I had to learn the ropes myself – why should I have to help the latest hires? Survival of the fittest is the best way to weed out the duds."

Clearly, his firm had failed to clarify how the new joiner would add value to him and the rest of his practice group – and he felt no accountability for anyone's success other than his own.

Despite these all-too-common refrains, the data on collaboration's benefits is irrefutable – for the sake of lateral hires, the firm more broadly, and ultimately for clients. Below, we offer a roadmap for firms to both hire collaborative partners and make sure that they are sufficiently integrated into the core client work. We also explore how to lay the foundation for both stages.

Solutions for integrating smarter collaboration into lateral hiring – for maximum performance

Clearly, firms need a well-constructed plan, a relentless focus on execution, and clear accountability processes if they expect to help laterals achieve two-way collaboration quickly and efficiently. To keep up, law firms must hire the kinds of partners who have the skill and the will to collaborate with peers with the goal of building multi-threaded client relationships. Firms need a robust infrastructure to help integrate lateral talent into client service teams and relevant sector groups. Finally, incumbent partners – especially the leaders of the practice groups and sector teams who wanted to hire the lateral – need to have laterals' success on their scorecard, with direct links to their bonus. These need to align closely with the lateral partners' scorecard. The remainder of this chapter lays out these steps for success.

Figure 3: Core stages and steps for successful lateral hiring

Source: Gardner & Co.

Stage 1: Lay the foundation for hiring collaborative talent
Robust planning, backed up by data-driven analytics and sufficient capability building, *before you start the recruitment process*, will help create the necessary foundation to hire collaborative people and get them integrated deeply and rapidly into your core work.

Create a data-driven business plan
Strategic considerations and financial models should make it crystal clear how the new hire will be accretive, rather than cannibalize business from existing partners. Opportunities may include penetrating strategic

prospects, entering specific geographic markets, filling expertise gaps from partner turnover, and building a new practice or sector (or expanding an existing one).

Engage your financial and business development experts to collect and dissect both internal and market data to calculate anticipated return on investment (ROI) for each proposed candidate and produce a business plan toward that end. The plan should include client-specific and firm-building objectives with a named individual responsible to see each objective through to completion in collaboration with any new joiner. For example:

- What sector/industry-based experience is critical for the firm's port-folio aspirations?
- Which clients have an identified need where a lateral's practice will be important?
- Which thought leadership initiatives would benefit from a lateral hire's fresh expertise?
- Who is responsible for helping the lateral build their internal network?

Assign clear responsibilities to those people who will need to support the new hire and make it clear that this is part of their performance evaluation. The partner(s) responsible for each new hire will work actively with the lateral partner(s) to take this general business plan and tailor it to the newcomer's situation.

Objectively gauge each group's readiness to absorb the lateral. Has that office or practice just hired a cohort of other laterals who are consuming all the integration attention and energy? Is the practice group appropriately leveraged, such that the lateral will have adequate associate support? Are other resources (business development support, marketing budget, etc.) sufficient to support a new partner? Your ability to answer these questions ties directly to your ability to help a newly hired lateral succeed. The level of resourcing for each new hire should be part of the business plan, socialized with incumbent partners – their buy-in to "sharing" resources boosts their commitment to helping the newcomer succeed.

Track pockets of churn and burn

Few firms get this right. You need hard data to uncover which practice groups and business functions have a track record for successful lateral hire integra-tion. Firms are anecdotally aware of pockets of lateral lawyer "churn and burn" – an office or a specific practice group that continuously hires lateral lawyers and cycles through them quite rapidly. We have seen very few firms, however, that routinely or systematically collect that data and report on it or use it as a basis for resource allocation going forward.

Despite analyzing why some lateral lawyer hires have succeeded or not, focus tends to be more on the individual lawyer – whether the lateral came as part of a group or had niche expertise – and not the group that the lawyer joined. In other words, they typically fail to examine the firm's role in creating conditions for success or failure across practice areas, offices, sectors, departments, and so on.

Gather and review your lateral hiring data from the last five years or so:

- Who pushed for or sponsored each hiring request and how well did each of those laterals fare once hired?
- Who interviewed the candidate, and what did their interview notes identify as strengths and risks? (Come on, you do maintain an archive of interviewers' notes, right?)
- What was the track record of integration – how many incumbent clients did they serve in the first three, six and 12 months?
- How well did each of those laterals perform? (i.e., length of time at the firm, time until they achieved profitability, leadership roles attained).

You may discover a strong correlation between certain partners' or practices' attempts at lateral hiring and their success rates. Initially, treat evidence of churn and burn as a growth opportunity. Dig into the root causes. Gaining a full understanding of exactly what is broken helps a firm to pinpoint a sustainable, practical, and long-term fix.

Build collaborative know-how
Collaboration is not a narrowly defined skill in its own right, but rather a set of mindsets, behaviors, and abilities that collectively equip someone to engage in effective cross-silo working.

Through our research, we have defined nine major categories of those foundational capabilities (see Figure 4 below).[9] Groups that are guilty of "churn and burn" are likely to be deficient in many, if not most, of these skills.

Figure 4: Nine core smarter collaboration skills

Responding and initiating. Ability to collaborate or refine others' work, as the situation demands	**Applying conceptual and practical thinking.** Ability to embrace discussions about both complex ideas and the execution of them	**Getting involved in the work.** Ability to flex between being actively involved in work versus empowering others to get work done
Assessing and managing risk. Ability to assess and mitigate the downside(s) of a situation while seizing opportunities to capture upside potential	**Building collaborative relationships.** Ability to create a postive environment where people actively work with each other to achieve better outcomes	**Balancing group and individual work.** Ability to use collaboration at the right times (not too much, not too little), involving people across a broad spectrum of views and roles
Demonstrating trustworthiness. Ability to demonstrate both the character and competence that encourages others to work with you	**Showing trust in others.** Ability to show an appropriate level of trust in others	**Communicating collaboratively.** Ability to draw in and integrate a diversity of perspectives, even conflicting views

Source: Gardner & Co./Smarter Collaboration International

Developing these collaborative skills in law firms can't be left to chance and needs to be put in place before hiring so that the new joiner enters a collaborative team. Our research has uncovered three problems that arise from a *laissez-faire* approach to partners' professional development:

- Informal processes like peer coaching and mentoring tend to be inconsistent – and extremely rare for partners – which can create unfair advantages for a lucky few and major capability gaps for the rest.

- Lack of a feedback culture (disguised as "respect for others' autonomy") means that partners rarely get the constructive pointers they need. All too often, instead of providing direct feedback on how to improve, a partner will simply choose never to work again with a colleague who made a mistake.
- Opt-in training often captures the people who need it the least because it scoops up the believers who are already acting collaboratively.

So, what approach does work to develop and embed collaborative capabilities? We have found that the best program designs for building collaborative capabilities use ongoing, experiential learning in the context of real work. For example, this could be used with a practice group while partners are refreshing their plans for strategic client building, a sector group debating thought leadership priorities, or a key client team tailoring a new offering. All techniques should be guided by learning and development professionals, and/or external coaches who provide some formal training that builds and reinforces specific collaborative capabilities.

These initiatives run the gamut from highly ambitious to relatively simple in nature. Either way, here are a few tools that can enrich the learning experience:

- *Peer inputs.* Structured feedback from colleagues is a powerful way to gain insights into one's collaborative skills – and the work that remains to be done. The best development programs therefore incorporate colleagues' perspectives to help people understand their behavior and blind spots using tools like 360s (see below for more details).
- *Video-based feedback.* Video partners while they are engaged in collaborative group work, like developing a new pitch idea. When people see their own performance (guided by a respected coach or learning professional), they can self-diagnose issues – like how often they tend to interrupt – and are much more receptive to making changes. Provide them with a post-session, bullet-point list of behaviors they commit to improve plus access to the videos to remind themselves – in a compelling way – about changes they need to make. Schedule a three-month check-in to help them see the progress they have made toward that goal.
- *Live simulations.* Run simulations (and do not call them "role plays")

so that participants are not only exposed to concepts, but engage in actual decision-making, team launches, conflict resolution, and other key collaborative approaches. Simulations are inherently valuable (most of us would rather fly an airline where the pilots practiced using flight simulators, in addition to classroom learning).

Once again, all the approaches listed above need to sit upon a foundation of effective performance management and development. When the right recipe is achieved, it makes recruiting and fostering collaborative talent all the easier.

Stage 2: Build smarter collaboration into recruiting and interviewing
Firms spend the most time on this stage of lateral recruiting, but they often do it wrong. It's essential to screen for a candidate's collaborative capacity – that is, a candidate's skill and will to truly leverage your firm's full set of expertise in order to solve clients' most complex, high-value problems.

Use behavioral-based interviews to uncover collaborative track record
The best practice in creating interviews is to use behavioral questions, which target how someone acted in a specific situation, rather than hypothetical questions. Behavioral questions elicit a more realistic picture of candidates' problem-solving approaches and emotional intelligence – skills important for partners, business professionals, and associates alike. As the backbone of a structured interview approach, they are also helpful in overcoming implicit bias. As Iris Bohnet, Roy E. Larsen professor of public policy and behavioral economist at Harvard Kennedy School, advises, *"[Unstructured] interviews should not be your evaluation tool of choice; they are fraught with bias and irrelevant information".* [10]

The best predictor of future behavior is past behavior in similar circumstances, ideally recent ones that reflect long-standing behavior patterns.[11] Candidates are asked to describe particular situations they have faced, how they handled them, their personal emotional response, and what they learned from the experience. The objective is to break the candidate out of predictable and standard responses, allowing the interviewer to understand the candidate's behaviors and how well aligned those are to the firm's strategy, how the context shapes their actions, how reflective they are, how much credit (or blame) they give to others, and similar critical variables.

If you have used one of the many available psychometric tools with the candidate, then you will have a better understanding of them and can focus your question specifically on how they used the characteristics or attributes that the tool highlighted. This allows you to uncover their track record of collaborative client service.

For example, the Smarter Collaboration Profile[12] psychometric would indicate if someone is more comfortable focusing on highly complex problems, or they are more concrete in nature – preferring to understand how to get things done, like building action plans.

If they are highly complex, you could ask questions like:

- Share a time when you were able to develop an innovative idea that propelled your client relationship forward.
- Who did you work with?
- How did you explain the idea, especially to people who are focused more on details than the big picture?
- What resistance did you encounter and how did you get others on-board with the idea?

Conversely, you could ask a highly concrete person these kinds of questions:

- Give an example of time when you were able to take a complex or abstract idea that emerged in a client situation and translate it into a concrete action plan and then execute it.
- Who did you work with?
- What roles did you and others play?
- If you encountered roadblocks along the way, how did you resolve them?

The point is for the interviewer not to explore the result of the psychometric per se, but rather to understand a candidate's past collaborative performance – whether or not they are conscious of a specific attribute and have strong examples of constructively engaging with others (especially people who are different) to achieve better outcomes.

Each behavioral interview question should have a learning objective behind it. The question should be crafted to assess a technical, collaborative, or cultural capacity or behavior. Whoever creates the question should produce a "best practice" answer to the question with delineated criteria. Interviewers can then structure the interviews by organizing these questions into an agenda, walking through the questions with the candidate, and simultaneously scoring the candidate's answers against the "best practice" criteria. In addition to the numerical scores, firms should encourage interviewers to submit a qualitative, holistic assessment of the candidate that can be considered along with the metrics.[13]

Identify and train people to conduct behavioral-based interviews
Decades ago, when we were consultants at Bain & Company (Ivan) and McKinsey & Company (Heidi), we undertook a full day of mandatory training before we were allowed to interview candidates. Law firms must likewise equip their partners and other interviewers with the training and tools necessary to assess somebody through an interview for particular competencies (like collaboration) – a more precise process than walking away with only vague impressions of the "cultural fit".

What often happens in firms right now is that partners rely heavily on intuition, or observations of working on the opposite side of a deal from someone. They think their legal skills can be directly applied to hiring – with no training needed. As one litigator proclaimed, *"I'm brilliant at taking depositions. Obviously, I know how to ask questions! How hard can it be to interview somebody?"* But there is a real science behind the interview process, to discover how a person usually operates.

Interviewers should primarily understand not only *how* to ask behavioral questions, but also why – they are the best predictor of future performance. That said, interviewers can also surface important insights from other types of questions. This includes "case studies" where the candidate is asked to present their approach to solving a particular problem that represents the firm's typical client work.

When hiring for a specific role, you need a structured interview plan to ensure consistency, comparability, and thoroughness across interviewers. In addition to structured questions that are either standard or more customized in nature (e.g., grounded in distinct psychometric results), this plan should contain qualification scores on specific metrics, and guidelines for interview debriefs. One best practice is to submit interview data through standardized reports almost immediately after an interview. The data can be tallied and then used as the primary input for hiring. Any deviation should be examined for bias or other untoward influences.

Brief the recruiters and hold them accountable
Whether you are using an external search consultant or internal recruiters, make sure they are well briefed on your demands for collaboration and are

prepared to prescreen candidates for this quality. They must be prepared to question candidates about their teamwork experiences, both as leaders and as followers, and understand that they won't be considered strong applicants unless they have a strong collaborative track record with demonstrable outcomes. That said, recruiters must understand you are not talking about collaboration as a characteristic of being nice or collegial. This is instead about the ability to value and enlist other people's diverse views to tackle complex problems, in pursuit of shared strategic goals.

Recruiters must be able to articulate what aspects of the firm's strategy demand that people operate collaboratively. For example, if the firm is intent on pursuing prestigious global corporations and helping them resolve their most complex matters, the candidate will have to be open to collaborating not only across multiple legal disciplines and practice groups but also with colleagues from international offices. If you are hiring a candidate to serve private equity firms, they need to be comfortable not only doing deals but also seeking out colleagues across the firm who have deep industry-based knowledge – to bring specific expertise about the asset that is being acquired or disposed.

Provide recruiters with specific, successful collaboration examples they can share, and details on how collaboration will be measured and rewarded – both financially and otherwise. By being this explicit about the kind of behavior the firm is seeking, they can help the candidate understand what the role entails. This helps weed out non-collaborative candidates through self-selection – a very efficient way to weed.

Stage 3: Integrate new hires through smarter collaboration

Collaboration helps new joiners get integrated and become productive members of the firm – and ultimately thrive and stick around. But they must be integrated into the firm's core work quickly. This is a two-way street – the receiving practice group and other stakeholders must actively draw the new joiner into their projects, and that newcomer needs to actively seek ways to involve new colleagues in his or her work.

While many law firms claim to have a solid integration system, on closer inspection this typically isn't much more than an onboarding checklist.

Indicators that your integration system lacks robustness, institutionalization, and a long-term focus are shown in Table 1 overleaf (along with the opposing best practices).

Table 1: Indicators your integration system lacks robustness, institutionalization, and a long-term focus

Problem indicators	Best practice
1. It's focused on admin matters, like getting passwords and a security badge.	It's focused on bringing the lateral hire into the core, strategic work of the firm, through making the most of their unique strengths.
2. It's handled by admin staff or people in non-client-facing roles.	It's handled by client-facing leaders in the organization, including the lateral's manager.
3. It doesn't have direct client-related measurable outcomes.	It has direct client-related measurable outcomes that apply not only to the new joiner, but also the hiring partner and peers.

Source: Gardner & Co.

The following provides provides proven methods for strengthening firms' integration systems, so that lateral hires stay and thrive.

Create mutual accountability through a tailored two-way business plan and scorecards
Using the data-driven business plan created in Stage 1, work with the person that you've hired to tailor it to their specific situation. Without a concrete agreed-upon business plan with projected ROI, it is impossible to hold anyone accountable for results. Include the following items (and more) in the plan:
- Which particular clients have an identified need where the lateral's expertise will be important?
  - Which partner is responsible for introducing the newcomer to which specific person at the client?
  - When will those meetings take place?
- Which thought leadership initiatives will the lateral participate in to

build internal relationships, showcase their knowledge, and make a splash in the market?

- Who is responsible for helping the lateral build their internal network? Specifically, who does this person need to meet across offices, sectors, and practice groups? How is the lateral getting acquainted with those colleagues' work and clients such that they show up prepared to offer support in a compelling way?

The business plan should be revisited at least semi-annually, to make sure it's still aligned with firm strategy, goals, and resources.

Scorecards go hand in hand with the business plan, holding the new joiner, the hiring partner, and peers accountable for success. Base part of their performance assessment on how successfully they integrate each new joiner. Leaders must make it clear to groups that their ability to hire future laterals will depend on how successfully they integrate each newcomer.

Firms must also set expectations that the integration process will be three to four years, and create goals for what is expected to happen in each of those years. Responsible partners need to check in with the lateral hire with respect to their business plan, individual development plan, and other agreed-upon metrics at quarterly intervals to identify and remedy issues before they escalate.

Use an integration toolkit to set them up for success
In line with the business plan, managers and other "allies" can set new joiners up for success – early on – in multiple ways. Create and actively use an "integration toolkit" to systematically and effectively bring them into the firm's core client work. A collaboration-focused integration toolkit has three key elements:
1. An individual and team psychometric profile;
2. A formal team-launch workshop; and
3. Collaboration skills training.

Using a robust validated psychometric (not all of them are) will help the lateral hire understand their strengths and the composition of the team they are joining. A collaboration-focused psychometric can provide insights into one's collaborative profile, strengths, and watchout areas. Because collaboration is a team sport, it is not sufficient for the lateral to understand just their own profile.

The entire team needs to understand how the lateral's collaborative profile fits in with the group. Areas where the lateral hire is very different from the team can be a powerful complement and bring valuable perspectives to discussions. Differences can also be a source of tension if they aren't understood and valued. For instance, their new practice group may comprise only people who are highly wary – that is, people who want to see evidence of professional competence and good character before granting their trust. Likewise, the lateral hire might be highly trusting – that is, they assume competence and character and grant their trust from the beginning. The lateral hire might naturally wonder why the team is hesitant to collaborate. By understanding the team's natural wariness, the lateral can focus on how to build trust with colleagues.

Armed with an understanding of the team's profile, the group can focus on integrating the lateral hire through a formal team launch workshop. A typical workshop covers:

- Each members' expertise and client base. Teams often wrongly assume that the group, especially the more tenured members, knows everyone's background and expertise when in reality they might be familiar with the latest few projects someone has worked on at best.
- Opportunities for collaboration with the lateral hire – client work, client development, thought leadership, etc.

Assuming the organization is regularly hiring laterals, these workshops will be held frequently and therefore warrant investing in developing materials to lead them consistently.

Orient new joiners on the key principles of smarter collaboration, ideally using a self-guided learning platform that is scalable and dynamic (refreshed periodically to align with both latest research and the firm's evolving strategy). Foundational elements include the business and talent case for collaboration,[14] understanding how to use one's collaborative profile for gaining influence without authority, and developing a personal "business case", which clarifies how their own work contributes to larger goals.

Conduct data-based check-ins

Leaders must measure each lateral's integration progress from day one. Financial results (such as revenue from new client matters) are a "lagging indicator" – that is, they take time to emerge. It is therefore essential to measure some "leading indicators" to show whether the new joiner is on track, developing relationships and engaging in collaborative ways to become integrated and successful. For example, how many partners have used the newcomer's expertise to develop joint pitches or to create new IP such as white papers?

When partners do create these opportunities, celebrate them across the firm. Recognition for good behavior not only encourages more partners to engage in it, but also helps to spread the newcomer's reputation as a collaborative, value-adding asset within the firm.

Using a formal feedback process is also critical. For example, use a structured 360 feedback tool (like the Smarter Collaboration 360)[15] to do a self-assessment, plus receive inputs from several colleagues specifically about how well they are engaging. Use a 360 tool that is tailored to show people their strengths and growth opportunities so that they can quickly course-correct. These behaviors are particularly relevant for new joiners:

- *Articulates the value they bring in a clear, compelling way*. To gain the trust of other partners, a new joiner needs to succinctly communicate their unique expertise and perspective – at the right moments.
- *Works effectively in teams, even under pressure*. Trust is further enhanced by a new joiner collaborating successfully during times of stress, leading to high-value referrals and invitations to join client teams earlier on.
- *Encourages debate to surface different perspectives*. A newcomer who is comfortable with varying views not only will be pulled onto important projects sooner, but also will develop a network of eager contributors more quickly.

Results of the 360 will provide firm leaders with evidence for understanding each lateral's current level of integration. Crucially, these interim behavioral assessments should be used for coaching and development, not as inputs to anyone's performance assessment – otherwise, it is too likely that neither the lateral nor the raters will be completely honest in their assessment.

We recommend that a firm deploy this feedback process at the three-month stage to get very early warning signals. One advantage of a collaboration-focused 360 in particular is its focus specifically on behaviors that underpin collaboration, rather than more general ways of acting that might not be evident so early after joining. Re-running the process (it takes only about ten minutes to complete the survey) six months later shows important trends.

To supplement it, we recommend using a regular pulse survey (just three or so questions) to get the individual's input on how things are progressing. For example, a monthly pulse check may indicate that their colleague is micromanaging a team, and as a result, they don't feel empowered. Or they might share a feeling of being pulled in too many directions. These can serve as early warning signs and calls to action for specific changes – to ensure the new hire is integrated and thriving in their new role.

Another way to gauge a new hire's sentiment and integration is through analyzing communications within the company. Digital workplace platforms (Microsoft Teams, Slack, Symphony), email, and calendars contain extensive data on who is communicating or meeting with whom, and how often. We can see how many "communities" a person is engaged in. How often are they reaching out to the broader organization, and how extensively do their peers respond? How frequently are others reaching out to them? Not only is this data powerful for integrating new hires, it can also be used for analyzing inclusivity. By using technology to analyze collaboration almost in real time, firms can flag emerging problems of exclusion before they escalate.

Conclusion

In today's competitive marketplace, your firm's ability to attract, integrate, and ultimately retain lateral hires is critical. To retain your expensive lateral hires, ensure their productivity, and ultimately enhance your firm's viability, analyze your current efforts using the three-stage, collaboration-focused process outlined above. Then recalibrate and build your program to incorporate the best practices that align with your firm's strategic objectives. The firms that get it right – that is, those that discover the talent mix that is aligned with the overall firm strategy and develop an effective plan to locate, lure, and lock in that talent – will emerge the victors.

References

1   Groysberg, B. and Abrahams, R., "Lift Outs: How to Acquire a High Functioning Team", *Harvard Business Review*, December 2006.

2   Boushey, Heather & Glynn, Sarah James, Cost of losing talent, Center American Progress, 2012.

3   The Law Society (UK), Private Practice Solicitor Salaries 2016; Jonathan Prynn, Average pay for top partners at London law firm Linklaters smashes £1.5 million, *London Evening Standard*, 30 June 2017.

4   www.nytimes.com/2024/07/01/business/law-firm-pay-salary.html

5   Gardner, H.K. and Matviak, I. (2022) *Smarter collaboration: a new approach to*

breaking barriers and transforming work. Boston, Massachusetts: Harvard Business Review Press; Gardner, H.K. and Gillespie, A.E. (2018) *Smart collaboration for lateral hiring: successful strategies to recruit and integrate laterals in law firms*. Woking, United Kingdom: Globe Law and Business; and Gardner, H.K. (2017) *Smart collaboration: how professionals and their firms succeed by breaking down silos*. Boston, Massachusetts: Harvard Business Review Press.

6   For empirical results showing the effects of smarter collaboration on business and talent performance, see *Smarter Collaboration: A New Approach to Breaking Down Barriers and Transforming Work*; "By Failing to Collaborate, Law Firms Are Leaving Money on the Table", American Lawyer, www.law.com/americanlawyer/2018/10/04/by-failing-to-collaborate-law-firms-are-leaving-money-on-the-table/; and "When and Why Clients Want You to Collaborate", American Lawyer, www.law.com/americanlawyer/almID/1202757856001/

7   www.law.com/americanlawyer/2019/02/11/integrating-lateral-hires-the-key-to-retention-and-productivity/

8   Gardner, H.K. and Matviak, I. (2022) "Performance management shouldn't kill collaboration", *Harvard Business Review*. https://hbr.org/2022/09/performance-management-shouldnt-kill-collaboration.

9   Gardner, H.K. (2024) "Do you measure up? Equipping leaders to promote smarter collaboration", *Modern Lawyer*. https://globelawonline.com/article/730/do-you-measure-up-equipping-leaders-to-promote-smarter-collaboration

10 Iris Bohnet, "How to Take the Bias Out of Interviews", *Harvard Business Review*, 18 April 2016, https://hbr.org/2016/04/how-to-take-the-bias-out-of-interviews.

11 https://psycnet.apa.org/record/2004-19200-006

12 www.gardnerandco.co/insights/smarter-collaboration/

13 How to Improve the Accuracy and Reduce the Cost of Personnel Selection, *California Management Review*, https://journals.sagepub.com/doi/abs/10.1177/0008125617725288?journalCode=cmra

14 Gardner, H.K. and Matviak, I. (2020) "Implementing a Smart Collaboration Strategy, Part 1: Building the Case for Change", Harvard Law School, https://clp.law.harvard.edu/wp-content/uploads/2022/10/Gardner-Matviak_Implementing-a-Smart-Collab-Strategy_Part-1.pdf

15 www.gardnerandco.co/insights/smarter-collaboration/

Chapter 4:
Producer-Manager-Leader-Owner – how partners can tackle a changing landscape

By Joel Barolsky, principal, Edge International, and founder, Barolsky Advisors

Bob Andersen is a hands-on, high-billing, star partner at the Cambridge Consulting Group. He also has deteriorating relationships with his fellow partners, his team members, and his family. Anyone who has been through Harvard Business School's Leading Professional Services program knows Bob well.[1] The Cambridge Consulting Group case study is used to illustrate the tensions in the role of partner in being both a successful "producer" and busy "manager". The producer builds client relationships, wins new business, and is hands-on in delivering projects. The manager recruits and supervises team members and oversees operations.

The Harvard faculty makes much of the producer-manager concept in distinguishing professional service firms (PSFs) from other types of organizations. It states that in most non-PSFs, like major corporations and government agencies, the senior people are full-time managers and do little or no producing. To illustrate, it claims (correctly) that you typically would not find top-level executives of a large agricultural business spending their days milking cows.

From a law firm partner performance management perspective, the terms "producer" and "manager" are somewhat limiting. The role of partner in the modern law firm is much more nuanced, and as discussed in detail later in this chapter, it will become more complex and demanding as the legal landscape shifts.

A better shorthand description of the role of a law firm partner is that of a Producer-Manager-Leader-Owner (see Figure 1). Each partner's performance expectations should be orientated around all four dimensions, not just one or two. The roles are complementary but also conflict with each other, especially when it comes to allocating time and focusing energy.

Figure 1: The four key roles of a law firm partner.

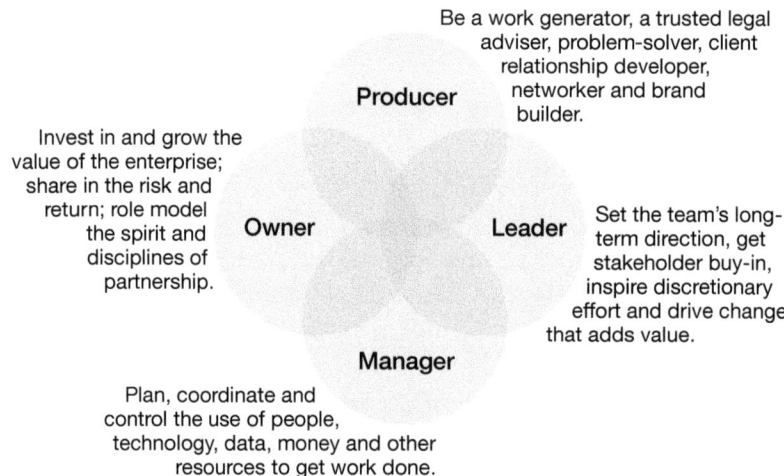

Producer

Be a work generator, a trusted legal adviser, problem-solver, client relationship developer, networker and brand builder.

Owner

Invest in and grow the value of the enterprise; share in the risk and return; role model the spirit and disciplines of partnership.

Leader

Set the team's long-term direction, get stakeholder buy-in, inspire discretionary effort and drive change that adds value.

Manager

Plan, coordinate and control the use of people, technology, data, money and other resources to get work done.

The performance management system that is set up needs to address the firm's and the individual's needs, both now and in the future. The system needs to be adaptive to take account of the many market-related changes at play, some of which are known and predictable, but many others remain quite uncertain.

This chapter explores many of the external forces that are likely to impact the partner role over the next decade. These externalities will obviously vary from firm to firm and from market to market, but the analysis is useful to fully understand the breadth and complexity of partner performance management in the years ahead. We'll look at these forces throughout the chapter from the lens of partner performance in terms of the four roles of producer, manager and leader, and owner.

Partners as producers
Looking out over the next decade, the challenges ahead for partners as producers fall broadly into two broad categories – client demands and competitor pressures.

Client demands
The biggest structural change in the legal market over the past 30 years has

been the growth of the in-house legal function. In 2022, 29 percent of all practicing solicitors in Australia worked in in-house roles for corporations and government agencies.[2] This same percentage was estimated to be less than five percent in 1990.

The growth of these roles has meant that some of the work that was previously briefed to outside counsel has been "in-sourced", consequently reducing the demand for private law firms. This trend has meant that law firm partners are now dealing with buyers who are legally trained and, quite often, former senior practitioners in top law firms. In addition, many larger client organizations involve their procurement functions in legal panel appointments and price negotiations for major matters.

Due to all these factors, buyers of legal services in mid-sized and larger organizations have generally become much more sophisticated, discerning, and demanding. Client expectations have risen and will keep getting higher. Partners, as producers, cannot rest on their laurels and will have to continuously seek to improve their clients' perceptions of the service experience, the depth of their legal specialization, the commerciality of their advice, cost-consciousness, and overall value.

It is worth noting that there is likely to be a slow trickle back to private law firms from senior in-house roles over the next few years. The pendulum won't swing completely the other way, but law firms now mirror many of the advantages that in-house roles have had in the past. This includes more flexible work arrangements, comparable workloads, and better diversity and inclusion practices. Private firms are also outpacing in-house in investing in new legal technology, and many (not all) offer better income opportunities.

Over the next decade, law firm partners will also need to become much more sensitive to demands in the environment, social, and governance (ESG) space. At a base level, this means compliance with minimum standards, but in some instances, clients and staff will ask for firms to be proactive advocates for social change. Some partners may be forced to decline certain matters for the firm to retain its "social license" or to maintain its brand position. In Australia, Corrs Chambers Westgarth had to cope with front-page headlines[3] for three months as it tried to deal with the fallout from asking some of its partners to decline to assist the Catholic Church in childhood abuse claims.

Competitor pressures

The late Alan Hodgart, a leading UK-based law firm consultant, introduced a strategic model that mapped the competitive landscape in most mature legal markets (see Figure 2). The Hodgart model highlights four broad types of legal work ranging from scarcer, price-insensitive, high-value BTC (Bet-The-Company) and CYB (Cover-Your-Back) work, and more abundant low-value work types, Operational and Commodity. It identifies four sustainable strategic groups – Full-service transaction-driven firms, Full-service business law firms, Specialist or Focus firms, and Commodity specialists. Hodgart argued that those firms in the last group, the Undifferentiated generalists, are unsustainable over time.

Figure 2: The Hodgart model of market competition.

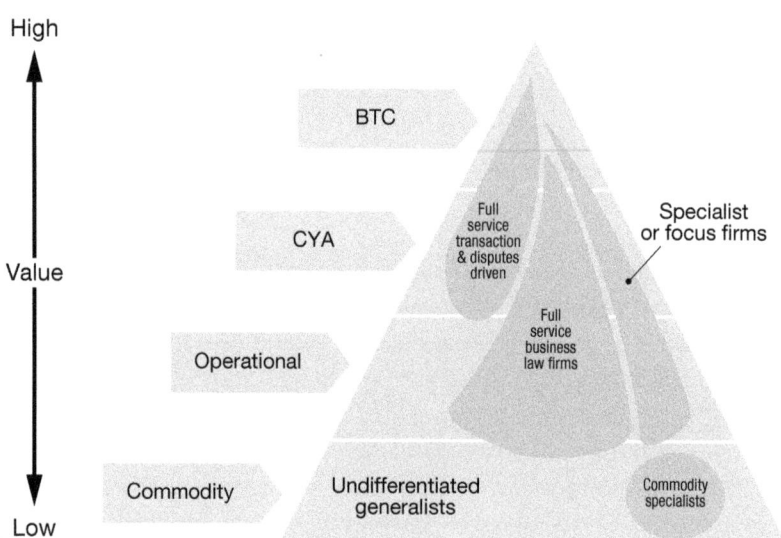

Applying this model, partners as producers will face different types of competitive pressures depending on three factors:

- The nature of the work they are primarily contesting – BTC, CYB, Operational, or Commodity.
- The strategic group and competitive position of their host firm – the firm might be a clear market leader, a challenger, an aspirant, or a laggard.
- The capability and personal brand of the individual partner and their team.

For example, an early career partner in an Undifferentiated generalist firm seeking to do high-end Bet-the-Company work will most likely have a tough road ahead, given the plethora of formidable competitors contesting the same space. In contrast, it will be an easier path ahead for a senior Commodity specialist partner leading a team with a dominant market share and a fine-tuned delivery model. Assessing individual partner performance needs to consider this competitive context.

In the Commodity specialist space, the decade ahead will continue to see some new entrants and growth of the incumbents. This growth will be driven by three factors – step improvements in enabling technology, increased client demand for routine regulatory compliance work, and premium-priced law firms shedding lower value commoditizing work to focus on specialisms. As these firms become more accomplished in global service delivery and develop deeper expertise, they are also likely to seek to move up the value curve and compete for some Operational and CYB work. The 2023 Thompson Reuters report into Alternative Legal Service Providers[4] revealed ALSPs as having aggregate revenue of $US20.6 billion and a compounded annual growth rate (CAGR) of 20 percent from 2019 to 2022.

Much has been written[5] about the entry of Big Four accounting and consulting firms into the legal market. The Australian experience is that these large multi-disciplinary PSFs have struggled to create a foothold. Firstly, they have been hamstrung by commercial and legal conflicts. Second, they have been unable to attract a critical mass of heavy-hitting partners from Tier 1 firms. And lastly, sophisticated clients don't place much value on a one-stop-shop proposition and prefer a "horses-for-courses" approach when it comes to their most critical matters.

Producer bias

From a performance management perspective, firms should ensure that partners don't spend an inordinate amount of time and energy on just winning and doing legal work at the expense of the other roles, such as Manager, Leader, and Owner. This phenomenon is known as Producer bias and is a common challenge, especially in early-career partners.

There are several personal and cultural reasons for Producer bias:

- Professionals become professionals to practice, solve client problems, and master their craft. In other words, to produce.
- Producers get quick and visible results, while managers see results gradually, and progress is often vague and ambiguous.

- The producer's task is intellectually challenging. Managers deal with complicated, intangible, and frustrating people problems.
- Production sustains credibility with other professionals and clients.
- Production keeps people in the know, in the market, and close to clients.
- Production is often what really counts in career advancement.

Production bias can mean that, as managers, partners risk not attracting and retaining good people. As leaders, there is a greater likelihood they will not focus on long-term strategy and innovation. As owners, a production bias may limit the opportunity to connect with and earn the trust of their peers.

The counterweight to these risks is that partners still need to produce. Most clients demand partner input on their matters and for partners to be immediately accessible. Partners also must ensure that all legal advice and other output is produced without errors and meets client expectations. Like most things, it's about achieving the right balance across the four roles.

Partners as managers

The second key role of partners is as managers. A core component of this role is attracting, retaining, and developing good people. Having good people means the practice can deliver the service at the required standards and be profitable and sustainable.

Looking ahead, there are four main external challenges likely to impact a partner's performance as a manager:

- Winning the war for talent.
- Coping with diverse multi-generational teams.
- Working with a flexible operating model.
- Embracing new technologies like Generative AI.

Winning the war for talent

The labor supply chain in the UK, US, and Australian legal markets works in a similar way. It starts with law schools that produce an abundance of graduates. A relatively small percentage of these graduates enter the private law firm apprenticeship system. Each law firm recruits and trains a set number of graduates that they imagine will meet their firm's future requirements. In aggregate, this is way less than the total market demands because a significant proportion of the trainees (over 50 percent in Australia) leave legal practice after a few years. This attrition then results in a major shortage in the three- to eight-year PQE cohort, which in turn drives up salary costs and makes it much harder to find and retain good people.

The future doesn't look any brighter. While it might ebb and flow, the war for top talent will continue.

In this context, it follows that partners as managers should be judged on their ability to attract, retain, and engage their team members. The evidence suggests good people will stay on when:

- They are paid fairly.
- Their manager is respectful and supportive.
- Their manager lives up to their expectations regarding career development, learning, and ongoing feedback.
- Their manager sets and expects high standards from everyone.
- Their manager doesn't foster a "dog-eat-dog" highly politicized team sub-culture.
- Their manager embraces change and improvement.

The firm should have an active performance management approach that helps partners develop these skills and behaviors. "Sink or swim" worked in some instances a decade or two ago, but it is a risky and insensitive way to help partners succeed in an environment where the war for talent is as fierce as ever.

Active support for partners would include a combination of formal training, self-assessment diagnostics, personalized coaching, and ongoing feedback from superiors, peers, and team members. The firm should also ensure the overall practice management system supports, rather than hinders, the desired outcomes. Key elements of the overall system often include measurement, reward, practice resources, workflow design, and technology.

Coping with diverse multi-generational teams

The legal team of the future is likely to be even more diverse than the present in terms of age profile, gender identity, ethnicity, and race. Diversity is an asset, but it also brings some degree of managerial complexity. For example, each generational group has its own idiosyncrasies, communication preferences, and expectations. Managers need to be able to be sensitive to these differences and play to people's strengths, but at the same time, treat everyone equitably and consistently.

For example, in introducing a new practice management system, Gen Z and Gen Y team members might feel very comfortable using the new software and pick it up very quickly but perhaps be less inclined to follow all the protocols, i.e. seek more independence or agency. Gen X and Baby Boomers, on the other hand, might struggle to learn to use this new tool but are happy to comply with all requirements. Partners as team managers need to be given clear guidance and support on handling these differences to ensure the new practice management system is implemented successfully and consistently.

Working with a flexible operating model

COVID-19 restrictions in 2020 and 2021 resulted in most law firms jumping to a full-time work-from-home operating model. To the surprise of many, efficiency and productivity over that period did not decrease. In the post-COVID era, many legal teams have returned to a model with some flexible working options. These might be set days per week working out of the office, different start and end times, or other hybrid working arrangements.

Many firms have now locked in a flexible or agile operating model by redesigning their offices with reduced floor space and below full capacity, i.e. it is impossible for everyone to physically work in the office simultaneously.

It appears that flexibility will continue to be a feature of the legal workplace of the future.

Managing a flexible hybrid team has some additional challenges over and above an "all-present" model. Even simple tasks like ensuring everyone has a desk on all-in-office days will take longer. Optimizing work allocation is trickier in a hybrid model. There is no doubt that fostering a deeply collaborative team culture with a dispersed team is a tougher job than with everyone co-located.

Team managers need to be supported with the right training and feedback to limit any proximity bias and be more deliberate in engaging with people who work remotely. They need tools to ensure full visibility of who is doing what and be able to connect with every team member without delays or drop-outs. Managers also benefit from better workload planning and work allocation systems. For example, Allens,[6] one of Australia's leading law firms, uses the Trello Kanban system to track all matters across all operators in real time, regardless of where they work.

Embracing new technologies like Generative AI

In modern legal practice, most managers use "non-people" resources like data and specialized legal technology to accomplish tasks. This technology is advancing rapidly and promises to change many core activities like document review, legal research, summarization, legal analysis, and document preparation. In May 2023, Stanford Law School's Codex Index[7] revealed that there were over 2,370 legal technology companies operating across the globe. Ten years prior there were fewer than 230.

The most likely outcome of this digital revolution is that in high-volume, more commoditized legal practices, the technology will displace the work traditionally done by junior lawyers. In more specialized and bespoke practices, the new technology will enable all team members to be far more efficient.

One consequence of these advancements is that partners as managers must learn the basics of workflow and service design. They need to be comfortable in planning and implementing technology-driven change and have the smarts to price and position the service so the practice remains profitable. While partners may draw on the expertise of the firm's legal operations and pricing experts, they will need a base level of knowledge to co-create these new ways of working.

Let's look a one simple example to illustrate this point. Australian law firm Wotton + Kearney is experimenting with the idea of capturing value for the use of its Generative AI software by charging clients for an "AI hour". This is a timekeeping unit for the time it takes the AI to assist. The AI hour can be easily integrated into the established time-based operating and billing processes and be quite easily understood and used by partners and by clients.

Partners as leaders

As leaders, partners need to ensure "strategic alignment" across their practice, both now and into the future. The Chorn Model (see Figure 3) suggests sustained success comes from a good fit or alignment of the marketplace, strategy, culture, and leadership.

The model posits that there are three potential misalignment gaps or indicators where a practice might have some vulnerability:

GAP 1: The practice doesn't have a winning game plan. For example, the team's aspirations, capabilities, and reputation don't address the reality of key clients already wedded to many stronger competitors.

GAP 2: The team's culture doesn't fit the strategy. For example, the practice seeks to compete on being at the cutting edge of process and service innovation, but the culture is oriented around black letter lawyering.

GAP 3: The team's leadership style and capability don't engender the desired culture. For example, the team seeks a client-centric service culture, but the leaders are unwilling to hold everyone accountable for agreed client service standards.

Figure 3: Chorn Model of Strategic Alignment.[8]

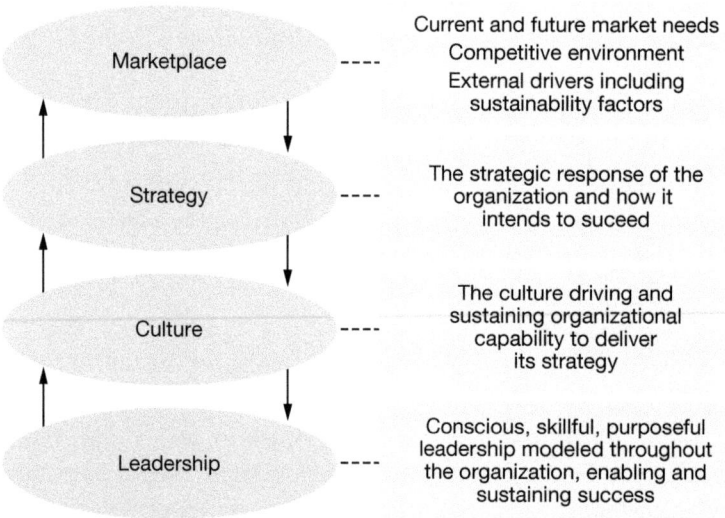

Strategic alignment is more difficult if the market is changing rapidly. A stable and predictable competitive environment allows leaders time to plan and fine-tune their strategy and culture. It also gives leaders a longer time frame to develop the requisite leadership skills and style.

Cultural alignment is also made more difficult if the practice has high staff turnover or frequent shocks to the operating model.

All indications are that the next decade will see accelerated change in the business and practice of law, largely driven by globalization, technological advances and the ongoing war for top talent.

From a performance management perspective, partners should be expected to finesse their practice so that it's strategically aligned. While it is difficult to formulate "hard" performance indicators to quantify strategy alignment, there are some proxy measures worth considering:

GAP 1: Practice revenue and profit growth. Market standing or brand position. Client satisfaction and advocacy, e.g. Net Promoter Score.

GAP 2: Staff engagement. Staff turnover. Employee Net Promoter Score.

GAP 3: 360 feedback. Self-assessment on leadership attributes.

Partners as owners

The base-level expectations of partners as owners usually include:

- Show up to firm events and key meetings.
- Contribute to firm strategy formulation.
- Communicate strategy and provide upward feedback.
- Provide input to major strategic projects.
- Share clients and connections.
- Help capture and leverage the firm's IP.
- Represent the firm externally – be a brand ambassador.
- Guard the firm's assets and financial interests.

Looking ahead, these roles and expectations are unlikely to change much.

One important dimension that is likely to shift in the years ahead is equity participation, particularly in the UK and Australian legal markets. The indications are that it will get tougher for partners to get equity and hold onto it. In the UK, leading American firms with "eat-what-you-kill" remuneration models are attracting top rainmakers from more traditional lockstep and hybrid firms. In Australia, top-end disrupters like Corrs Chambers Westgarth are having a similar impact. These competitive forces are putting pressure on all firms to lift their profit per equity partner performance and be "stingier" in offering equity.

Some firms are attempting to deal with this challenge by widening the ends of their profit bands – the top performers earn more, and the bottom earn less. This approach can work in the short-term, but if, over time, the rump in the middle earns, on average, substantially less than their peers, the firm will find it hard to hold onto their rising stars or attract new ones.

With equity harder to get, it seems as if the expectations around financial contributions are increasing and are unlikely to taper off.

Conclusions

For the sake of analysis, we have sought to discuss each of the four roles – the Producer, Manager, Leader, and Owner – individually. In reality, these are highly interrelated and interdependent. Looking at the partner role as a whole, we see complexity and ambiguity. When we take all the current trends and future developments, we see even more complexity.

Law firm leaders must be fully prepared for this challenge and craft a performance management approach that meets their partners' current needs but is also adaptive to change. Many things are coming down the pike that we can plan for, but there's a lot we can't foresee. Change is the only certainty. We need a system designed to flex and give partners the best chance of success – now and for the foreseeable future.

References

1   Harvard Business School: Cambridge Consulting Group, Bob Anderson case study, www.hbs.edu/faculty/Pages/item.aspx?num=16719

2   Law Society, 2022 Annual Profile of Solicitors NSW, www.lawsociety.com.au/sites/default/files/2023-06/2022%20Annual%20Profile%20of%20Solicitors%20in%20NSW%20-%20Final.pdf

3   www.afr.com/companies/professional-services/why-corrs-dropped-the-catholic-church-as-a-client-20220726-p5b4k6

4   www.thomsonreuters.com/en-us/posts/legal/alsp-report-2023/

5   www.lawgazette.co.uk/practice/big-four-increasing-share-of-legal-market/5115164.article

6   www.allens.com.au/insights-news/insights/2022/03/survive-and-thrive-using-tech-to-your-advantage/

7   http://techindex.law.stanford.edu

8   www.prescience.eu.com/success-is-for-those-who-seek-guidance/

Chapter 5:
The role of wellbeing in promoting performance

Bree Buchanan, JD, co-founder, Institute for Well-Being in Law and senior advisor, Krill Strategies, LLC

Introduction

In just the last decade, multiple studies have verified what we in the legal profession have known intuitively since stepping into the world of law – that the legal profession can be hazardous to our health. In particular, years of practice take their toll on our mental health, resulting in rates of depression, anxiety, and burnout that far exceed those in other professions and that of the general public. The difficult and often painful feelings arising from those conditions engender self-medication with alcohol and other substances that create the conditions for the onset of substance use disorders and addiction. While we have suspected these dangers for a long time, current research set out in the following section shows that behavioral health problems are impacting a significant percentage of members of the legal profession.

Law firm partners are best situated to deploy strategies that prevent behavioral health disorders, promote wellbeing, and enable members of the firm to seek help where needed. To provide context, this chapter begins with a global review of foundational studies that lays out the current state of knowledge regarding the prevalence of depression, anxiety, burnout, and substance misuse that plagues our profession. Next, the way these issues affect performance, unwanted attrition, and profitability are set out. Most importantly, the chapter will conclude with pragmatic strategies for partners to support individuals in the firm, as well as to become catalysts for effectively modifying systems, practices, and law firm culture that will support all members of the workplace.

Partners are best positioned to create the pervasive cultural change necessary to make the profession one that is more humane and less damaging to its members' health. Educational programming for legal professionals (which encompasses most of the current efforts to reduce ill mental health) and other strategies that place all responsibility on these individuals for fixing the "mental health crisis in the legal profession" will inevitably fall short of the goal. Only those who enjoy the privilege (and burden) of leadership possess the authority to mitigate the detrimental behavioral health effects imposed by our profession.

Behavioral health of the legal profession across the globe

Undoubtedly, a "wellbeing in law" movement has begun and is gathering steam as jurisdictions around the globe embark upon efforts to ensure lawyers' abilities to function at their very best, as well as to preserve the public's trust in the legal system. This section sets out foundational studies from multiple jurisdictions in order to provide the most current information related to the behavioral health of our world's legal professionals.

Australia

Australia was the first country to engage in and publish significant research regarding the levels of behavioral health issues affecting the legal profession. A 2009 study[1] of just under 1,700 legal professionals (barristers and solicitors) found that 62 percent of solicitors and 44 percent of barristers experienced significant levels of psychological distress compared with 37 percent of the population. A 2014 study[2] of 384 employed lawyers revealed 37 percent of respondents experienced moderate to extremely severe depressive symptoms and 31 percent experienced the same level of symptoms for anxiety. A questionnaire regarding the rate of alcohol consumption showed that 35 percent of respondents were drinking at a hazardous level. The eye-opening rates of behavioral health concerns revealed in these studies served as catalysts to the wellbeing in law movement that began to take hold in North America and the UK in the mid-2010s.

United States

Until the mid-teens, the US lacked solid statistical evidence of the prevalence of behavioral health issues. The first of a series of well-designed foundational studies conducted with a large population sample was published in 2016. In the study of 13,000 lawyers,[3] the profession was put on notice that 28 percent of its members were struggling with depression, over three times the rate of the general population. Over 36 percent were drinking in a manner consistent with "hazardous drinking or possible alcohol abuse of dependence", again at a rate of over three times the US population. This study also revealed the incidence of these conditions were consistently highest among the youngest members of the profession, a finding consistently echoed by later studies in the US and globally.

Another large study[4] conducted in 2021 by the same researchers, confirmed the high rates of hazardous drinking and revealed a gender disparity in this trend. Of the female respondents, 34 percent screened positive for hazardous drinking while male respondents showed a rate of 25 percent. Over one-third of test-takers reported that their drinking had increased during the pandemic. When asked diagnostic questions related to depression, 19 percent of women and 14 percent of men reported moderate to moderately severe depression. One finding – that lawyers with high stress were 22 more times likely to consider suicide than those with low stress – gave insight into the potentially deadly nature of lawyers' chronically elevated levels of stress.

At the time of writing, the most recent window into the wellbeing of the US legal profession is given by ALM's Mental Health Survey of the Legal Profession[5] (published in 2024), which annually collects data points that reveal behavioral health trends. In response to the question, "Do you feel depressed?" just over one-third indicated that they did, a slight rise over pre-pandemic levels of 31 percent. In answering a similar question regarding anxiety, a little over 70 percent responded positively.

In 2023, ALM's researchers started asking whether test takers were experiencing "physical and mental overwhelm and fatigue" (a strong indicator of burnout and a precipitator of more serious behavioral health issues), with two-thirds replying "yes". Regarding feelings of loneliness – another powerful driver of ill health – just over one-third replied that they did feel detached and alone in the world. Disturbingly, 20 percent reported feeling a sense of hopelessness about their future.

United Kingdom
The most significant study in the UK[6] was conducted from 2020-2021 and involved 1,713 legal professionals. Respondents were simply asked if they had experienced issues related to behavioral health in the last 12 months. Their responses categorized as "very often" to "all the time" for depression were 16 percent, and for anxiety were 39 percent. The average score for burnout was 42 with 35 being the cutoff for "high risk of burnout". Researchers also noted a high correlation between those experiencing burnout and those getting fewer than seven hours of sleep per night. When inquiring as to alcohol consumption, over one-quarter responded that they were having three or more drinks per night.

Canada

In 2021, data was collected from 7,300 participants who represented all members of the Canadian legal system (lawyers, Ontario paralegals, articling students, Quebec notaries). This national study[7] estimated that psychological distress (an unpleasant psychological state that is not attributed to a specific pathology) was at 57 percent for all lawyers. Groups in which both depressive and anxiety symptoms are at the highest included legal professionals with fewer than ten years of professional experience and with legal professionals under 40 years of age. Those with the highest proportions of suicidal ideation were among those lawyers most isolated (professionals working in the Canadian territories) at a rate of 29.7 percent, all lawyers (24.4 percent), and those legal professionals who identify as non-binary (61.9 percent). These results came from Phase One of the study, with Phase Two to be conducted later in 2024.

International

In 2020, the International Bar Association (IBA) administered the first-ever global survey of 3,256 participants from 124 jurisdictions, the findings of which were reported in *Mental Wellbeing in the Legal Profession: A Global Report*.[8] Using the World Health Organization's measure of mental wellbeing in which a score below 52 percent is an indicator of the need for a profession-ally administered screen for depression, researchers found that the average overall score of respondents was 51 percent. Over one-third of respondents indicated that their work had a negative or extremely negative impact on their mental wellbeing. Findings also showed that respondents in law firms of 51-100 employees experienced the most detrimental effects (44 percent), with associates (46 percent) and paralegals (39 percent) being the specific roles most negatively affected. The most consistent and marked differences in wellbeing appear to be based upon age, gender, disability, and ethnicity, which suggests a probable connection between problems with equality, diversity, and inclusion, and poor mental wellbeing. Finally, the survey showed the impact of ignoring mental health issues on productivity (and, hence, profitability) with 46 percent of respondents considering time off, 26 percent making mistakes, and 32 percent feeling unable to perform.

Making the business case for greater wellbeing in the profession

Although the law was once considered a "noble profession", we have undoubtedly moved to an era in which the legal profession is a business, one that is driven by the pursuit of profits. While strong humanitarian and ethical reasons exist for why the wellbeing of its members should be made a priority, these arguments have failed to move law firms to make meaningful changes. Consequently, a more persuasive argument[9] for changing the business of law lies in the profound effect that wellbeing can have on the bottom line. Researchers have long shown that unwell and unhappy workforces underperform, burnout, and leave their jobs at accelerated rates. Conversely, lawyer wellbeing is a form of human capital that provides a competitive advantage.

Lawyers, particularly those of the Gen Z and Millennial generations who prioritize mental health and wellbeing, are drawn to workplaces where their humanity is respected. When work demands far exceed the ability to tend to any part of their lives outside of work, these legal professionals often "vote with their feet" and move to employers who offer the promise of greater work–life balance. Although the law firm model is built upon recruitment of large associate cohorts that are intentionally whittled down over their early years, *unwanted* attrition costs dearly. According to one estimate,[10] the cost of replacing a departing associate ranges from $200k to $500k, or roughly one-and-a-half to two times the lawyer's annual salary. These figures do not account for the implicit cost of turnover that includes lost productivity and opportunity costs covering the work of the departed lawyer, and disrupted intrafirm and client relationships. Aside from unwanted attrition, the ability to onboard the most highly prized associates and laterals will likely be impacted for those firms who fail to prioritize the wellbeing of their people.

Lowered productivity caused by poor behavioral health also cuts deeply into law firm profits. A US study published in 2015[11] showed that businesses lost $102 billion annually due to absenteeism and presenteeism caused by depression. A 2023 study by Unmind[12] (UK) of 3,800 lawyers in six large US law firms showed that law firms lose an average of ten percent – or $22 million – in staffing costs due to poor employee mental health. Studies have also shown the undeniable fact that depressed employees have trouble concentrating, difficulty in making decisions, and decreased engagement at work. These issues diminish work productivity and quality, cutting into profits while impacting client satisfaction and retention.

In addition to the negative impacts of unwanted attrition and reduced productivity, diminished wellbeing increases risk and, therefore, costs associated with operating a law firm. When a legal professional's mental health is suffering, the likelihood of costly errors increases. US organizations responsible for disciplining lawyers who run foul of ethical guidelines routinely report high levels of substance misuse and/or depression among their case-loads. In fact, research is showing that burnout is associated with dishonesty, ethical lapses, errors, and a general decline in client care. Not only do these underperforming lawyers pose a potential risk-related liability, but they are also at increased risk of violating their jurisdiction's rules of professional conduct. In the US, some states (California, Utah, Massachusetts, Vermont, and Virginia) are now linking wellbeing (and the lack thereof) directly to their rule that lawyers must provide competent representation. In effect, their new rules provide that maintaining one's wellbeing is a part of maintaining one's competence to practice.

The vital role of law firm leaders in promoting wellbeing

The behavior of partners sets the tone for the entire firm and is the most definitive influence – for ill or otherwise – on their members' quality of life. These leaders are also primarily responsible for creating the firm's culture. Because their words and deeds are scrutinized by everyone at the firm, they have an outsized role in communicating whether the firm values individual members' wellbeing or it merely values members as cogs in a billing machine. In fact, how lawyers believe they are valued by their firm is highly determinative of their overall wellbeing. In a 2020 study of 2,000 lawyers,[13] researchers conclusively found higher levels of mental health among those who worked for firms that valued their skill, professionalism, and human worth. Conversely, the lowest levels of mental health and the highest levels of stress were found among those who felt unvalued by their firm and/or who experienced little to no feedback. In all cases, firm partners were the ones primarily responsible for communicating these value judgments about employees.

The most successful lawyers rise to partner and on to firm leadership but, unfortunately, their legal education and experience in substantive law in no way prepares them for the leadership skills essential to maintaining a healthy – and wealthy – practice. As a result, firm leadership training with a focus on empathetic communication, establishing psychological safety, and effective motivation strategies is essential. Firms would also benefit from teaching partners about strategies to promote wellbeing, team building, and conflict resolution, as well as how to support the professional development of their staff. The overall wellbeing of the office will be lifted, productivity increased, and client satisfaction enhanced.

Leadership strategies for partners seeking to improve wellbeing in the workplace

Given the indispensable role that partners play in creating a workplace that prioritizes the wellbeing of its people, the following sets out a series of practical steps for making meaningful advancements in promoting wellbeing and limiting the development of behavioral health issues.

Assess how policies and practices impact wellbeing

Partners and leaderships should first make a clear-eyed assessment of how their workplaces' policies, practices, and culture play a role in defining the wellbeing of their legal professionals. Valuable questions to consider include the following.

- What behaviors are incentivized by policies and/or practices? If these incentives (compensation, increased autonomy, promotion) are encouraging unwell behavior (excessive hours, lack of sleep, increased self-medication to cope with chronic high stress), can the harm be mitigated by institutionalizing incentives for healthy behavior?
- Can some guardrails be placed on policies that promote excessive work? For example, instituting a regular review of excessive hours worked, as well as a lack of leave taken, can help identify those with work habits that are moving them towards ill health.
- How well do partners model the behavior desired of their legal professionals? Has leadership shown through their actions how they want others to act regarding their physical and emotional health?
- Is the workplace one that is psychologically safe such that employees feel they can talk about declines in mental health with their supervisor?
- If an employee is concerned about the behavioral health of a co-worker, do policies include direction on what they should do, to whom they should report their concern, and that they will be protected from retaliation?
- Are behavioral health issues ever discussed in firm communications, preferably by firm leaders? Or is the workplace one in which the stigma of these issues is so high that people are not willing to seek help when it's needed?

Institutionalize wellbeing into firm structures and culture.

While some large US firms have created a "director of wellbeing", those making a real commitment to improving the behavioral health of their staff have created a wellbeing committee. This group is ideally composed of a cross-section of employees and led (or at least overtly supported) by a firm leader or partner. In addition to sponsoring educational programming to support employees, the committee should also be consulted on firm bene-fits, policies, and practices to determine their impact on wellbeing. Additionally, this group is ideally situated to provide a review of the firm's behavioral health resources with an eye towards quality and availability of services provided, as well as the firm's utilization rates of each resource.

Another aspect of embedding wellbeing into workplace practices concerns communications from firm leadership and human resources. To signal that behavioral health is an acceptable topic of conversation and not one so stig-matized that it dares not be mentioned, it should be made a regular part of firm communications. A member of the leadership team or a partner who has had some life experience with these issues and who would be willing to share that experience can play a pivotal role in reducing the stigma attached to behavioral health disorders. Time for discussion of these topics should also be woven into standardized processes such as onboarding, in-house training, performance reviews, and exit interviews. For example, reviews could be an opportunity to talk about whether the member is thriving mentally or needs services or other support, and if they are experiencing barriers to improving their wellbeing, getting adequate rest, or having sustainable balance between their work and home lives.

Cultivate connection, high-quality relationships, and a sense of belonging. Lawyers who feel connected to their work, their employers, and their colleagues are apt to experience less stress and a greater perceived sense of wellbeing. A perceived lack of belonging (that one is not accepted, respected, or supported) is strongly correlated with depressive symptoms. Of note, those historically kept outside the profession's circles of power are often thwarted in their basic human need for inclusion, connection, and belonging, leading these individuals to experience elevated rates of behavioral health distress. Hence, efforts to promote diversity, equity, and inclusion (DEI) also have the effect of promoting the overall wellbeing of those targeted by these efforts.

Feeling isolated and disconnected at work also sets up employees for expe-riencing loneliness, a seemingly low impact but unpleasant experience that actually has profound consequences for behavioral and physical health. The first alarm was sounded in 2018 when the *Harvard Business Review* shared findings of a wide-reaching study[14] of the perceived sense of isolation and loneliness among US professionals. Lawyers were found to be the loneliest professionals, closely followed by members of other professions such as doctors and engineers. This finding was buttressed by a 2023 study by ALM,[15] which found that 45 percent of firm lawyers felt isolated at work and 35 percent felt detached and alone in the world. Also, in May of 2023, the US Surgeon General issued an alarming report[16] in which he declared a "loneliness epidemic" among the US population. In his report, Dr Murthy highlighted research showing that those experiencing unwanted disconnection from others experience a 26 percent increase in risk of early death and are twice as likely to experience depression.

Some specific strategies for partners and firm leadership seeking to reduce loneliness and disconnection can include:

- *Create and adequately support affinity and peer support groups.* Employees with common interests (e.g., the future of AI, people of color, or parents with young children) can find community and a sense of belonging, This practice is even more important for those from marginalized populations who may find supportive connections with others in the group. In doing so, they may discover means to address isolation and form meaningful relationships with those facing similar challenges.

- *Develop a strong sense of belonging among staff.* Having a deep connection to a workplace is the number one desire of employees (desired more than an increase in pay, better benefits, or a better work–life balance) and its absence is the second most often cited reason for quitting. Given its importance, surveying staff about how connection, inclusion, and belonging can be heightened is a great foundational step toward creating those conditions. Leaders should remain vigilant about creating opportunities for staff to learn about one another as people and be scrupulous about making sure everyone is included in these efforts. Some straightforward tactics to create a sense of belonging among teams or practice groups include:

  - Setting team goals and reviewing progress made toward them;
  - Soliciting, and listening to, feedback;
  - Engaging in personal or professional development training;
  - Strategizing together to help manage time and provide support to one another;
  - Encouraging equitable participation by all team members; and
  - Taking time to acknowledge one another as people with lives outside the office, as well as to celebrate personal and professional milestones and achievements.

- *Create opportunities for meaningful work.* Researchers in the 2018 Harvard Business Review study found that the single most impactful leadership behavior to counteract loneliness is to build shared meaning with colleagues. This finding is based upon the truism that people want to feel they matter and that they are part of something bigger than themselves. To achieve a widespread sense of meaning among staff, partners should ensure that staff understand the reason for a project and how it comports with the mission of the firm or the client. Communicate with team members working on a project about why the work matters to the firm, the client, and/or society. Often this means making sure people understand how a particular project affects the larger goals.

Adopt policies that promote work flexibility

Addressing work–family conflict is vital for firms concerned about the wellbeing of their lawyers as studies[17] have consistently shown that elevated work–life conflict is related to higher depression, anxiety, emotional exhaustion, illness symptoms, and alcohol misuse. This much sought-after balance is also of increasing importance to associates and – likely – the generations to follow. As evidence of this trend, 2021 research[18] into 3,700 mid-level associates at large US law firms showed that 60 percent would consider leaving their current firm for better work–life balance, while only 27 percent would leave for higher compensation. A recent ABA study[19] shows that younger generations highly value flexibility and freedom to balance their work and personal lives in a fluid manner. Additionally, these Gen Zs and Millennials look to – and expect – that their employer will support them in these efforts.

Policies to promote flexibility can include:

- Seeking input from one's practice group or team members on how they believe their work and home lives can be better balanced and conflicts reduced.
- Offering scaled hours matched to scaled compensation, while maintaining paths to leadership and equity partnership. A growing number of firms report[20] allowing reduced-hours tracks that still lead to partnership.
- Continuing to permit hybrid or remote work whenever feasible. Even as the pandemic is in our collective rear mirrors, many firms maintain hybrid workforces with lawyers and staff continuing to work remotely at least part of the time. A 2022 survey of Am Law 200 firms[21] showed that

79 percent of firms expect all or most of their workforce to be eligible for a hybrid work arrangement, and 80 percent have completed or were developing formal assessments of roles and individual workers eligible for full remote work in perpetuity. Allowing at least some telework days can help improve employee job satisfaction, whether by giving parents more family time in lieu of commute time, allowing minority lawyers a break from majority-white office environments, or simply allowing lawyers a more comfortable and safer workspace at home.

Protect people's ability to rest and disconnect.

A 2023 US survey of the legal profession[22] revealed that 88 percent of lawyer respondents got seven or fewer hours' sleep a night, which is below the minimum needed for physical and mental health, as well as for adequate functioning. Other studies[23] have shown that being awake for 24 hours puts one at the same level of cognitive ability as someone whose blood alcohol level is 0.10 percent. To avoid increased risk, errors, and poor performance, as well as decreased productivity and client satisfaction, partners, and the firm leadership must take responsibility for creating conditions under which its members can get adequate sleep. In addition, professional staff must be able to psychologically disconnect from their work. Preoccupation with work-related thoughts and work–life conflict are significant contributors to poor mental and physical health.

To ensure adequate time for rest and rejuvenation, partners should endeavor to build flexibility into time management practices. Creating a culture of respecting lawyers' personal time will require firms to communicate their philosophy with clients, while reassuring them that their needs will be met by refreshed and engaged lawyers during reasonable work hours. Even more important than clients, firm leaders and those with supervisory functions must fully buy in to the importance of placing some guardrails on expectations of around-the-clock availability. The US Bank[24] has developed best practices around this thorny topic, as has the Mindful Business Charter,[25] a corporate wellbeing pledge campaign in the UK that includes many large law firms.

Some general ideas for building more flexibility into team time-management practices include:

- Establishing norms that limit emails and calls after-hours, on weekends, and during vacations to actual emergencies.
- Clearly communicating response-time needs in emails, especially if the

sender chooses to send the email after-hours or on a weekend. When nothing is communicated, the risk is that achievement-oriented lawyers will believe that they must respond immediately and that every project is due as soon as possible.

- Specifying deadlines and expressly stating when projects are not urgent.
- Routinely consulting with affected persons (whenever possible) before setting and agreeing to deadlines.
- Designating one day each week as "meeting free" to allow for periods of uninterrupted deep focus. When possible, consider allowing a "cameras off" virtual meeting from time to time as the constant self-monitoring that occurs with cameras is the primary driver of "zoom fatigue".
- Identifying common work practices that may be at the root of significant work–life conflict and ways to improve. Examples may include "over-selling" (taking on too much work on too short of a deadline) and "over-delivery" (promising more than the client needs just to increase hours on a project or to impress the client to highlight one's exceptionalism).

Finally, partners should enable associates and professional staff to take vacations and to disconnect while on them as much as possible. To do this, partners can:

- Articulate clear expectations by creating a policy or protocol to convey expectations that lawyers who are away on vacations or medical leave should only be contacted in a real emergency (and not because it's more convenient).
- Convey supportive messages that tell associates and staff it is ok to disconnect, and that responses to emails are not expected.
- Ensure that substitutes are designated to cover for lawyers and professional staff who are away on vacation.

Actively manage the most severe threats to wellbeing.

Bullying, harassment, and incivility all pose particularly toxic threats to the wellbeing of those on the receiving end of these actions. Targets of these behaviors often experience psychological distress, burnout, and depression. In 2019, the International Bar Association conducted the largest-ever global survey[26] (7,000 respondents from 135 countries) on bullying and sexual harassment in the legal profession. It found that one in two women and one in three men had experienced bullying, while one in three women and one in 14 men had experienced sexual harassment in their legal workplace.

Researchers also reported on the great reluctance to report these behaviors due to the status of the perpetrator, fear of repercussions, and the simple fact that these behaviors are endemic to the workplace. These actions affect the bottom line of firms due to increased behavioral health concerns and attrition. The study found that 65 percent of those bullied and 37 percent of those sexually harassed had left or were actively considering leaving their workplaces.

While not as extreme, acts of incivility permeate the legal profession and include disrespectful speech or attitudes, rudeness, cutting sarcasm, and belittling of – or complete disregard for – co-workers. Partners must not turn a blind eye to these acts and the conflict it often engenders, even when engaged in by top performers. We know the ripple effects of this degradation extend far and likely last as long as the affected employees (which includes those who witnessed the acts) remain at the firm. Studies have clearly and consistently shown that such actions diminish motivation and performance, reduce productivity, discourage help-seeking by the affected individuals, and increase burnout, depression, substance misuse, and anxiety.

To stem the tide of incivility and unacceptable behavior, all partners and those in leadership positions must act as role models for respectful communication and interaction. All firms should adopt a code of conduct that prohibits harassment, bullying, and discrimination, and that establishes the process for immediately dealing with violations. Aside from codes and policies, firms should also foster a culture of teamwork, based upon mutual respect, collaboration, and open communication. In today's workplace, where psychological safety is paramount, all members should feel they can speak their mind, ask for help, and admit mistakes.

Conclusion

The wellbeing in law movement is still new and its potential for making the law a more humane profession is yet to be realized. Cross-jurisdictional guidance is still needed on law firms' duties and best practices, lawyers' and professional staff's responsibilities for their own wellbeing, and how the international legal community can positively influence workplace wellbeing. By skillfully implementing strategies set out in this chapter, partners and law firm leadership can become catalysts in making the legal profession one that is more sustainable, meaningful, and – of course – profitable.

References

1   Courting the Blues: Attitudes towards depression in Australian law students and lawyers https://law.uq.edu.au/files/32510/Courting-the-Blues.pdf

2   Australian Lawyer Well-being: Workplace Demands, Resources and the Impact of Time-billing Targets, www.tandfonline.com/doi/full/10.1080/13218719.2013.822783

3   The Prevalence of Substance Use and Other Mental Health Concerns Among American Attorneys, www.ncbi.nlm.nih.gov/pmc/articles/PMC4736291/

4   Stress, drink, leave: An examination of gender-specific risk factors for mental health problems and attrition among licensed attorneys, https://journals.plos.org/plosone/article?id=10.1371/journal.pone.0250563

5   *American Lawyer*: Mental Health by the Numbers, www.law.com/americanlawyer/2024/05/17/mental-health-by-the-numbers-the-2024-survey-infographic/

6   Law Care: Life in the Law, www.lawcare.org.uk/media/14vhquzz/lawcare-lifeinthelaw-v6-final.pdf

7   Towards a Healthy and Sustainable Practice of Law in Canada, https://flsc.ca/wp-content/uploads/2022/10/EN_Preliminary-report_Cadieux-et-al_Universite-de-Sherbrooke_FINAL.pdf

8   Mental Wellbeing in the Legal Profession: A Global Study, www.ibanet.org/document?id=IBA-report-Mental-Wellbeing-in-the-Legal-Profession-A-Global-Study

9   Capitalizing on Healthy Lawyers: The Business Case for Law Firms to Promote and Prioritize Lawyer Well-Being, https://repository.law.miami.edu/fac_articles/899/

10 Walking the Legal Tightrope: Solutions for Achieving a Balanced Life in Law, https://digital.sandiego.edu/sdlr/vol47/iss2/5/

11 The Economic Burden of Adults with Major Depressive Disorder in the United States (2019), https://link.springer.com/article/10.1007/s12325-023-02622-x

12 Unmind, the State of Law in 2023, https://unmind.com/handbooks/the-state-of-wellbeing-in-law

13 People, Professionals, and Profit Centers: The Connection between Lawyer Well-Being and Employer Values, www.mdpi.com/2076-328X/12/6/177

14 Employees Are Lonelier Than Ever. Here's How Employers Can Help, https://hbr.org/2021/06/employees-are-lonelier-than-ever-heres-how-employers-can-help

15 www.law.com/americanlawyer/2023/05/18/mental-health-by-the-numbers-an-infographic-mapping-the-legal-industrys-wellbeing/

16 Our Epidemic of Loneliness and Isolation, www.hhs.gov/sites/default/files/surgeon-general-social-connection-advisory.pdf

17 Not Able to Lead a Healthy Life When You Need It Most: Dual Role of Lifestyle Behaviors in the Association of Blurred Work-Life Boundaries With Well-Being, www.ncbi.nlm.nih.gov/pmc/articles/PMC7786197/

18 Midlevel associates rated these firms tops for job satisfaction; survey finds hybrid work preference, www.abajournal.com/news/article/midlevel-associates-rated-these-firms-tops-for-job-satisfaction-survey-finds-hybrid-work-preference

19   2022 Practice Forward Report: Where Does the Legal Profession go From Here?
     www.americanbar.org/content/dam/aba/administrative/law-practice-
     division/practice-forward/2022-practice-forward-report.pdf

20   Some Big Law Firms are Giving Part-Time Associates a Path Forward to Partnership,
     www.law.com/therecorder/2021/10/25/some-big-law-firms-are-giving-part-time-
     associates-a-path-forward-to-partnership/

21   Major US Law Firms Invest in Non-Traditional Benefits for Attorneys and Staff,
     www.aon.com/risk-services/professional-services/major-us-law-firms-invest-in-non-
     traditional-benefits-for-attorneys-and-staff

22   https://therapyforlawyers.com/wp-content/uploads/2023/05/ALM-Attorney-
     Mental-Health-Article.pdf

23   NIOSH Training for Nurses on Shift Work and Long Work Hours,
     www.cdc.gov/niosh/work-hour-training-for-nurses/longhours/mod3/08.html

24   Making Well-Being an Expectation in Attorney-Client Relationships,
     https://lawyerwellbeing.net/2022/08/05/making-well-being-an-expectation-in-
     attorney-client-relationships/

25   www.mindfulbusinesscharter.com/the-charter

26   Us Too? Bullying and Sexual Harassment in the Legal Profession,
     www.ibanet.org/MediaHandler?id=B29F6FEA-889F-49CF-8217-F8F7D78C2479

Chapter 6:
The impact of substance abuse disorder on partner performance

By Jim Lawrence, partner, Bryan Cave Leighton Paisner

Introduction

Substance abuse disorder (SUD) is a critical issue that can significantly impact partner performance. As key decision-makers and leaders, senior partners are integral to the firm's success. When affected by SUD, their ability to perform optimally, maintain client relationships, and uphold ethical standards can be compromised, posing risks to the firm's reputation and financial stability, not to mention the partner's wellbeing. This chapter delves into the author's lived experience with SUD, the prevalence of SUD among lawyers, the signs of SUD in senior partners, appropriate responses, and the importance of destigmatizing SUD within law firms.

My story

I'm an alcoholic with 17 years of sobriety. I drank heavily from the moment I started, as a teenager. Attending university provided cover for my increasingly abusive drinking because all my friends partied, too. But after graduation, while most of them managed to balance partying with the increased responsibilities of adulthood, I landed a job at Atlantic Records in New York City – a perfect career choice for someone with a drinking problem and no interest in slowing down. I experienced a fair amount of success in the music business, but later, when I took on the new challenge of attending law school, I quickly discovered that partying like a rock star (and with rock stars) wasn't a viable option. So, I white-knuckled it, stopping without recovery, and ended up doing well. But that first post-graduation beer set my brain off like a rocket. More, please!

After law school, I worked for a large NYC-based firm where I bought into the romantic notion that "real" lawyers party as hard as they work. I performed well in my new profession, but that only hid the fact that I was depressed – and still drinking heavily. The hangovers started to take a measurable toll. I was newly married, and we had a baby girl. But while I kept up a good front at home, my life as an associate was chaotic and confusing.

After returning to live in the Midwest, in late 2001, I was fortunate to join BCLP's Kansas City office as a third-year associate. My wife and I were hopeful that trading our NYC lifestyle for homeownership and parenting in Kansas City would curb my erratic drinking habits. It didn't. I was a binge drinker. I never knew if that first cocktail would lead to a few more or a serious bender. My alcoholism was easy to hide (or so I thought) because I wasn't a falling-down drunk. Rather, I would just get quieter as the number of drinks increased.

By the time I was a seventh-year associate, alcohol had become an obsession. My first thought every morning was, "Damn, I did it again – but today is going to be different". By about noon, I would start the mental bargaining process – I'll just have a couple of drinks tonight. I hated the person I had become, but the first taste of alcohol washed away the guilt and bargaining until the next morning. And that was my life – day after day after day.

Being a lawyer with SUD was taking a toll on my marriage, my friendships, and significantly, my sanity. The therapists I saw for my substance-fueled depression told me I had a drinking problem, but I was in denial. What did they know? My relationship with alcohol had become so ingrained in my identity that I feared my legal career would be over if I had to stop drinking. How could I create client relationships if I was sober? Socializing would be painfully awkward, right? If I stopped boozing, I imagined, I would lose my drinking buddies at the office. According to my warped judgment, sobriety meant losing everything I had worked so hard to achieve. So, I kept drinking.

Because addiction is a chronic disease, my binges became longer and more frequent. Drinking socially just got in the way of serious drinking. The summer of 2007 was particularly dark. My inner conflict peaked – the thought of another drink was unfathomable, and the thought of never drinking again was unfathomable.

But after a particularly ugly episode one night (I'll spare you the details), I had had enough. I admitted that I needed help. The next morning, I attended an Alcoholics Anonymous meeting, and I haven't had a drink since. Much to my surprise and relief, my legal career didn't tank. I didn't lose my drinking buddies – today, I still count them as my best friends. People didn't treat me like a weirdo. I'm sharing this story because I wonder how different my life would have been if, while I was a young lawyer, an established partner in the firm had raised their hand and admitted that they, too, had been affected by SUD. Would I have sought help sooner, knowing that my career would survive sobriety?

Speculation aside, here are the facts. I've been with BCLP for almost 25 years, including 17 consecutive years in recovery. I have been a partner since 2008. As a well-established and "senior" partner, I had a platform to make the road to recovery less fraught for others. So, in 2020 I sent an email to the entire firm disclosing my experience with SUD. I figured that a few colleagues would appreciate the public acknowledgment, but I had no idea how eager my colleagues were for a safe space to share their own experiences with SUD. Within hours of hitting send on the email, I had received over 100 replies. Some people congratulated me on my recovery, but most people wanted someone to listen to their own experiences without judgment. I heard SUD-related stories about spouses, children, parents, and friends. Most importantly, I heard from colleagues in need. They asked, "How did you do it?" and "I've been thinking about sobriety for some time".

Statistically speaking, every large law firm likely has numerous employees currently needing help with addiction issues, but many of these employees are scared to seek help because of societal stigma and career concerns. The best way to eliminate the deadly stigma around addiction in law firms is for senior partners to openly discuss this all-too-common disease. Most law firms offer great resources to address almost any type of mental health concern, including SUD. But if law firm employees do not feel as if they can safely take advantage of these wellbeing benefits, then they are not working as intended. As a lawyer with SUD, I worried that showing vulnerability would crater my career. I feared that others could not relate to my condition and that I would continue to suffer alone. I could not have been more wrong. Being a leader in recovery and without shame has earned by colleagues' trust and admiration. I've also removed a bit of the deadly stigma that keeps so many of us unable to ask for help. SUD is incredibly complicated, but one way for partners and senior law firm leaders to alleviate the consequences is simple – make every effort to remove the stigma and share your own experiences if possible. Who knows – you might just save a life.

Prevalence of substance abuse disorder among lawyers
While my personal experience with addiction is limited to alcohol, many partners face issues with, among others, gambling, sex, and eating. Based upon my years of recovery, I no longer differentiate between various forms of addiction. The brain's reward system is triggered in similar ways, regardless of the addictive behavior. Compulsion, withdrawal, and chronic relapse are universal consequences of addiction. While SUD disorder is most notably

prevalent in the legal profession, this chapter can reasonably apply to other troublesome addictive behaviors.

According to a study[1] by the American Bar Association (ABA) and the Hazelden Betty Ford Foundation, approximately 21 percent of licensed, employed, attorneys qualify as problem drinkers, 28 percent struggle with depression, and 19 percent exhibit symptoms of anxiety. The study found that younger attorneys in the first ten years of their career or under the age of 30 were at an even higher risk, with 32 percent qualifying as problem drinkers. Furthermore, a survey[2] conducted by the National Institute on Alcohol Abuse and Alcoholism (NIAAA) revealed that attorneys experience a higher rate of problematic drinking compared to other professionals, with about 20.6 percent of attorneys showing signs of alcohol dependence and abuse, compared to 11.8 percent of other highly educated professionals.

SUD is particularly prevalent within law firm leadership. Senior law firm leaders face unique challenges that can increase their vulnerability to SUD. The legal profession is inherently high-stress, with tight deadlines, demanding clients, and high-stakes cases contributing to chronic stress. The more senior partners in a firm often work extended hours, leading to burnout and the use of substances as a coping mechanism. Constant client demands and the pressure to deliver successful outcomes can lead to immense stress and anxiety. In addition, the culture within many law firms often involves social drinking, making it easier for substance use to escalate. The more senior partners in law firms may also feel isolated due to their positions, lacking a support network within the firm to discuss personal struggles. When you add these toxic environmental factors to a genetic predisposition to SUD, it's obvious why addiction in all forms is endemic in our industry.

The impact of social stigma on SUD

Social stigma surrounding SUD often prevents individuals from seeking help due to fear of judgment or professional repercussions. Individuals with SUD may fear being judged as weak or incapable, particularly in a competitive and high-achieving environment like a law firm. Concerns about potential career damage or loss of professional standing can deter individuals from acknowledging their issues. Stigma can lead to isolation, as individuals may avoid discussing their struggles with colleagues or seeking support.

Removing stigma is essential for fostering a supportive environment where partners and employees feel safe to address their issues. Implementing regular training sessions to educate all firm members about SUD, its signs, and the importance of early intervention is crucial. Developing clear, supportive policies that encourage individuals to seek help without fear of negative consequences is also important. Creating an open culture where discussions about mental health and SUD are normalized and encouraged helps in destigmatizing these issues.

Leaders play a pivotal role in shaping the firm's culture regarding SUD. Demonstrating openness about personal challenges can significantly impact the firm's approach to addiction. When senior partners and firm leaders share their personal or indirect experiences with addiction or other personal challenges, they can inspire others to seek help. When leaders openly discuss their challenges, it breaks the silence and encourages others to share their struggles. Vulnerability builds trust within the team, making individuals more likely to seek help when needed. An open and supportive environment reduces fear and stigma, encouraging early intervention and support. Leaders who seek help and manage their SUD effectively model healthy behavior for others to follow. Leaders should consistently show empathy and provide support to those struggling with SUD. Advocating for and implementing policies that support mental health and wellness within the firm is crucial.

Identifying SUD

Recognizing SUD in partners and senior law firm leaders is inherently difficult. Established partners have significant autonomy over their schedules, which allows them to manage their time and mask SUD. Partners are often highly intelligent and sophisticated, which enables them to develop strategies to discourage scrutiny of their behavior. Partners are also able to hide behind their perceived success. Can someone that accomplished really suffer from SUD? As a result, it's not always possible to "see" SUD. Indeed, the disease is highly individualized, so there are no universal "tells" like you might find with certain physical diseases. If you suspect a partner or other senior leader is being affected by SUD, you should consult with human resource (HR) professionals to effectively respond. HR professionals have expertise in handling sensitive issues and can provide guidance on the best approaches. They can help maintain confidentiality and protect the privacy of the individual involved. Ensuring that the law firm's response complies with legal and ethical standards is critical to avoid potential lawsuits. HR can also facilitate access to resources, such as employee assistance programs (EAPs), counseling, and treatment options. My firm, BCLP, provides its employees with free access to an EAP that offers confidential SUD coun-seling, referrals to support groups and 12-step programs, support during the recovery process, and assistance with talking to a friend or loved one about SUD. Employees might find it easier to seek help or confidential information from a third-party EAP vendor as opposed to their actual employer.

Conclusion

SUD can severely impact partner performance, but by proactively removing the stigma of addiction, early identification, appropriate intervention, and a supportive, non-judgmental environment, these individuals can receive the help they need. By fostering a culture of openness and support, law firms can not only aid those struggling with SUD but also enhance overall firm performance and morale. Leaders should exemplify vulnerability and empathy to dismantle stigma and promote a healthier, more supportive work environment.

References

1   www.isba.org/ibj/2017/09/lawpulse/lawyersandaddiction
2   https://pubmed.ncbi.nlm.nih.gov/26825268/

Chapter 7:
Strategies to prevent burnout and create a sustainable law practice

By Paula Davis, JD, MAPP, founder and CEO of the Stress & Resilience Institute

I'd like to share with you a story of a partner's experience of burnout.

Four years after joining my law firm as a partner, I had a nervous breakdown. Doctors called it major depressive disorder with anxiety distress. My illness followed five years of accumulating professional burnout. What started as burnout could have ended much earlier in its progression, but at that time, no leader admitted to mental health problems.

I joined my law firm at the end of March 2004. I got married three weeks later on 18 April 2004, and that day, a Sunday, was my first day off in the year 2004. There was no honeymoon – I came back to a 12+ hour billing day on Monday. I continued to work that way after my younger kids were born in 2005 and 2007. I had no parental leave. I asked no other partner to cover for my practice during this time. I came back to work a day or two after each of my children was born.

In the spring of 2008, I lost my largest client at the time, just before it filed for bankruptcy. I did not know how I could replace that client. As you might suspect, my wife was at her wits' end, with two teenagers and two small babies, and a husband who rarely saw his kids or his wife awake.

As I became increasingly anxious, doing my job became more difficult; the anxiety increased and never seemed to let up. At one point, I was at one of my monthly practice group meetings listening to an associate talk about an M&A practice point. I was keenly aware of these types of issues, and yet when I tried to listen to this talk, I could not understand it. I just couldn't follow the topic through the fog of my anxiety. Unable to understand the presentation, my brain turned to wondering how I managed to convince the world I could handle this level of work when it was so obvious to me at that moment I could not.

A few days later, an AGC at a major firm client rightfully chewed me out for contradicting her on a call with her internal clients. And if that wasn't bad enough, I contradicted a statement she made where she simply repeated advice I had given her the day before! I apologized profusely to her, and I knew the game was up. Like a broken leg, my brain could no longer support the weight of my professional responsibility.

I wondered, when did this happen? And I wondered how long it would be until what was now obvious to me would be obvious to everyone. How long until the firm would ask me to leave, and I would be unable to support my family? I sought treatment that day.

After the screening questions one gets about suicidal thoughts and suicidal plans, I was asked if I was looking forward to anything. My answer was no. Then a surprising question – so what are you living for? My answer was, "I believe I'll get better". I was lucky that I hadn't yet reached the point where even that belief would evaporate. Many are not so lucky.

Fortunately, I did get better quickly with medication, keeping my leave to three weeks and doing my best to make it look like a vacation. When I returned, I changed my approach to respect the limits of my body and brain. After a while, I no longer needed medication. I still worked hard, but I was now aware that I had a breaking point, and I had to watch for it and stay clear of it. Believe me, it's totally doable to be a successful leader, do the hard work that's necessary, and still take care of your body and brain.

This partner is still at the same firm, and he's now the practice group leader of the firm's corporate practice group. I had the privilege of hearing him tell this story live, and it's a moment that will stay with me for a long time. Aspects of his burnout story reminded me of my own, and I hear similar sentiments regularly from lawyers at all levels, but increasingly from partners.

Partner mental health is a drastically under-explored aspect of the well-being conversation, and only tends to surface when a high-profile suicide or other mental health crisis makes the news. Legal leaders have reported to me an alarming increase in the number of partner leaves of absence, mental health issues, and early retirements, with burnout being a main and consistent culprit.

Preventing burnout at any level is a complicated task. It involves taking what I call a "me and we" approach because burnout is caused by a mix of individual and organizational factors. One-off wellbeing programs and apps aren't enough to help. You can't yoga your way out of burnout. Burnout is what stopped my law practice after seven years, and I have had to be very intentional in my own recovery efforts to keep it from returning. Much of what I talk about today in my work is about the "we" side of this equation. I help legal leaders, teams, and organizations learn the mindsets associated with leading in a way to create more engaged and motivated lawyers and legal teams. However, the focus of this chapter will be on the "me" side – specifically, the deep work that is involved in helping partners prevent and recover from burnout.

The burnout basics

The conversation about burnout increased exponentially during the pandemic, and any lengthy discussion about it needs to start with the basics. Burnout has become an overused word to mean all forms of stress, but it's really a very specific type of stress that exists on a continuum that consists of these three dimensions:[1]

1. Chronic exhaustion (feeling consistently physically and emotionally drained, tired, overwhelmed, and overloaded).
2. Chronic cynicism (feeling annoyed and frustrated with people, particularly your clients; you may start to distance yourself from your colleagues and clients, ignoring the qualities that make them unique and engaging, and the result is less empathy).
3. Inefficacy (feeling disengaged; it's the "why bother, who cares" mentality that appears as you struggle to identify important work resources and begin to feel ineffective and detached from your work).

While you may tend to think of burnout as merely chronic exhaustion, burnout isn't burnout until all three of these dimensions are present.[2] The most frequent question I am asked is how to know when stress is turning into something more significant. An easy first step is to evaluate where you are with each of these burnout dimensions.

While "regular" stress can come from myriad sources, the World Health Organization updated its definition of burnout to make clear that burnout refers to chronic stress associated with work and should not be applied to describe experiences in other areas of life. The WHO's definition of burnout also reiterates that burnout is the combination of the three dimensions listed above.[3]

The interplay between engagement and burnout

As more legal organizations seek to figure out how to engage their lawyers, it's important to note that engagement is not the opposite of burnout.[4] Another profile has emerged that legal leaders need to monitor – their "engaged-exhausted" lawyers. This is one I see with increasing frequency in my own work – especially at the senior lawyer level. These are lawyers who likely show the following profile – high exhaustion, high cynicism, but high professional efficacy. High professional efficacy sounds like, "I can effectively solve problems that arise from my work", "I feel effective at getting things done", and "I know I am contributing to my work and my team".

In a study in which more than 1,000 workers were surveyed, the results showed that 35.5 percent of the sample were moderately engaged-exhausted while 18.8 percent of the sample were highly engaged-exhausted. The engaged-exhausted group was still passionate about their work, but they had strong mixed feelings about it – high levels of interest and still feeling connected to it (the high professional efficacy dimension revealing itself), but also high levels of stress. Notably, the engaged-exhausted group showed the highest rate of turnover intention in the study, even higher than the study participants who were most burned out.[5]

Many legal leaders assume that engaged lawyers are happy and functioning well at work. That may not always be true because, for some, engagement and stress (and aspects of burnout) co-exist. The absence of burnout does not imply the presence of engagement or vice versa. To illustrate, an attorney workload and hours survey published by Bloomberg Law showed that 29 percent of respondents said they were currently experiencing burnout while also reporting a satisfaction score of seven or higher out of ten.[6] It's not uncommon for the corporate legal teams I work with to report high rates of burnout while also earning top tier scores in organizational engagement surveys. Building engaged legal teams is an important and worthwhile endeavor for firms and legal organizations, but as to its impact on burnout, it's important to think about engagement as a positive counterpoint to it.

The importance of the Core Six

Burnout is more likely to happen when you have an imbalance between your job demands (aspects of your work that take consistent effort and energy) and job resources (aspects of your work that are consistently energy-giving and help you achieve your goals).[7] There are six key job demands that have been identified as the root causes of chronic stress and burnout as follows (I call them the Core Six):[8]

1. Unmanageable workload (you have so much work that you feel like you're treading water from day-to-day and you might sink at any moment).
2. Lack of recognition (no positive feedback – you rarely, if ever, hear thank you from either colleagues or clients; you don't feel appreciated or valued).
3. Lack of leader/colleague support (not feeling a sense of belonging at work; there is little community or trust on your legal team; and I think it's fair to give some thought to what community means now given the prominence of hybrid work).
4. Unfairness (favoritism may govern important decisions; arbitrary decision-making may be present, along with lack of transparency).
5. Values misalignment (what you find important about work doesn't align with your legal organization's values).
6. Lack of autonomy and control (having little choice as to how and when you perform the tasks related to your work).

Even though the strategies I will talk about below are individual in nature, legal organizations must also address the Core Six.

New research about burnout in the legal profession

In 2023, I partnered with American Law Media (ALM) to conduct a survey about burnout in the legal profession. Specifically, I wanted to understand, in a more nuanced way, how frequently lawyers and legal professionals were experiencing different aspects of the three burnout dimensions – exhaustion, cynicism, and inefficacy. I created 17 statements and asked respondents to rate how frequently the statements applied to them. There were 887 responses to the survey, a mix of lawyers and legal professionals, with most respondents being lawyers. The respondents practiced/worked at law firms of all sizes.

The first thing that troubled me when I looked at the data was how frequently lawyers feel tethered to their work, to the exclusion of time with family and friends, and spent on hobbies. See the table overleaf for more information.

STATEMENT	RESPONSE
I have so much work to do that it takes away from family and friends.	63.3 percent said they felt this way a few times a week or more.
I have so much work to do that it takes away from hobbies and personal interests.	69.5 percent said they felt this way a few times a week or more.
I don't think about my work much at the end of the day.	60.8 percent said they could detach from their work a few times a year or less or never.

The data showed that this is not a BigLaw problem – this is a legal profession problem. Our survey included a significant number of responses from lawyers and legal professionals at all firm sizes, based on the following categories: 1-200 lawyers; 201-500 lawyers; 501-1,000 lawyers; and firms with 1,001+ lawyers. While the percentages reporting these same frequencies were higher in the largest law firms, they weren't wildly higher. The one exception is firms with 201-500 lawyers. While their percentages weren't good, they were markedly better than the other three categories.

Below are the results specific to partners and counsel. The percentages are those who responded by answering, "a few times a week or more" to the first two statements and "a few times a year or less or never" to the last statement.

STATEMENT	EQUITY PARTNER	NON-EQUITY PARTNER	COUNSEL
I have so much work to do that it takes away from family and friends.	65.1 percent	69.4 percent	53.9 percent
I have so much work to do that it takes away from hobbies and personal interests.	69.7 percent	75.9 percent	56.5 percent

continued on next page

STATEMENT	EQUITY PARTNER	NON-EQUITY PARTNER	COUNSEL
I don't think about my work much at the end of the day.	66.4 percent	63 percent	52 percent

This has consequences. To be sure, this level of time spent away from family, friends, and personal interests, coupled with the fact that work is almost always on your mind, isn't good for relationships or for personal health and wellbeing. And you're feeling it.

The below percentages reflect those who responded, "once a week, a few times a week, or every day". For example, 63.3 percent of respondents said they felt overwhelmed by the amount of work they had at least once a week, a few times a week, or every day.

STATEMENT	RESPONSE
I am overwhelmed by the amount of work I have.	63.3 percent
I have a hard time concentrating at work.	64.9 percent
I have become less interested in my work.	63.4 percent
I have become more cynical about my work.	68 percent
I feel emotionally drained on a regular basis from my work.	68.7 percent

In the table overleaf are the specific partner and counsel results, using the same response frequency of "once a week, a few times a week, or every day".

STATEMENT	EQUITY PARTNER	NON-EQUITY PARTNER	COUNSEL
I am overwhelmed by the amount of work I have.	55.4 percent	65.4 percent	52 percent
I have a hard time concentrating at work.	51.5 percent	63.9 percent	61.3 percent
I have become less interested in my work.	51.5 percent	65.8 percent	65.7 percent
I have become more cynical about my work.	55.8 percent	64.8 percent	65.7 percent
I feel emotionally drained by my work on a regular basis.	61.4 percent	72.3 percent	65 percent

Think about these results for a minute. These are the most senior lawyers in your firm tasked with representing your clients on the most complex and nuanced matters that they have. Half or more are feeling drained, distracted, cynical, and disinterested at least once a week, and for many, multiple times a week to every day. What does this mean for your clients? For the lawyers' family and friends? For partners' wellbeing? In addition, the combination of chronic stress, work overload, and loneliness – all known issues in the legal profession – is a particularly toxic trio for lawyer mental health and wellbeing.[9]

Strategies to help

The following are some examples of deeper level strategies that I have used in my own burnout recovery, taught to many others, and/or the research is learning can be effective in the fight to prevent burnout.

Acknowledge the producer-manager dilemma

One area of struggle for partners is managing their dual roles. While this duality starts much earlier in their careers, I don't think it's fully acknowledged or taken as seriously until they reach the partner level. It's called the producer-manager dilemma and is explained in more detail in chapter four.. Once you make partner, you are truly seen as a leader in the firm; however, you must also continue to produce work and bill hours. Added to that, the expectation for developing business comes fully into play and you are balancing two very heavy loads in two very different worlds. In addition, associates are now looking to you for guidance, mentorship, and coaching and feedback. And when the producer-manager roles come into tension with each other, partners often favor the producer role as more important. You must manage people – a skill set very different from the practice of law that rarely gets enough training and development attention. As a result, you must effectively manage your clients, your teams, and yourself. The table below sets out some ideas to help.[10]

MANAGE YOUR CLIENT	MANAGE YOUR TEAM	MANAGE YOURSELF
Take time to align interests and find the best way to manage the matter.	Delegate as appropriate to your team (see the icebergs section below).	Reframe tasks – spending time to coach a senior associate may enhance business development potential later.
Know the client's priorities and preferences.	Co-create a check-in schedule with associates working on your matters to limit micromanaging.	Know your most critical business objectives on both the client- and team-building fronts.
Manage task expectations and ask specifically about timing.	Set clear goals and expectations with associates, and give them enough latitude to figure out how to get from Point A to Point B (based on level of knowledge).	Build a network of support (see leverage relationships section below).

Wrestle with your wiring

To prevent and recover from burnout, you must go deep. You need to understand your mindsets and "wiring" – the traits, styles of thinking, and behaviors that have influenced your leadership style, how you form relationships, goal achievement, and your mental health and wellbeing. These are your core values and beliefs, or your rules, about how you think you and others should operate in the world. They are called your Icebergs or rules (and I use the terms interchangeably).[11] These rules exist at the individual, team, and organizational/institutional level, and everyone has them. Your core values and beliefs often operate outside of your conscious awareness (the iceberg part "hidden under the water") as you go about your day, but they can be triggered in certain circumstances, such as when you overreact (or underreact) to something, notice a pet peeve was triggered, or when you keep thinking about something days after the event happened. Control, achievement, and relationships are all big iceberg themes, and these beliefs can be rooted in fear of failure, worrying what others think, and not feeling good enough. Examples, like saying yes to everything, working at a relentless pace, feeling like you can never let anyone down, that you must produce perfect work, that you must always have the answers, and thinking that your self-worth is tied to your role as a lawyer are all common icebergs I hear from partners.

It's important for you to surface your rules so you can evaluate them. Once you surface the belief, you can evaluate it by asking these questions:

- Is this rule helping or harming? Is it getting me closer to, or further away from, the goals I want to achieve? Is it too strict or rigid? Most of your icebergs are inflexible.
- How did the rule develop? Was it part of how you were raised? Did it develop in law school or by virtue of your time practicing law?
- What is the payoff for following this rule? I ask you to resist the urge to label your icebergs as "good" or "bad". They just "are". They operate in ways, though, that either push you closer to or pull you further away from what you want. One of my icebergs is "Taking a break is a sign of laziness". This iceberg developed from my family of origin and the way I was raised. My parents owned a plastic injection molding company, and I worked in the factory during my high school and college summers. On one particularly hot summer day, I took a break in the corner of the warehouse five minutes before my shift ended. My dad found me "hiding" and said, "If you have time to sit you have time to sweep" and handed me a broom. Having a strong work ethic has helped

me tremendously in life, yet it's part of the reason why, when I have a few moments to relax, I often revert to answering a few emails or completing a task, rather than taking a break (pulling me further away from my desire to rest).

- What alternative rule might be more helpful? I've reshaped my iceberg to be, "Taking a break is a sign of self-care". It doesn't always work, but the point is that it's much more flexible and I'm much less hard on myself.

A big problem, though, is that legal organizations continue to hire for and reward these traits and mindsets. Partners get promoted to partner, in part, because of this wiring. And yet, they are also the traits and mindsets that can be part of what leads to burnout.

Improve "anti-burnout" behaviors

Australian leadership researcher Nick Petrie[12] and his team have spent the past few years interviewing thousands of professionals about their burnout experiences. They discovered that a small percentage of people who they interviewed performed at a very high level but didn't burnout. In reviewing their notes, they found that the low burnout group displayed certain behaviors that seemed to protect them from burning out. I list those behaviors in the chart on the next page and invite you to think about the areas in which you need to improve. Take some time to think about the strategies you might use. Note that your icebergs may be present in a big way as you work through this list. It's a great spot to invite the help of a coach.

One specific strategy Nick and his team found that was particularly useful by the group who worked very hard, yet didn't burnout, was to have an "opposite" world. One clear takeaway from my study is that lawyers at all levels are exhausted. They are depleted and consistently find themselves being pulled toward work and away from family, friends, hobbies, and fortifying activities, with an intense frequency. It isn't sustainable. For many lawyers, work has become their identity. Who are you when you aren't practicing law? Are you an avid reader? A master gardener? A competition level baker? You need to be able to answer this question. Having an "opposite" world to visit with regularity acts as a powerful burnout buffer and, importantly, contributes to work detachment and recovery that is necessary to manage high levels of stress.[13]

"ANTI-BURNOUT" BEHAVIORS	STRATEGIES TO IMPROVE
Create clear boundaries between work and home.	
Have rituals for switching between work and home.	
Make peace with not getting everything done each day.	
Develop other outside of work roles and identities (who are you and what you love to do when you're not lawyering).	
Have a phone strategy in place to become more intentional about phone use at home.	
Have a clear understanding of what works for you each day in terms of how you get your work done.	

Track progress

One of the single biggest things you can do to create energy and motivation is to make progress in your work.[14] While it's nice to win a big trial or close a big deal, those big wins don't happen all the time. What does happen, though, are the minor milestones, breakthroughs, and small wins along the way, and it's these small wins that often evoke outsized positive psychological reactions. Another wonderful byproduct of progress is self-efficacy. Small wins help fuel the belief that you are on the right track and have the power to accomplish your goals. You can support your daily progress by making sure that the right types of resources, including relationships, support your work.

Progress looks like small wins and breakthroughs, forward movement, and/or goal completion. Try listing three to four events from this week that demonstrate progress for you:

1. _____

2. _____

3. _____

4. _____

Next, put a check mark by those factors that were present in your work this week.

Checklist of factors that make progress more likely:
- I had clear goals.
- I had enough flexibility and control to do the work.
- I had sufficient resources.
- I had sufficient time to do the work.
- I had someone to talk to when I felt challenged.
- I felt recognized for my efforts.

Tally up your check marks. The more you have, the more likely you felt energized and motivated by your work and the progress you made this week.

Build a stronger relationship bench

While many lawyers are part of practice groups and teams of various sizes, lawyering can often feel like a siloed and, at times, isolating job. At the partner level, you are essentially building your own business, and if you work at a firm, you're a business owner among a collection of other business owners. Research has shown that partners are in the 12th percentile in sociability[15] and lawyers generally have the highest rates of loneliness of similar professions measured.[16] This doesn't necessarily mean that lawyers don't like other people. Given partners' analytical nature, they often tend to form relationships based on facts and thinking and may gravitate more toward to the relationships where they've already done that hard, getting to know you, work.

The problem with this is that strong relationships represent a critical way to manage stress and prevent burnout. It has been shown that friendship groups outperform acquaintance groups on a variety of work tasks – whether it's a more thinking-type cognitive task or a hands-on model building task.[17]

Decades-long research by Gallup has shown that if you have a best friend at work, you are more likely to engage your clients, get more done in less time, and innovate and share ideas. Unfortunately, only 30 percent of employees report having a best friend at work, but those who do are seven times more likely to be engaged in their job.[18] The evolution and growth of friendships at work is a critical part of a healthy workplace, and one that the legal profession needs to significantly amplify in importance, particularly for lateral partners.

A partner recently reached out to me after I presented a program at his firm. He wanted to ask me a few questions and talk about his concerns about his stress levels, which were driven by increasing business development pressures. He had been at the firm for several years, joining as a lateral. As we talked, I asked him whether there was another partner who he felt he could talk to, even if only to ask some basic performance-related questions. He said no. In addition to the struggle lateral partners may feel in forming and building new relationships at their new firm, the legal profession in general needs to improve how it talks about relationships.

Focusing on your relationships and interpersonal interactions become a critical pathway for helping you better manage micro-stress. Micro-stressors are the small moments of stress in your personal and professional life that accumulate over time, and the accumulation can have a significant impact on your wellbeing, health, and resilience.[19] Researchers identified more than a dozen influential micro-stressors, such as misaligned roles and priorities, insufficient communication practices, surges in workload and responsibilities, confrontational conversations, and personal values conflicts. One occurrence of a micro-stressor might not register as a threat to your wellbeing, but over time, the effects of micro-stress grow.

Researchers found that the connections you make provide important pathways to thriving and resilience and, in particular, help to diffuse the intensity of accumulated micro-stress. Specifically, they suggest you need to have the right people in seven different categories. As you review the seven categories below, write down the name of someone you can rely on or turn to in each.

- *Category 1: Providing empathetic support.* Who lets you vent and helps you feel like they are there to listen?
  Name(s):

- *Category 2: Identifying a path forward.* These people give you good, practical advice and help you see options. They are also good at explaining how they handled a similarly tough situation.
  Name(s):

- *Category 3: Offering perspective.* When you over-think, this person gives you some much-needed perspective to help you realize it's likely not as bad as you might think.
  Name(s):

- *Category 4: Managing the surge.* Unpredictable client demands, business development efforts, and new projects are all factors that might lead to a surge in the amount of work responsibilities you have. This inevitably spills over into other areas of your life. Who are the people you can count on when you are overwhelmed with demands?
  Name(s):

- *Category 5: Taking a break.* Who helps you take a break or a pause from your stress?
  Name(s):

- *Category 6: Providing levity.* These are the people you can count on to provide humor and lightness during a challenge.
  Name(s):

- *Category 7: Making sense of people and politics.* Who gives you a broader team or organizational view and can give you a better understanding of others' behavior?
  Name(s):

Now review your list.

Do you have the same person listed for each category? Many people smile and admit, "yes". It's often a significant other, spouse, or close friend on repeat. Know that you're asking a tremendous amount of that one person, and he or she likely isn't the best person to support you in every category. Think about ways to increase your relationship "bench".

For some people, it's hard to think of a name for every category. I realized that I struggled to write down names for categories two and three, and that helped me realize that I need to hire a business coach to give me the perspective that I need as I grow my business.

Law is a competitive profession, and that pressure only escalates as you ascend the ranks. Many partners tell me that they don't want to appear weak, or aren't sure they can trust certain people, so they don't seek out new friendships among their partner colleagues. While I understand the hesitation, I also think it's a huge, missed opportunity to help each other in these strategic ways. After all, you're "partners". Think about what that word means. Bigger picture, having a well-designed network allows you to flexibly reach out to the right people in small but powerful ways for the right kind of support, both personally and professionally.

In order for lawyers to lead well and lawyer well, they need to be well. I received the following email from a partner at a large law firm recently supporting this notion:

> "It seems to me that one of the main obstacles to happier teams [and lawyers] at law firms is the prevailing culture of our profession. We're expected to behave like cool and rational professionals all the time. On some level that clinical detachment is what our clients need from us, but I would argue (1) it's not what they most want from us and (2) focusing on it causes us to de-emphasize and de-value some of the things that matter most to us. It's skills like listening [and] empathy that differentiate the most successful lawyers from everyone else. Those aren't the analytical or technical skills we learn in school and develop throughout our careers; they're the skills that make clients feel we care about their problems."

And make us feel like we care about each other.

References

1   Christina Maslach (2017), Finding Solutions to the Problem of Burnout. 69(2) *Consulting Psychology Journal: Practice & Research,* 143-152.
2   Christina Maslach & Michael P. Leiter (19 March 2021), How to Measure Burnout Accurately and Ethically. *Harvard Business Review.* https://hbr.org/2021/03/how-to-measure-burnout-accurately-and-ethically.
3   World Health Organization (28 May 2019). Burnout an "occupational phenomenon." www.who.int/news/item/28-05-2019-burn-out-an-occupational-phenomenon-international-classification-of-diseases.
4   Toon W. Taris, Jan Fekke Ybema, and Ilona van Beek (2017), Burnout and Engagement: Identical Twins or Just Close Relatives? 5 *Burnout Research,* 3-11. *See also,* Sarah-

Genevieve Trepanier, Claude Fernet, Stephanie Austin, and Julie Menard (2015), Revisiting the Interplay between Burnout and Work Engagement: An Exploratory Structural Equation Modeling (ESEM) Approach. 2(2) *Burnout Research*, 51-59.

5   Julia Moeller et al. (2018), Highly Engaged but Burned Out: Intra-Individual Profiles in the US Workforce. 23(1) *Career Development International*, 86-105.

6   Linda Ouyang and Jacquelyn Palmer (11 March 2021), ANALYSIS: Hours Data Show the Sweet Spot for Lawyer Satisfaction. https://news.bloomberglaw.com/bloomberg-law-analysis/analysis-hours-data-show-the-sweet-spot-for-lawyer-satisfaction.

7   Arnold B. Bakker, Evangelia Demerouti, and Ana Sanz-Vergel (2023), Job Demands-Resources Theory: Ten Years Later. 10 *Annual Review of Organizational Psychology and Organizational Behavior*, 25-53.

8   Christina Maslach (1998), A Multi-Dimensional Theory of Burnout in Theories of Organizational Stress (Cary L. Cooper ed). 68. Oxford. Christina Maslach, Wilmar B. Schaufeli, and Michael P. Leiter (2001). Job Burnout. 52 *Annual Review of Psychology*, 397-422. Christina Maslach and Michael P. Leiter (2008), Early Predictors of Job Burnout & Engagement. 93 *The Journal of Applied Psychology*, 498-512. Omer Aydemir and Ilkin Icelli (2013). *Burnout: Risk Factors in Burnout for Experts* (Sabine Bahrer-Kohler, ed.). 119-143. Springer. Christina Maslach and Michael P. Leiter (2022), *The Burnout Challenge: Managing People's Relationships with Their Jobs*. Harvard University Press.

9   Patrick R. Krill et. al (2023), Stressed, Lonely, & Overcommitted: Predictors of Lawyer Suicide Risk. 11 *Healthcare*, 536.

10   The ideas on this chart come from a combination of ideas put forth in Heidi K. Gardner (20 July 2015), Juggling the Producer-Manager Roles. *Professional Collaborations* blog. With inspiration from the US Bank Guidelines, developed in part by Ben Carpenter, Senior Vice President and Deputy General Counsel at US Bank, and the Mindful Business Charter, Richard Martin, Chief Executive Officer. You can read more about each of these initiatives at Jessica Cherry (27 October 2023), Fostering Attorney Well-Being by Humanizing Attorney-Client Relationships; The Mindful Business Charter & US Bank Well-Being Guidelines offer Pathways to Change. Practical Law – Thomson Reuters.

11   The information in this section about icebergs comes from Karen Reivich and Andrew Shatte (2002). *The Resilience Factor*. New York, NY: Broadway Books.

12   www.nicholaspetrie.com/

13   David B. Newman, Louis Tay, and Ed Diener (2014), Leisure and Subjective Well-Being: A Model of Psychological Mechanisms as Mediating Factors. 15 *Journal of Happiness Studies*, 555-578. *See also* Sabine Sonnentag, Bonnie Hayden Cheng, and Stacey L. Parker (2022), Recovery from Work: Advancing the Field Toward the Future. 9 *Annual Review of Organizational Psychology and Organizational Behavior*, 33-60.

14   The ideas in this section come from the work of Teresa M. Amabile, Steven J. Kramer, and their colleagues. I used the following resources: Teresa M. Amabile and Steven J. Kramer (May 2011), The Power of Small Wins. *Harvard Business Review*. Teresa Amabile and Steven J. Kramer (2011), *The Progress Principle: Using Small Wins to Ignite Joy, Engagement, and Creativity at Work*. Boston: Harvard Business Review Press.

15　Dr Larry Richard (2002), *Herding Cats: The Lawyer Personality Revealed*. Altman Weil. www.managingpartnerforum.org/tasks/sites/mpf/assets/image/MPF%20-%20WEBSITE%20-%20ARTICLE%20-%20Herding%20Cats%20-%20Richards1.pdf

16　Shawn Achor, Gabriella Rosen Kellerman, Andrew Reece, and Alexi Robichaux (19 August 2018), America's Loneliest Workers, According to Research. Hbr.org. https://hbr.org/2018/03/americas-loneliest-workers-according-to-research

17　Karen A. John and Priti Pradhan Shah (1997), Interpersonal Relationships and Task Performance: An Examination of Mediating Processes in Friendship and Acquaintance Groups. 72(4) *Journal of Personality and Social Psychology*, 775-790.

18　Tom Rath (2006), *Vital Friends: The People You Can't Afford to Live Without*. New York: Gallup Press.

19　All of the ideas from this section come from Rob Cross & Karen Dillon (2023), *The Microstress Effect: How Little Things Pile Up and Create Big Problems – and What to Do about It*. Boston, MA: Harvard Business Review Press.

Chapter 8:
The costs of partner underperformance to the profession

By Graham Browning, director, Arrisan

Partner performance is a subject close to my heart. As Freshfields' troubleshooter for hard people issues for 20 years, I dealt with the fallout of partner underperformance at all levels. If I learnt one thing, it is that performance is in the eye of the beholder. We are human and we all have blind spots. While we strive for excellence, we will inevitably fall short sometimes. It is what we do next that counts. Can we face discomfort and change, or do we go on the defense? We all have a choice to make and a part to play, for better or worse. My hope is to help you play your part well, rise to the challenge, and give you a framework for action.

This chapter focuses on how slippery slopes begin, the damage they cause when they are not addressed, and what firms can do. We will peek into a day in the life of three fictional partners. Speaking from 30 years' experience, I've focused on the behaviors that most commonly create issues. I highlight the impact so you can identify these behaviors and know how to tackle them in your own workplace. Talking about "costs" may make it sound dry or abstract when it's anything but. It affects people, performance, and firms in profound ways. A firm that does not address these behaviors effectively will create a culture ripe for fear, silence, distrust, breakdowns, bullying, harassment, discrimination, wasted talent, underperformance, and censure. Clients want to be associated with well-managed firms that reflect well on them. Societal and commercial pressures have increased the complexity and jeopardy involved in these issues. To rely on yesterday's solutions is to invite trouble.

Ace – the line partner

Poor people management skills
Entering the office with her morning decaf cappuccino with oat milk, Ace decides not to attend the team's people management training. She is too busy, and always prioritizes hard lawyering over soft people management.

Costs

It spells trouble when leaders of a people business lack people management skills. This skill deficit will have consequences, because Ace will either shy away from situations or deal with them like the novice she has chosen to be. Delegation, feedback, motivating, sensitive conversations, and nipping issues in the bud are essential skills, dismissed as "soft" by those who lack them. She may be a fantastic technician, but Ace's lack of skill with people has serious implications. At best, individual and team performance around Ace will be sub-optimal and there will be an over-dependence on others to plug the gap. As performance expectations rise and new joiners' needs become more complex, cracks will appear and her shortcomings will cause major problems.

Bad manners

In the corridor, Ace passes associate Adam. He smiles at her – she ignores him. Adam recently spent two months working with Ace, but he is not one of her core team and her mind is elsewhere. At a deeper level, there is something about Adam that plays on Ace's insecurities; as a result, she does nothing to encourage him and is prone to having a dig. Adam feels the snub and tells his friends that he will do all he can to avoid working with her again.

Costs

Slights send a clear message that someone does not count, and neglect is a good example. Digs and discrimination are close cousins. From my experience of leading employee engagement and employee relations, marginalized people are more likely to actively work against the firm's interests than any other group. Expect Adam's productivity and commitment to drop – he is spending time that could be productive chewing over Ace's behavior instead. There is also the impact on the team – stories like this are blots on the firm's reputation. Fueled by her baseless animosity towards Adam, the in-out dynamic Ace has created is the bedrock of all kinds of organizational strife. Manners matter. I once asked a high potential associate why she was leaving. "To go somewhere where they say hello to you in the corridor." What a waste.

Caring only about profit

Ace sits down and reads two emails. The first is an all-partner email from Wolf in the leadership team, saying, "Market conditions remain challenging. We must focus relentlessly on billing to achieve our targets. I will attend review meetings to support partners as necessary."

The second is Wolf's request for partners to get involved in a diversity program. The email says this is a "valuable non-chargeable" activity. Ace used to get involved. Now she mutters, "All that matters are the numbers these days" and presses delete.

Costs
People are guided by what their leader is seen to value day-to-day. If a leader's preoccupation is individual financial performance, then many partners will prioritize chargeable over non-chargeable activity, whatever the implications for the future of the firm. Over time, everything non-financial becomes held together by the goodwill of a handful of people. The pressure to increase profitability more than anything else also increases the likelihood of personal misconduct and unethical business decisions.

Poor delegation
A client messages Ace, requesting the firm to make a filing. She messages junior fee-earner Bea to tell her to contact the client urgently and be available for a call any time over the weekend. Unlike others, Bea's hours exceed full capacity because she is excellent and therefore the preferred choice of several seniors. She cancels personal plans in order to work over the weekend, checks her phone constantly, and sleeps badly. At one point she panics about what to do – she wants to call Ace but is afraid to do so because of her reputation of "not suffering fools". In a state, Bea makes a mistake. The next week, Bea worries about what she did but is afraid to say anything. Ace does not check-in or give the matter another thought.

Costs
Individual issues are normally produced by systemic issues. Here, the work allocation system punishes Bea for her high performance, with risks to her health, to the client, and to the firm. With no effective controls, partners are free to dump work and disappear without regard to the individual's capacity or wellbeing. Bea's fear of annoying someone senior compounds the problem. Depending on the nature of the mistake, Bea could be in regulatory trouble. If investigated, Ace and the firm will hope that a regulator will not ask why a junior was overloaded, unsupervised, exhausted, and afraid to ask for help.

Silencing
Counsel Cam asks Ace for her opinion on a client matter. The client is a

company defending litigation about a product. Cam has received a claim from a member of the public saying that the product has made them seriously ill and their situation is desperate. Cam says the claim is well founded and advises early settlement. Ace says they should delay. The additional work will help meet her revenue target. Cam feels uneasy about this and asks whether they should consult the client partner on the environmental, social, and governance (ESG) issues. Ace tells him that he is in the business of law, which means keeping the client happy while making a profit.

Costs
Covering up bullying, harassment, and discrimination. Tax evasion. Biased investigations. Prosecuting the innocent. There are many examples of lawyers playing an essential role on the wrong side of scandalous behavior. Most firms talk about their values and ESG commitments. It plays well when hiring, but how true they are is revealed by the decisions about money, clients, and people. Even if time does not judge Ace, Cam will, and all the people he tells. The incoming generation expects higher standards, and past decisions have a habit of coming back to haunt firms. In an increasingly transparent world, wise partners remember that what is said behind closed doors is less likely to stay there.

Weak feedback skills
It is the deadline day for contributing feedback for associate performance evaluations. Ace has little time for feedback. Of 15 requests to provide feedback, Ace completes two – Danni's and Eddie's.

Ace's feedback on Danni is, "Needs to be more responsive and manage expectations. This will demonstrate the required commitment." The first time Danni hears this is when it is read out during her review meeting. She does not know what Ace is referring to.

Ace's feedback on Eddie is, "He is doing well and is on track". Eddie is a member of Ace's core group. The partners have decided that Eddie is too error-prone and will not make partner. This has never been discussed with him and he is known to be sensitive to criticism. After a spate of resignations, Ace cannot afford for Eddie to leave, so she persuades the other partners to give him a top performance rating and bonus.

Costs
Ace's assumption that "feedback" means criticism is a common basic mistake. Starving people of the information they need to gauge their performance is the

root of so many problems I have dealt with. Confidence is eroded. Opportunities to change are lost. Insecurity increases. Effective partners normalize discussion of how their people are doing so that bad feedback doesn't come out of the blue. Delaying feedback reduces its currency and allows facts and motives to be challenged. I have known badly handled feedback to create six figure liabilities – figures that dwarf the cost of equipping people to do it skillfully.

For feedback to be useful, it needs to help someone improve their performance. For that, they need to accept it. Ace's feedback will be rejected as unfair. Danni's trust in Ace and the firm will be damaged, especially because this is on the record and may affect reward and prospects. It is remarkable how viscerally people remember unfair feedback and performance reviews. Betrayed people never forget.

The "You're fabulous, you're fine – oh, now you're fired" approach to people management is something I have fought against throughout my career. It is neither honest nor wise. It is the opposite of a high integrity, high performance culture. The first issue is the unfairness. Over-rewarding performance is a waste of resources that also demotivates higher performers. The second cost stems from allowing a significant gap to appear between how the firm sees the individual and how they see themselves. Partners are less invested in those with no future at the firm. The individual gets frozen out long before the tap on the shoulder. In that time, work dries up and confidence evaporates. During the period of mis-matched perceptions, something may happen that complicates matters. I am not the only person in HR to have received the call that goes like this: "Sam is useless, always has been. Has not done any work for months and we decided a month ago they need an exit message at tomorrow's appraisal. No record of any of this, of course, but anyone could have read the signals. One trifling detail, barely worth mentioning, but they just told us they are [stressed / depressed / anxious / ill / pregnant / gay / filing a complaint]. Send me a script.' If HR cannot stop this conversation from going ahead without fear of criticism, then brace yourself for a bumpy ride.

Solutions

The keys for underperforming line partners are to increase their:

- Resources to meet the expectations on them, including wellbeing support;
- Awareness of themselves and of their effect on others;
- Ability to manage themselves and others; and
- Accountability for their behavior.

Bill – the rainmaker

Not collaborating with partners

At his desk early after a session in the gym, Bill downs a protein shake. He opens an email from Fatima, a partner from another practice in an overseas office that reads, "Hi Bill. Just want to make sure that we talk before you pitch to BigCo. I spoke to them recently – we need to be joined up and I have some useful intel. Best, Fatima." He replies, "There is no need to send me emails like this. I saw BigCo yesterday and it went very well. If there is an opportunity for you, I will let you know."

BigCo's general counsel (GC) decides to test the firm with a small instruction. If Bill had worked with Fatima, the GC would have instructed the firm on a large cross-practice multijurisdictional mandate. On hearing that he has won some work, Bill emails his practice and sector group, saying, "I met BigCo's GC, and he has asked me to lead on a critical project. I am delighted. It shows what a little bit of proactivity achieves." Senior leader Wolf replies, "Well done Bill. This is exactly what we need!" Bill celebrates with his associates, during which he shares his negative views about Fatima "off the record".

Costs

The costs of not collaborating are almost too obvious to state but happen too often to ignore. The firm misses opportunities that it may not be aware of. Lack of mutual respect puts sand into the firm's engine. Self-advancement harms the collective and management can fuel the problem by promoting the me-first self-promoters. Partners share damaging opinions and information, relationships sour, and competition breaks out. It becomes a rat race, where only rats win. People get hurt, but nothing is done except to reward and protect the perpetrators. The solution? Look hard at how your "stars" achieve their results and address toxic behavior.

Not collaborating with other professionals

Bill is waiting for the client acceptance team to approve a new client. He sends an email demanding same day clearance. When he does not receive a reply within five minutes, he leaves voicemail after voicemail. Grayson in client acceptance replies after ten minutes, and politely reminds Bill that he's not provided the information required for client acceptance to progress the matter. Bill previously ignored two requests. A furious Bill calls Grayson and bawls him out, calling him a "fee-burner". He forwards Grayson's email to the head of the department, editing out the part that reflects badly on himself, and slams Grayson's competence. The head of the department sympathizes with Grayson and tells him not to take it personally. She takes no further action as partners and their favorites are protected species at the firm.

Costs
If there is one thing partners hate, it is process. If there is one thing partners expect, it is to be in a well-run firm. Business services get squished when those wishes collide. This is the world where rules and people get broken, reputations are trashed, turnover is high, and toxic game-players rise. If the firm tolerates Bill's behavior, it systematizes the problem. The root cause is a culture that demands servility towards partners, treats "non-fee earners" as inferior, and fails to support them with the demands they face. The higher up the firm's management this attitude goes, the greater the damage.

Promoting toxic behavior
Bill bumps into Hero, his favorite member of business services and for whom he recently lobbied for uniquely favorable treatment. Bill likes throwing his weight around for his favorites. He rates Hero because she dishes the dirt about colleagues, helps Bill find workarounds for the firm's systems, and echoes Bill's opinion that most support staff are a waste of space. Hero is a ruthless careerist and, with powerful patrons like Bill, her rate of ascent has outstripped her abilities. This has been no impediment, as her signature strength is her ability to thrive despite gross misconduct levels of bullying and manipulation. People are scared of her. The chief people officer and other seniors are aware of Hero's impact but do nothing. As a result, the problems she causes are swept under the carpet. This suits Hero perfectly – with HR and leadership on her side she is secure.

Costs
Hero is a major risk to people and the firm. She is a threat to the health and career of her team and peers. Her psychological games can lead people to contemplate taking their own life. Complaints and turnover will rise. The firm's reputation will take a hit. Performance will be hampered as collaboration withers under her influence. The firm will pay a heavy price for providing safe harbor to Hero. Putting aside the ethical, legal, regulatory, and financial ramifications, the firm will find itself drawn into the drama of managing one incident after another. Until the firm removes Hero, she will play the firm for

all it is worth. If the firm decides to manage her out, Hero will be prepared and the firm may further reward her toxicity with a large payoff, a false narrative about her departure, and failing to report her to the regulator.

Solutions
The keys for underperforming rainmakers are:
- Ensuring their reward is affected by how collaborative their behavior is;
- Control any exception seeking for themselves or their favorites;
- Face into their damaging behavior in a way that gets their attention; and
- Never allow them to become semi-detached from the rest of the firm.

Wolf – firm leadership

Leaders doing other people's jobs
Wolf marks up some documents from a specialist team in the firm. He does not need to do this and it creates unnecessary delays and work, but he enjoys it.

Costs
Over-involving yourself in other people's work may not look like underperformance, but wasting time on the wrong things is exactly that. One of the hardest things for a partner in management to do is to avoid the temptation to involve themselves unnecessarily, for example in topics where they have technical expertise. Fiddling about like this is a favorite refuge for some; the dopamine hit of improving syntax is a nice reminder of simpler times. Devious leaders do the opposite to getting involved and create scapegoats by making sure that someone else holds the pen on anything risky while they flag vague concerns. The costs are significant – wasted time that could have been spent listening to neglected parts of the business and showing appreciation rather than leaving experts feeling second guessed, unsupported, and demotivated. The solution? Ask your experts what they need from you and what they do not. Ask them whether they feel supported by you and reflect carefully if you hear anything other than a wholehearted, "Yes".

Uncontrolled financial decisions
Wolf approved the budget last week, but now emails the C-suite and says he

wants a further five percent reduction by the end of the week. He puts a line through the proposed spend on anti-harassment training (he does not like consultant spend) but does not cut the $5,000 for the Associate Equestrian Dressage society or the $50,000 for consultants to help him prepare for his session at the partner conference (some consultancy spend he likes a lot). Regardless of their performance, he gives special bonuses to the people he relies on the most, to keep them onside and avoid awkward conversations. He rails against financial exceptions in all parts of the firm except his own.

Costs
Money talks, and Wolf's decisions speak volumes. First, he is fickle. Changing the budget at the last minute creates pain and poor decisions. Second, there are the decisions themselves. These show the firm's true values and lack of accountability. There would be no integrity issue for the firm if Wolf's words matched his deeds. They do not.

Bad appointments
Wolf emails Ace to say he is appointing her to management, against HR advice. He tells himself the move will upskill her. Wolf also emails the firm to announce the recruitment of Indiana, a high-profile hire. Indiana was terminated by his previous firm and has a "good brain/nasty character" reputation in the market. Wolf would have discovered this if the firm applied the same rigor to partner/senior business services recruitment as for all other roles. The truth is that Wolf would have hired Indiana even if he knew he was bully, justifying the decision based on the lie that he would "manage it". Sadly, the hire damages the firm's reputation.

Costs
Wolf has created a future headache for the firm. The best guide to how Ace will behave in the future is how she has behaved in the past. The promotion will not improve her management skills by magic. The morale in Ace's team will take a tumble, driving disengagement, and complaints. It sends the message that people management skills do not matter.

As for Indiana, it is difficult to get senior lateral hiring right and many do not live up to the promise. There are several reasons for that, but a big one is that firms are happy to offload their problems, and the receiving firm does not do proper due diligence. This creates a circus, with a merry-go-round of underperformers at the center.

Unjustified exceptions

After partner lobbying, Wolf agrees to exempt one practice group and one region from an initiative to improve the firm's culture.

Costs

When I look back to the root causes of the biggest shambles I have dealt with, they all began with management making a political exception from training, policy, control, or change. Firms that permit an individual, team, or region to be semi-detached play with fire – a "them and us" mindset ensues, and the foundations of the firm crack. In that gap lurks things like fraud, harassment, bullying, discrimination, and bad practices.

Echo chambers

Wolf meets his direct reports. He says he has heard about negative comments in the media. He also says that complaints are increasing. Wolf is not concerned about the legal or financial risk, as partner Wily oversees investigations. Wolf knows he can rely on Wily to be "commercial" and investigate just enough to have a presentable defense, but not enough to uphold serious concerns.

Nevertheless, these trends go against the image Wolf wants to present, so he says he is curious to hear his team's thoughts on what is happening. There is silence. Giving Wolf unwelcome news is a risky business. He is a terrible listener and does not react well. A brave voice pipes up that there has been a negative reaction to some recent decisions. Others nod in agreement and mention a few names – Ace, Bill, Hero, and Indiana. Direct report Toady sees an ingratiation opportunity and says he strongly disagrees with this – it is not about the firm, it is about "snowflakes and troublemakers". Wolf thanks Toady for the "common sense". He says the others do not understand – a consultancy told him that all is well. Toady makes Wolf feel good; in return, Wolf will increasingly turn to him.

Costs

Wolf silences people, except people like Toady. The cost to Wolf is his experience of the firm detaches from reality. Leadership depends on being able to hear uncomfortable information and having the courage to do something about it. Wily's "commercial" approach is a barrier to change. It is a triumph of short-termism over long-term value, trust, and integrity.

No accountability

That evening, Wolf is to deliver a speech on the firm's new values of Fellowship, Accountability, Kindness, and Excellence. Joy, his EA, has stage managed every aspect of the event so that Wolf comes across extremely well. Before he heads off to the auditorium, Joy tells him that she has accepted a role elsewhere. Wolf loses his temper and shouts that he forbids it. He storms off to deliver his speech. Another partner in the leadership team, Luna, overhears and says that she will speak to Wolf. She never does.

Meanwhile, Wolf – an industry icon – wows his audience of future talent with a wonderful speech about the firm's collaborative culture and the importance of inclusion and diversity to him personally. He never apologizes to Joy.

Costs

No one holds Wolf to account directly but that does not mean there are no consequences. Joy's resignation has already materialized. The story will affect how others see Wolf, Luna, and the firm. Such events are remembered and are more likely than ever to surface. The odds of complaints being made have shortened, and managing those complaints has become more demanding. Regulators focus on behavior more than before, and regulatory action can take years to resolve. And Wolf's speech on the firm's FAKE values? Raising false expectations in the next generation sows the seeds of disappointment, betrayal, and resentment. The firm has until those joiners start to align rhetoric and reality.

Solutions

The solutions to underperforming senior leaders are:
- Individual and collective upskilling, support, and accountability on the issues set out in this chapter;
- Ensuring they are focused. It is always concerning to see someone running a huge business prioritizing client work or their next move; and
- Create strong speaking up channels and information flows to the firm's governance board, without undue influence.

The costs of complicity

When I sit down with people like Ace, Bill, or Wolf it is normally because they are in trouble – or at least at risk. They sometimes wonder, "Why didn't someone tell me before?" Often, part of the answer lies with them, as they were not ready to hear. But part of the answer lies with the people who could have said something and chose not to – other partners, the C-Suite, Wily and Luna, for example. If these folks had done the right thing rather than play along, then the issues could have been surfaced and addressed. The skill and/or the will to act was missing.

I am not appealing to anyone's better nature or sense of guilt. If you are a partner and you know that a peer has a seriously negative impact, why not check your regulatory obligations? You may well find that your future could turn on doing something about it. Whatever the rulebook says, those who are – or should be – aware of misconduct and do not take effective action will be seen by others as part of the problem. There are no observers of bad behavior, only people who help and those who enable the behavior to continue.

How to upscale what is good and downscale the costs of underperformance

Looking back over 30 years' experience, I have found that firms need to tackle three things – a skills gap in how to nip issues in the bud on the ground, effective controls, and a gap at management level that allows high-risk issues to go unaddressed.

Table 1 overleaf sets out seven actions that will help. None of them involve a new policy. Too often I have seen leaders try to write their way out of problems they have behaved their way into. It never works.

Actions individuals can take

What to do if you see something out of line? Here are my top dos and don'ts:
- Do:
  - Understand your obligations – both regulatory and firm policy. If you are – or should be – aware of a conduct or capability issue, you may be obliged to do something.
  - Talk to the most trustworthy person in a position to act.
  - Get support – as someone who once blew the whistle, I know how hard it can be to rock the boat. Look after yourself.
- Do not:
  - Feel guilty – you are not causing trouble. You are trying to help and do the right thing. Be guided by your needs, obligations, and the truth.

Table 1: UPSCALE actions to reduce the costs of underperformance

U	Upskill everyone	Equip everyone to set the right tone and navigate key moments skillfully. Invest in extra love for those who deal with these issues day-to-day, such as HR and Legal.
P	Partner management	A partner once advised me, "Partners don't tell partners what to do." That was terrible advice – partner to partner support and accountability is the bedrock of firm culture. There also needs to be a strong infrastructure of good management practice – too often in law firms, basic HR practice falls apart at the partner/senior business services level. Make sure you press for clear and effective expectations, resources, and accountability systems.
S	Strengthen trust	Put trust at the heart of how the firm manages, investigates, and resolves all people issues.
C	Controls that are seen to work	Ensure the following are known to work for key people matters: controls, processes, resources, and governance. How long do issues fester? Can politics and profitability undermine your firm's values?
A	Align messages with reality	Aim to eliminate gaps between what is said and done, remembering that the firm is not just experienced by fee-earners.
L	Learn from mistakes	There can be magic in the wake of a fiasco, but only for those who ask the right questions and are willing to change. Avoidance fosters fragility.
E	Exit toxic people	Do not assist them to find a job elsewhere and report misconduct to the regulator to protect the profession.

- Gossip – rumors and speculation are never helpful when dealing with sensitive people issues.
- Get stuck in your thoughts – what you do counts, not what you think.

Final thoughts

Experience has given me a great deal of empathy for the hard-pressed partner – and for the hard-pressed associate or member of business services. It has helped me to understand the many costs of underperformance.

- Individual (distraction, disengagement, underperformance, lack of collaboration, and costs to wellbeing).
- Team (contagion, conflict, underperformance, hits to reputation, negative impact on turnover).
- Firm (clients, systems, performance, innovation, resources, reputation, talent, retention, regulatory, strategy, and ESG).
- Profession (standing, purpose, and social contract).

I have presented a range of issues related to underperformance through the lens of three fictional partners and sought to explain what firms can do to upscale their performance. Although some of the scenarios and behaviors may seem far-fetched, they are true to life and a long way from the most extreme cases I have seen. The fundamental issue is nipping issues in the bud in a way that strengthens relationships. I hope that I have helped to clarify your role in a wide range of situations and the practical steps you can take.

Chapter 9:
Performance management strategies

By Krystal Champlin-Gerage, CEO and law practice management consultant, RJH Consulting

Dealing with an underproductive or underperforming partner ranks highly among the challenges faced by law firms. When forming a partnership, the initial goal is that all parties will do their best to perform and produce equally for the success of all involved. But what begins with the best of intentions does not always last. Distractions and issues such as entitlement, mental health challenges, burnout, family situations, and substance abuse can cause attorneys to fail in providing the way they intended or committed to the firm. The stress of unequal workloads, unfair distributions, and even navigating the personal issues of colleagues can strain a law firm to the point of fracture, if not dealt with quickly and thoroughly.

This is not an isolated or rare problem. Gallup's 2023 workplace survey of American workers[1] revealed that the rates of engagement in all industries has stagnated at 33 percent, leaving the rest either actively or passively engaged in their work, both in-person and in hybrid settings. In his January 2024 breakdown of the findings on the poll service's website, Gallup writer Jim Harter states:

"Each percentage point gain or drop in engagement represents approximately 1.6 million full- or part-time employees in the US. Trends in employee engagement are significant because they are linked to many performance outcomes in organizations. Not engaged or actively disengaged employees account for approximately $1.9 trillion in lost productivity nationally."

In addition, as a population, lawyers are at higher risk of countless debilitating problems, such as a higher prevalence of alcohol and drug use – 21-36 percent report issues of alcohol abuse[2] as well as fatigue, stress, and depression due to the pressure to work long hours under high-pressure circumstances. This positions them to burn out, to lose momentum, or puts them at increased risk of health issues.

The problem of underperformance needs to be handled delicately and navigated with care. On the one hand, underperformance can carry ethical concerns about a firm's responsibilities to its clients. On the other, unraveling the source of underperformance can be challenging, since the level of potential problems a firm is dealing with can range from mental health issues, undisclosed family or personal strife, a concealed substance abuse problem, or even simple laziness.

Although confronting underperformance is difficult and often uncomfortable to face, it is not impossible. This chapter will explore how and why underperforming partners are a problem, the various reasons why people underperform, how to protect a firm contractually and otherwise from underperforming partners, how to handle underperformers, and how to interact with clients in the midst of these conflicts. The prevalence of substance abuse and burnout in the industry will be addressed, as well as navigating communication issues arising from generational differences with regard to work–life balance.

Most importantly, a case will be made for the need for firms to prioritize regular earning and goal-setting meetings and engaging coaches or consultants to ensure that underperformance is caught quickly.

Risks of underperforming partners

Along with causing stress and frustration, underperforming partners can – and do – put a firm at greater risk. This risk has ripple effects throughout a firm. It never just stays isolated to one person.

The obvious risks of underperforming partners have to do with attaining clients, retaining clients, and serving clients. A partner who is negligent in their business development efforts will leave the firm off-balance, causing strain or overwork for the others or allowing the firm's bottom line to struggle. An underperforming or distracted partner might miss important details, behave unprofessionally, or in other ways lose the business its potential clients. At worst, this behavior and negligence could leave the firm open to malpractice accusations. Regardless, a firm's reputation among clients – especially in the world of online reviews within easy access – is easily lost and difficult to repair, and the actions of one partner can have long-term, damaging effects.

One less obvious place where the impact of underperformance can be the most insidious – yet easily overlooked – is in staff morale. When a member of the team is not contributing, it greatly impacts the workplace culture. These problems can be contagious, especially if the source of the problem is a senior partner. Their underperformance can cause support staff or younger attorneys to feel frustrated or jaded at work, leading them to underperform themselves as an act of frustration or retaliation, or simply to find employment elsewhere. If this underperforming partner is in a position of authority, they can also create roadblocks for their associates by standing in the way of promotions. Support staff may find themselves in awkward positions if they know someone is underperforming but are not sure what others know or who to tell or what to say.

If the issues are not addressed in a timely manner and partners turn a blind eye for months or even years, people will talk and the firm will develop a negative reputation, impacting recruitment efforts or the potential for mergers. Top talent, on both the legal and support staff side, will want to be in a place where they feel motivated, inspired, and excited to advance their careers. If they sense that the firm doesn't take underperformance seriously, they may not trust the structure that they're putting the future of their career in. People want a tangible road forward to advance their career, but will not want to do so if it is unclear how this will happen.

Underperformance in a corporation vs partnership

Dealing with underperformance in a corporation structure can be less complex than within a partnership, and often comes with fewer dangers to all concerned. In a corporate structure, it is more likely to find the traditional hiring and firing policies, performance improvement plans, and hierarchy that are found in other industries. Performance is often tied to compensation and termination in a different way that is easier to enforce.

A partnership is different in key ways. Much of the time, a partnership is built on a nonobjective system in which everyone shares the profits. The basic idea – in theory – is that everyone does equal work, and therefore deserves equal share. There is an assumption of shared effort, shared reward.

The obvious pitfall with this system is that it decreases the incentive for partners to match each other's pace and work ethic, to ensure they are keeping up their end of the deal. If everyone knows they will be getting an equal section of the profits, no matter what they do or don't do, there's no external reason to apply themselves to match the effort of their peers. Similarly, it can be challenging to move these people along from the firm if they fall behind, since partnerships do not always have a clear, objective rubric for termination or discipline.

The erosion of trust can leave partnerships open to the "partner run" – a common factor in examples of law firm collapse, both on large and small scales. In an article for Harvard Law School's *The Practice* magazine, John Morley explains that the unique way that partnership-based law firms are structured can leave them open to a spiraling decline. When one partner leaves – or is removed, for any reason – it impacts profits for the other partners, and can have a ripple effect. He writes:

> *"If partners were paid in fixed salaries, they would not care about the declining profits. But because they are paid in profits, departures become self-reinforcing. As each partner leaves, the benefits of staying decline for all those who remain. This is a direct consequence of partner ownership."*[3]

Because of this worrying potential, the structure of a partnership-based law firm should be taken very seriously to prevent such issues from plaguing – and possibly ruining – a firm's ability to function properly and to the benefit of all concerned.

This can be a strong case for structuring a firm as a corporation rather than a partnership. While a partnership has its benefits and can work very well in the right circumstances with the right mix of partners, the structure of a corporation can function as a protective measure for all involved.

Safeguarding your firm from suffering the consequences of underperforming partners

The key to solving underperformance problems lies in their prevention, and prevention begins with making sure that every single member of the team feels accountable, engaged with, and included in major meetings and decisions. Proactivity in this area is vital, and can make or break the level of engagement of the firm's partners.

While many firms only meet annually to review their numbers, assess and reassess their goals, and take care of other important housekeeping, they would be much better served by meeting monthly or at least quarterly.

In these quarterly meetings, the firm should be covering present and impending expectations, setting and reviewing benchmarks (i.e., whether or not they were hit) – along with what distributions will look like. Many firms wait until mid-year or year-end to do their distributions, so that it ends up being a surprise. This is a mistake. As much as possible, surprises should be eliminated from a firm's operation. Regular, quarterly, meetings ensure that everyone is on the same page.

Accountability becomes a much more nebulous thing when there aren't clear benchmarks to compare performance to. If everyone is meeting regularly and all are responsible for their own reporting on their individual performance – and if everyone is already on the same page about what good performance looks like – it becomes obvious when someone is underperforming. And, for a little added weight, everyone in the room finds it out at the same time, including that individual. There is no hiding or shirking in this situation, no excuses. In this scenario, partners always have to present what they're working on and explain why their results are not coming along as planned. They are responsible for not only their results, but for explaining them. This is what a firm should all agree to do from the beginning, so there is no misunderstanding.

These regular meetings are also where the firm can examine whether its marketing and business development efforts are effective. If a firm is tracking its current strategy accurately, it can take a closer look at the rate, return, and ROI of that strategy and make adjustments where necessary that everyone is aware of and agrees to.

When business development efforts are handled in these regular meetings, everyone is given a chance to be accountable for what they are responsible for, so there are no excuses for not hitting the marks. Gaps and areas where you could need outside expert advice become easily identified, and the firm can see – all together as a unified team – what is working and what is not working. A proactive and collaborative atmosphere makes it very difficult for underperformance to thrive.

This proactivity and collaboration should also extend to the setting and meeting of goals, both individually and as a team. On an individual level, each person should be responsible for setting their own goals, instead of having a goal handed to them by someone else. This will make goals feel more attainable to that person and will eliminate excuses for not meeting them. Similarly, firm-wide goals should involve everyone's input, because a person who helps to build something is more inclined to be attentive to it. If someone puts time and energy into building a tower, they are going to put much more care and attention into preserving that tower to keep it from toppling.

For added support, it can really help to hire a coach or consultant to help the firm outline this structure together and agree together how everything will look. The basics of running a meeting and effectively communicating should be intuitive, but everyone has blind spots, and objectivity can be nearly impossible. Having an outside observer in the room can be to everyone's benefit.

How to confront an underperforming partner

Confrontation regarding another person's performance, particularly a peer, can be an uncomfortable challenge. But in issues of underperformance, time is of the essence. Proactivity and a strategic approach can lessen the discomfort of handling this situation.

The most ideal way for an underperformer to be revealed is in regularly scheduled meetings, so that accountability can be a collaborative process rather than something that has to be investigated on the back-end. When a partner's contributions or reports in the meeting are vague or feel incomplete, ask follow-up questions. If things aren't matching up with collectively set goals, partners can and should openly express concern. Initially, it is best to question one another with a curious tone rather than an accusatory one.

That said, if the firm has not had a regular practice of consistent meetings, or if handling underperformance in a meeting setting has not been effective up until this point, more formal action may be required. This will likely require a one-to-one confrontation.

It can be helpful to send a more senior partner in the firm to confront the underperformer, especially if there is a tenure difference. This can mitigate any peer-to-peer ego issues or even help alleviate embarrassment. But regardless of who is doing the confrontation, it should be done professionally and with no ambiguity.

First, present the facts. Utilize the documented data that was previously collected. Explain to them what you understand to be true, and allow them the opportunity to correct where they think it is needed. For example:

"For the last x years your fee production has been significantly and consistently lower. You have not provided a significant contribution to business development or leadership in the firm to make up for this deficit. Could you explain this pattern?"

After presenting the facts, take time to listen. If the individual has corrections to make about the data that has been presented, take them into account.

They may also give additional context for what is going on with them – divorce, mental health issues, illness, or other problems outside of work. If they do not offer this information, it is appropriate to ask if there's anything in their lives putting on pressure or giving them added stress. If they say that there is, make sure they know that the firm wants to support them.

After discussing any corrections or additional context, do not leave the conversation without planning a course of action. Invite the person to share what they believe should happen next, and genuinely listen to their ideas with an open mind. There may be details that the firm is unaware of, and people will respond much better to a collaborative approach than if they feel they are being cornered. No one wins when everyone's defenses are at their highest. It is difficult to be reasonable when a person feels attacked, and this will only lead to stress for all parties and an unsuccessful encounter.

If the person does not come to the conclusion on their own, be straightforward about proposing that compensation should be adjusted based on the data presented. (In situations where pay and performance are already linked, this action may not apply.) Whenever possible, refer back to any agreements, especially the partnership contract. Ensure that communication is assertive and clear, leaving no room for misunderstanding.

The person may quickly make promises to turn around performance and ask for time to improve. If the period of poor performance has gone on for some time, understand that they are unlikely to follow through on rashly made promises.

Make sure that the road forward is mapped out. Initial conversations on the topic can be more casual and relational, but that cannot last forever if there is no change. If there are no underlying personal issues and it appears a lack of effort is the issue, be clear with the underperformer. This is a problem, and it is not going away. The person needs to know when they walk away from that conversation that it wasn't just a high-level, hypothetical conversation. Action *needs* to be taken or action *will* be taken on their behalf. The steps along the road forward need to be quantifiable. The person should not be left in a position where there is any possibility of confusion regarding what is expected of them.

After every conversation, follow up with an email. Make sure it is congenial, but also outlines and debriefs the exchange. For example, *"It was nice to talk to you today. Thanks for listening, and thanks for sharing. This is what I understand you are about to do, and this is what I plan to do..."*

Offering support

There are a myriad of support avenues that can be extended to struggling attorneys, depending on what is at the root of the issue. Particularly when partners are younger or inexperienced, they may need continuing education or training to improve in areas outside their natural aptitude. Meticulous contract lawyers may need resources to be successful in their business development efforts, while passionate and visionary lawyers may need support staying organized and tracking deadlines.

Formal mentorship should always be woven into the culture of a law practice, no matter the size. More experienced attorneys can provide a listening ear, words of wisdom, and stories from the trenches that pave a way for those coming behind them. If you have a small firm, consider facilitating cooperation with another local firm in order to get mentorship needs met.

Coaches who specialize in the legal profession can also help lawyers upskill in a number of different areas, including goal setting, organization, work–life balance, and prioritization. One advantage of using a third party in this case is confidentiality – lawyers struggling with personal issues or who feel embarrassed about their failings may feel more comfortable confiding in someone outside of their workplace. Coaches can help bolster confidence and deal with any imposter syndrome that partners may be facing.

If the issue appears to be related to burnout, the firm may encourage vacation or sabbatical to allow the person to become refreshed and recalibrated. This is particularly relevant when a historically high-performing individual has a sudden change in behavior.

Sometimes it takes time for younger attorneys to find a place to thrive. Just as younger people sometimes need time to settle into a profession that suits them, lawyers need time to settle into a specialization. It may be that the work the person has been assigned does not match their mastery or passion, and trying other kinds of work may pique their interest and cause them to show more enthusiasm about their work.

Involving a coach or consultant

Proactive involvement of coaching or consultancy firms is one of the most strategic preventative actions a firm can take when it comes to performance. It is advisable to do a holistic assessment of all of your infrastructure every two to three years. Firms often practice this when it comes to refreshing their website and marketing, but consider expanding this assessment to include relational calibration, goal setting, and long-term planning.

Involving coaches and consultants early on can also ease the process down the road when you face underperformance issues because the relationships have already been established. The underperforming party is less likely to feel that the coach was hired specifically to deal with them, causing them to feel they're under scrutiny too soon. The coach(es) can be involved in ongoing conflict resolution, so that when and if problems escalate, they are already a trusted party.

External consultants and coaches will have an eye to blind spots and have many pointed questions to ask, providing valuable insight that is difficult to attain when one is too close to the problem.

Addressing substance abuse

Substance abuse in the workplace is a highly challenging topic to address. Often, substance abuse issues go unnoticed or covered up for long periods of time due to the person's ability to function despite the addiction.

Jim Lawrence's contribution to this book (chapter six) offers the perspective of someone who is a recovering alcoholic who overcame his addiction many years ago, and who is now a senior leader in his law firm. What follows is my personal perspective.

The first person to suspect or recognize an attorney's substance abuse issue is often a staffer working closely with that person. This places the staffer in a difficult position, because they may feel uncomfortable discussing their suspicion with anyone, fearing retribution or that they are mistaken. This is one reason it is important to develop strong relationships with staffers – they have a unique perspective that should be sought and respected.

When the firm suspects an attorney has an addiction issue, it can be helpful to address their performance rather than the suspected addiction. *"We have noticed a change in billable hours and collections and we have complaints that work hasn't been done correctly. We want to see improvements in 60 days."*

Offer support without overtly presupposing or prejudging what the person's problem is. Consider asking something like, *"Is there anything going on that we can support you with?"* The hope is that they will see the lifeline and grab it, but whether or not they do, avoid accusing anyone of a substance problem.

Do not turn a blind eye to a potential substance problem. These situations can be awkward to navigate and it can feel easier to avoid dealing with the confrontation, particularly if everything seems like it's functioning pretty well, but take seriously the threat of malpractice claims. This is a time to watch closely. Begin by discretely evaluating this person's work and documenting any known issues. Make sure deadlines are being met and that the firm is not otherwise compromised.

If potential malpractice issues arise, alert the insurance carrier of a potential claim. When doing so, do not voluntarily disclose that substance abuse might be at play. It is not a requirement to do so, and if the carrier discovers the abuse, they may not pay the claim.

If nothing improves and the person refuses to reveal that they have a problem, it is important to quickly transition the attorney out for the protection of the firm. This is another example of a circumstance where it is important to have clear contractual provisions in the partnership agreement for expulsion. If the partnership agreement requires a unanimous or high percentage vote, the situation could become more complicated if the partnership is not unified in its approach.

If the person does reveal their struggle and the firm is capable of doing so, consider helping the person find an attorney-specific recovery program. Though it is an expensive route, some firms will pay for inpatient programs and have found success in doing so.

Protecting the firm

While navigating these issues, stay committed to protecting the firm at all costs. Fighting for the individual, when it is evident that they can and want to improve, is also a worthwhile endeavor, but do not do so at the cost of malpractice risks or client loss. Do not allow avoidance or fear of confrontation to delay handling any suspected underperformance – the quicker things are addressed, the clearer they will be for everyone going forward.

If someone is showing signs of being uncoachable or not immediately taking steps to rectify the situation, make clear that the firm intends to take the issue seriously and is not afraid to take drastic action if necessary. Along the way, put every decision in writing so there is no misunderstanding from any party. Involving outside legal counsel will assist the firm in considering its contractual obligations to the partner, and can bring a fresh set of eyes to the situation.

If the conflict escalates, the partnership agreement is unclear and the firm's partners are divided about how to move forward, it may be necessary to vote to dissolve the partnership and form a new one with those who are committed to reforming things.

Communicating transitions to clients

If a decision is made to oust the partner, be intentional about how this decision is communicated to clients. Setting strong emotions aside, even if the person has made the firm look bad, avoid making defamatory or derogatory remarks about the person. You do not want to put the firm at risk of being accused of slander or libel. This does not guarantee that the person being expelled will uphold the same level of honor, but unfortunately there is not a lot that can be done to prevent someone from saying negative things about the firm.

Do what you can to protect that person from further career damage, though it may have been their decisions that brought them to this point. Do not share more than is needed with clients, and frame things as, *"We have mutually decided to go in different directions".*

Detail the path forward to clients, including all changes in communication channels. Make sure those clients feel prioritized and not lost in the shuffle.

Fostering a performance culture

Making sure individual attorney (and staffer) wellbeing initiatives are woven into the fabric of the firm's culture is one of the most effective ways to prevent underperformance. The youngest generation of attorneys has become savvy to the importance of work–life balance and burnout concerns, and it is important to take these issues seriously at your firm. These generational differences can cause divisions in any organization, but fostering an environment of collaborative conversation and decision-making will prevent future resentments.

Build sabbaticals into partnership contracts and keep an eye on billable hours. Do not create a culture that values billable hours above all, as this is not sustainable and leads to long-term physical and mental damage. Always keep the long game in view as you are building a successful partnership that is designed to last the test of time.

References

1   Jim Harter, "In New Workplace, US Employee Engagement Stagnates," Gallup, 24 January 2024, www.gallup.com/workplace/608675/new-workplace-employee-engagement-stagnates.aspx.

2   Krill PR, Johnson R, and Albert L. February 2016. *The Prevalence of Substance Use and Other Mental Health Concerns Among American Attorneys.* https://pubmed.ncbi.nlm.nih.gov/26825268/

3   John Morley, "Why Law Firms Collapse", Harvard Law School, March 2016/2017. https://clp.law.harvard.edu/knowledge-hub/magazine/issues/why-law-firms-collapse/why-law-firms-collapse/

Chapter 10:
The role of coaching and mentoring in partner performance management

By Jonathan Middleburgh, principal, Edge International[1]

Introduction

Alex has been a partner for several years in a mid-sized firm in the mid-West of the United States. The firm is highly profitable, and Alex has a well-deserved reputation as a star corporate lawyer. She is technically brilliant and popular with clients both in New York and Silicon Valley for her solution-oriented advice. Within the firm, the situation is somewhat different. She is known for being short-tempered and extremely difficult to work with. Associates and trainees do not want to work for her.

Brian is head of department in an international law firm where he has spent his entire career. He is about to turn 57. He has periodically discussed with the firm's senior leadership setting a date for his retirement but has always backtracked. He has confided with a couple of close colleagues that the future scares him.

Caroline is a tax partner in a large law firm in Australasia. She was made up two years ago and her practice has stalled. She receives regular plaudits for her technical skills and the support she gives to colleagues internally, but she has had no real success winning business for the firm. Her numbers are poor.

The above situations are doubtless familiar to anyone who has managed a large law firm. Perennial problems present themselves – how does a technical specialist redefine herself as a winner of work? How does a successful partner transition towards retirement? How best to help someone who struggles with people management?

Coaching claims to provide a solution to these problems. But does it? Does it offer a panacea or is it just an expensive placebo? How do coaches measure their impact? At a more fundamental level, what is coaching and how does it claim to shift entrenched behaviors?

This chapter provides an overview of coaching principles for those unfamiliar with coaching, as well as a discussion of issues of interest to those more familiar with coaching but perhaps unconvinced as to its efficacy.

Starting with a working definition of coaching, the chapter sets it in context amongst other approaches to the development of partners (and other lawyers) in law firms (and other organizations), such as technical skills development, postgraduate qualifications such as MBAs, and learning through reading (e.g., books on management / leadership etc.).

The chapter goes on to discuss how the external coach typically starts working with a partner in a law firm – setting up a coaching "contract", agreeing on the number of sessions, and ensuring that the relationship does not end up with the client (or "coachee") becoming dependent on the coach.

Using examples from the three scenarios presented above (coaching clients of mine, with the facts heavily adapted to preserve confidentiality), the chapter illustrates how coaching works (and sometimes doesn't), and how it drives outcomes. The chapter describes how the coach works with a law firm partner to set goals, typical topics covered during coaching, and what common outcomes look like. Coaching is distinguished from other approaches, in particular mentoring, and the value of mentoring is explored.

The difference between external and internal coaching is also addressed. The chapter explains how internal coaching relationships work best for partners – and when it would be preferable to retain an external coach. There is a brief discussion on mentoring and the value of mentoring in developing partners.

What is coaching?

There is no widely accepted definition of coaching. Nonetheless, many definitions contain similar elements.

Tim Gallwey, author of the best-selling *Inner Game* series of books, which he began writing in the 1970s, defines coaching as, "The art of creating an environment, through conversation and a way of being, that facilitates the process by which a person can move towards desired goals in a fulfilling manner".[2]

Philippe Rosinski similarly defines coaching as, "the art of facilitating the unleashing of people's potential to reach meaningful, important objectives".[3] Anne Scoular, co-founder of the well-known Meyler Campbell coaching program, aptly describes coaching as concerned with "pulling out the capacity people have within".[4]

For practical purposes, most definitions encompass the following elements:

- Coaching is a learning activity.

- The coach does not teach the coachee.
- The coach facilitates a learning process.
- This process typically involves the coachee acquiring additional understanding or insight into his or her actions or behaviors.
- The learning process is frequently goal-oriented – that is, successful coaching will help the coachee get closer to the attainment of his or her stated goals. Indeed, I would argue that, in the case of coaching partners in the context of performance management, coaching should always be goal-oriented.

Of these elements, the second is probably the most important to grasp. The coach does not teach the coachee. Coaching can be more or less directive or non-directive, but all "best practice" coaching starts from the premise that:

- The coachee must take responsibility for the outcomes of the coaching process; and
- The focus is on the coachee acquiring insight and learning (in the context of partner coaching, the aim is for the partner to improve his or her performance, often around management of leadership objectives), rather than the coach primarily dispensing knowledge to the coachee.

Take the example of Brian, the head of department approaching retirement. Most coaches will not tell Brian how to plan for his retirement or provide him with financial advice or strategies for how to spend his newfound leisure time. What the coach will do is help Brian think through his goals for the next stage of his life, acknowledge and address his anxieties, and then plan for the future. Similarly, a coach will not typically "teach" Caroline business development or tell her what to do. He or she will help Caroline to reflect on her current approach and to work out some new strategies to improve her success in winning new work.

Coaching creates a safe environment in which the coachee can reflect on the goals that he or she brings to the coaching. It is a space for reflective learning where the coachee can receive and process feedback from both the coach, colleagues, and sometimes clients. That said, coaching of partners should be a purposive, goal-based activity, and a good coach will not have done a good job without helping the coachee to move towards the attainment of those goals.

Contrast coaching with more traditional forms of learning and the differences stand in sharp relief. Traditional skills training for lawyers is aimed at the acquisition of technical or quasi-technical skills. The prevailing method is "chalk and talk" with the transmission of knowledge from teacher to learner. "Chalk and talk" has its place, of course, usually where the learner needs to acquire some defined knowledge. Even in that case, research into learning suggests that we remember only roughly 20 percent of what we see or hear, 50 percent of what we both see and hear, and 70 percent of what we see, hear, and discuss. By contrast, we remember around 90 percent of what we see, hear, discuss, and practice. Coaching is active learning, in the sense that coaching always involves practice, both within and outside of the coaching sessions.

Above and beyond this last point, "chalk and talk" cannot help where the goal is the acquisition of insight or self-awareness, the development of understanding, or the need to make behavioral change. Consider the case of Alex, whose managerial skills are poor / dysfunctional. Does Alex have any insight into the impact of her behaviors or real self-awareness? Her performance review might have flagged a broad area for improvement, but she may benefit from – indeed need – detailed textured feedback from relevant colleagues (including juniors) to develop an understanding of the effect of her behaviors. Having received that feedback, what is she to do with the feedback? Does she have the tools to become a better manager of people? "Chalk and talk" might cover the basics of management and some usual frameworks for becoming a better manager, but it will never address needs as complex as those presented by Alex. Chalk and talk will not help Alex to develop insight into her behaviors, still less help her to practice a changed mode of behavior. Coaching can help to do all this and more.

Coaching shares some similarities with mentoring. Mentoring, like coaching, has become increasingly popular over the last 20-30 years. The International Bar Association (IBA) promoted a mentoring scheme as part of its service to members around 10-15 years ago. But mentoring is somewhat different to coaching, as is explored more fully below.

How to get started
A relationship with an external coach typically starts either when an individual feels that he or she has a need for coaching or when an organization recommends coaching for that individual.

An individual does not always know what she needs. She may know that she needs help but does not know what help looks like; she might have heard about coaching from a colleague or friend, but not know the full extent of what coaching involves. A law firm recommending coaching may be a sophisticated purchaser of coaching services and the coach may be known to it. Often this is not the case. The potential coachee may well have little or no prior experience of coaching. In either case it is the coach's professional responsibility to explain what the potential coachee can expect from the coaching process.

Very early in the coaching engagement, the coach needs to discuss and agree the ground rules for coaching. Who is paying? Who is the sponsor? What are the rules about confidentiality and information? Is there to be a report back to anyone within the organization and, if so, what are the rules around this? It is important for the coachee to know that anything highly personal will "stay in the room" – this is vital if the coach is to develop a relationship of trust and confidence with the coachee. That said, most law firms will want some sort of report back – to understand what the coaching is achieving. This is completely understandable as coaching is very expensive and it is legitimate for the law firm to understand whether the goals are being achieved and whether it is seeing the desired level of return on its investment. It is important to set rules around the specificity of report back and for everyone involved to be on the same page about these rules.

If the ground rules are discussed and agreed at an early exchange, in my experience problems almost never arise in practice. Most coaches understand that the law firm is paying for an expensive type of learning. It is ideal that the ground rules be recorded and signed by all parties involved.

Personal chemistry is of paramount importance in choosing a coach. In theory, the coach herself might decide that the chemistry is not right, or that the coachee is not ready for coaching, or does not have the mindset to benefit from coaching. Sometimes the coach will discern that the paying law firm is foisting coaching on an unwilling partner. In that situation, a good coach will usually decline to proceed as an unwilling coachee will not engage constructively with the coaching process.

If coach, coachee, and law firm all decide to proceed, they will need to agree on the number and frequency of sessions. These will depend on the issues. If they are complex, they are likely to need around six to eight sessions and to take place over a few months. If the issues require behavioral change – as they often do – it is important to realize that changing behaviors takes time. I remind my coachees that the habits they are trying to change have formed over a long time, often decades. It is unrealistic to expect them to change overnight.

Equally, a good coach will put boundaries around the length of the coaching relationship. Coaching can develop into a dependency and coaching is about self-enablement. Any coach who suggests a very long-term coaching relationship is unlikely to have the coachee's best interests at heart.

How does coaching work?

Once the preliminaries are out of the way, coaching can begin. While it is important to stress that every coach has a distinctive style and approach, there are certain "common" approaches to coaching. The approach described here is the well-known and relatively basic GROW model of coaching.[5] "GROW" is an acronym for the stages of the coaching process:

- Goal setting.
- Reality checking.
- Reviewing Options.
- Identifying What will be done.

At the first stage of the process, the coach will explore what the partner (and the law firm / sponsor / line manager) wants to get from the process and help the partner to formulate goals. Typically, the coach will ask the partner a range of questions aimed at defining these goals. A skillful coach will use a combination of insightful questioning (usually starting with open questions, then probing as needed) and active listening.

Take the example of Brian, the head of department who is a few years away from retirement. Brian might initially formulate some limited goals around planning for his leisure time in retirement. Insightful questioning from the coach might elicit that Brian is feeling anxious about the future and his loss of partner status. The coach might suggest that Brian frame some wider goals for the coaching. Very different goals might emerge – for example identifying what Brian would like to get out of his life for the next five to ten years and determining whether he does in fact want to retire or wants to explore the possibility of a part-time consulting role or similar within the firm.

At the second stage of the process, the coach explores reality with the partner. In Brian's case this might cover several areas:

- What motivates him? Where do his core interests and values lie? Is working a fundamental motivator? Could Brian envisage a lifestyle where he is no longer working? Is he putting off retirement due to fear, e.g. about loss of status / meaning in life?

- What is the financial reality for Brian? Can he afford to retire? Most law firm partners in good firms can afford to retire (possibly with some adjustment to lifestyle) but fears about money are often a proxy for deeper anxieties about the future.
- How much of Brian's self-worth is invested in his work and current partner status? Lawyers typically underestimate how much of their sense of self-worth is invested in their professional status and role.

Often the partner will want to move swiftly from reflection to reviewing options and setting an action plan. Lawyers tend to prefer action planning to reflection. But coaching is a reflective process, and it is often the reflection that underpins the breakthrough or "lightbulb" moment. The coach often has to hold the partner back from action planning before he or she has done the groundwork required for effective action planning.

That said, coaching is not just about reflection – it is about shifting from reflection to action. The skillful coach will stimulate reflection but at the right moment pivot to action planning. The third stage of the process – reviewing options – typically involves the coach working with the partner to generate some options that are explored and refined.

In stage two of the coaching process, Brian might recognize for example that he is not ready to give up work entirely. He may have seen retirement in black-and-white terms but might now be willing to explore a portfolio retirement with a mix of work (paid and unpaid, volunteering, and leisure. Stage three would then involve generating and exploring the range of options with Brian, e.g. finding a new role within the firm (BD or ambassa-dorial; consultancy), a role in a new firm, non-exec roles, leisure options, voluntary work, more time with family, etc.

Sometimes the partner will find it difficult (at least initially) to generate options. It is key at this stage for the coach to open up the coachee's thinking, using the range of tools and techniques at the coach's disposal. A discussion of these tools and techniques are beyond the scope of this chapter but what is relevant is that a good coach will have a decent tool kit.

Once the options have been generated, these can be examined and whittled down. Some might be unrealistic, some might be fanciful, some will look attractive but need to be thought through. For example, many partners think they will walk into a series of interesting non-exec roles on retirement. In practice, it is quite hard to find good non-exec roles and the competition can be fierce. Lawyers are often not the preferred candidates for such roles as they are seen as more likely to be blockers than enablers. A skillful coach will help the coachee to review their options and test them out. This might take more than one session. For example, the coach might suggest that the partner research the practicalities of certain options between sessions.

The fourth stage involves action planning – identifying what is going to be done, when, and committing to an action plan.

It is important to correct any impression that the process is simple, simplistic, or linear. The process can sometimes be circular and is often iterative. Caroline might focus on business development outcomes at the start of the coaching process but gradually realize that she needs to make behavioral changes to build a reputation as a trusted strategic adviser, rather than as a back-room technical specialist, which is how she is currently viewed by most of her clients, and by the market. As a technical specialist, she might be very focused on results and outcomes and not realize that she needs to work on some of her client relationship skills (and softer skills at engaging with potential new clients). Sometimes, in my experience, the coachee has a lightbulb moment when she realises that her focus has been on the wrong issue – she has organized large numbers of technical presentations, for example, but not spent the time to connect on a personal level with attendees at those sessions.

Does coaching achieve results?

Prospective clients often ask whether coaching is anything more than an expensive conversation. How can one measure the impact of coaching and does the outcome justify the cost?

These questions are entirely understandable, especially within the context of performance management of law firm partners. Coaching is a "soft" process and outcomes can be intangible and quite hard to measure. However, there is a solid (and growing) body of science demonstrating the efficacy of coaching outcomes, and lawyers can be shown hard data providing evidence that it is not just a placebo.[6]

Nevertheless, the reality is that one cannot "prove" the efficacy of coaching in the same way as one can the efficacy of a medicine or vaccine. The nature of the coaching process means that it is impossible to conduct blind trials within control groups or to conduct rigorous experiments. Other variables might impact on the partner's growth – for example, mentoring taking place with a senior partner alongside the coaching.

That said, there is a very solid body of experience from sponsors in law firms that coaching does achieve outcomes – the willingness of law firms to invest heavily in coaching is itself an endorsement of the effectiveness of coaching, even if it is clearly not scientific evidence.

In practice, it is relatively straightforward to track whether coaching is making a difference and having an impact. One straightforward way to measure impact is to obtain 360 feedback data on the areas to be addressed in the coaching process towards the start of the coaching process, and to obtain repeat data during or at the end of the process. This can be – and usually is – qualitative data, but it also possible to obtain ratings (e.g., on a one to ten rating scale). The achievement of outcomes will be clear from the data – if the data shows that there has not been a shift, it is reasonable to conclude that the coaching has not had the desired results. This might be due to a range of factors – the partner's failure or inability to engage with the coaching process, his or her inability to make significant change, or the inefficacy of the coach. Whatever the reasons, one can say that the coaching has not made a significant difference.

In my experience, coaching will "work" to a greater or lesser extent in at least 80-90 percent of cases. In ten to 20 percent of cases it does not work, and this is usually due to the coachee having a rigid mindset, not being suited to what is a reflective process, or not being a constructive participant in the coaching process for other reasons. Sometimes it is because the chemistry between coach and coachee doesn't gel for whatever reasons. In the work I do with clients, I think it sometimes (I believe rarely) is because I can't find the right modality with which to work with the coachee. Any good coach will acknowledge that he or she sometimes can't find the right way to break through with a particular person.

Internal vs external coaching

This chapter focuses primarily on external coaching, reflecting the fact that my primary expertise and experience is providing coaching as an external coach to law firms and in-house legal departments. I have coached many partners in a wide range of law firms internationally (across UK / Europe, North America, Gulf, Asia) and the enhancement of performance has usually been at the core of those coaching engagements, in one way or another.

Many firms either lack the resource to retain external coaches or have chosen – in the case of some of the largest firms in UK / US / Australasia etc. – to insource coaching (i.e., bring it in-house), often because this can save significant amounts of money when multiple partners and other lawyers are being coached.

Does internal coaching offer similar benefits to external coaching? What are the pros and cons of external vs internal coaching?

First, it is important to define who will provide the internal coaching. Nowadays, in the largest firms, this is usually an experienced, qualified coach – for example, someone in the firm's learning and development department or an HR professional – or less frequently a lawyer line manager. Herbert Smith Freehills, for example, insourced coaching many years ago and set up a coaching academy to ensure that coaching was being delivered to a high standard. I am aware of several other firms that have done the same, such as Allen and Overy (now A & O Shearman). The coaching function is often headed by someone who is himself or herself an experienced coach who coordinates the provision of internal and external coaching and ensures that it takes place to a good standard.

Often, though, when law firms talk about internal coaching, they are describing less formal coaching provided by a more senior lawyer (typically a line manager or senior partner) who has acquired some coaching skills through internal or external training or informally "on the job".

In theory, if internal coaching is provided by an experienced and qualified coach, outcomes should be broadly similar to those outlined above. Internal coaches can, however, lack the range of experience of an external coach, who may have worked with a wide variety of clients, and coached partners in a range of law firms. As in any field of endeavor, experience generally improves competence and an external coach who has many years of experience is likely to be (though not bound to be) more skillful than a freshly minted coach.

Even if the internal coach is highly experienced and well qualified, an additional issue presents itself. Partners are often highly reluctant to open up to internal coaches in the same way as they will to external coaches, regardless of assurances of confidentiality. My experience is that partners are particularly reluctant to open up to internal coaches. There can be concerns that personal information might leak or that data gleaned during the coaching process might influence other internal processes, in particular remuneration / bonus. These concerns are usually misplaced but they are a reality. Partners typically feel uncomfortable undergoing coaching from a line manager.

Finding and selecting a coach

Having identified coaching as an appropriate approach for a specific performance management need, the next step is to find someone suitable.

Some firms (particularly mid-tier and higher) will likely or certainly know coaches or have a tried-and-tested roster of coaches, but this is less likely to be the case for smaller firms. Questions such as "Where should I look?" or "How do I assess / validate expertise?" come into play.

The best approach is by personal recommendation. People within the legal community are generally willing to share experiences and make introductions. Professional networks and groups such as the IBA can be good sources of contacts.

A coach who works well with one individual or group of people in a particular context or situation may not necessarily be the best fit with another individual or group of people, given different personalities and different issues. Chemistry is key and it is therefore important to use recommendations only as a starting point.

There are several professional associations for coaches. Because there are so many, there are no commonly accepted standards. Nevertheless, professional associations can be a useful resource, and their websites can be informative. One of the best known is the Worldwide Association of Business Coaches,[7] which accredits training organizations such as Meyler Campbell and certifies their graduates. Other bodies include the Association for Coaching,[8] the International Association of Coaching,[9] and the International Coaching Federation.[10] There are also many good and highly experienced coaches who are not accredited by one of these associations but hold other professional qualifications, for example as in my case in occupational psychology.

As with any other procurement, it makes sense to be clear about the desired outcomes and to invite a few prospective coaches to explain how they would approach the assignment. Inquire as to their level of experience in dealing with similar situations. Depending on the number of coachees, there may be benefits in working with a specialist organization rather than just one individual.

It will be important to be clear how the coach or organization approaches issues such as confidentiality, initial chemistry meetings (as these free of charge?), and reporting, as well as cost. It may be sensible to try a pilot project first.

It is essential to have an initial chemistry meeting between the potential coach and the partner in question. It is often helpful to provide a choice of coaches. As pointed out above, chemistry is key and coaching simply won't work if there is bad chemistry between coach and partner.

Mentoring

The focus of this chapter is coaching rather than mentoring. Mentoring differs from coaching in that it is typically a less formal process than the structured type of coaching process discussed above.

Modern mentoring can be defined as a process that:

> *"Allows established professionals and less experienced professionals to meet and engage with each other, offering both parties the chance to succeed, progress and learn new skills. In contemporary mentoring, mentors do not give the answers, their role is to help the mentee come to their own conclusion."*[11]

A good mentoring relationship can be transformative and the springboard for transformational development and growth. Typically, one thinks of the mentor / mentee relationship as being between a more senior individual in an organisation and a more junior one, rather than the specific context being between a more senior partner and a more junior one – but mentoring relationships can be helpful within this context too. For example, new heads of department and new managing partners can benefit from having a mentor, whether internal or, in the case of a new managing partner, most likely external. It is also relevant to say that many mentor / mentee relationships are best viewed as two-way relationships, in the sense that the mentor can also benefit by being "reverse mentored" by the mentee. The mentor often has a lot to learn from the mentee (for example, a junior partner might help to keep the senior partner in touch with what is going on at the more junior levels of the firm, especially in larger law firms).

A detailed discussion of mentoring is outside the scope of this chapter. Advice can be obtained if a firm wishes to set up a mentoring scheme – there are some good resources about mentoring available online.[12] A number of law firms such as Milbank LLP and Simpson Thacher & Bartlett LLP provide details of their mentoring schemes online.

Inevitably there is some overlap between how best practice coaching and best practice mentoring takes place. Typically, mentoring is more directive in modality than coaching. A good mentor will invariably also be a good coach, whether trained formally as a coach or just understanding that the best type of learning occurs when the mentor helps the partner develop self-insight and self-awareness.

Conclusions

This chapter has articulated some of the benefits of using coaching as a tool in the performance management of law firm partners. It has explained how the coaching process typically works and how it can achieve outcomes relevant to the performance of partners in law firms.

Looking for the right coach can be a voyage into the unknown. I hope that this chapter has provided some helpful guidance as to where to go and what to look for, so that firms can continue to develop their partners so that they can achieve their full potential.

References

1   I am indebted to Simon Pizzey who was my co-author on a previous version of this chapter, which appeared in a previous title published by Globe Law & Business. Jonathan Middleburgh, Simon Pizzey, *Coaching*, pp. 41-52 in Rebecca Normand-Hochman (Ed.) (2013), *Managing Talent for Success: Talent Development in Law Firms*, Globe Law & Business Publishing, London. The bulk of this chapter is taken from that earlier chapter. Any errors in the additional content are my own.

2   W. Timothy Gallwey (2000), *The Inner Game of Work*, Thomson, p.177.

3   Rosinski, P. (2003), *Coaching Across Cultures*, Nicholas Brealey Publishing: London, p.4.

4   Scoular, A. (2011), *The Financial Times Guide to Business Coaching*, FT Prentice Hall: Harlow, England, p.7.

5   Whitmore, Sir J. (2009), *Coaching for Performance* (4th Ed), Nicholas Brearley; London, p.55.

6   See for example: De Meuse, K.P., Dai, G. and Lee, R.J. (2009), "Evaluating the effectiveness of executive coaching: Beyond ROI?" *Coaching: An International Journal of Theory, Research and Practice*, 2, 117-134. There are numerous other studies and several meta studies.

7   https://wabccoaches.com/

8   www.associationforcoaching.com/

9   https://certifiedcoach.org/

10 https://coachingfederation.org/

11 See abdo.org.uk, section on Contemporary Mentoring.

12 See for example the helpful overview of Mentoring provided in a Note on the PLC website by Emma Sharpe and Claire Debney, Founders of MOSAIC.

Chapter 11:
Effective performance reviews

By Ray D'Cruz, CEO and co-founder, Performance Leader

Introduction

Performance reviews are scheduled and structured assessments of partner performance. An effective review will assess contribution for a preceding period and clarify contribution expectations and objectives for the future.

While there is some debate about the value of formal reviews, as explored later in this chapter, reviews possess enduring relevance for partners because they provide a comprehensive and reliable assessment mechanism. A standard review process will draw together a range of assessment inputs, which include both the qualitative and quantitative, and the financial and non-financial.

Where a firm uses a merit-based profit allocation model, the performance review process will impact the partner's reward outcome. In managed lockstep firms, where performance evaluation may impact progression through gateways or positions in cohorts, the review process is an important evaluation mechanism tool. Merit-based and managed lockstep firms will often have a remuneration committee or similar group to connect performance assessment and reward determination.

Even in firms where performance evaluation seems less important, performance reviews are still useful. In a firm using a pure lockstep, the performance review can be used as a formal feedback tool to help partners improve their contribution in line with the increased expectations that come with progression through the pure lockstep. In some formula-based systems, such as equal share partnerships, the underlying expectation that all partners will perform effectively places pressure on leaders to extract some performance equivalence from partners. In this context, performance reviews can be useful for holding partners accountable for making an equivalent contribution.

Irrespective of the reward system, performance reviews provide an opportunity to recognize partners for their contribution, both individually and within the partnership. Partners, who are typically high achieving individuals, value recognition. Firms that don't offer regular recognition to their partners miss an engagement opportunity by instead relying on financial reward to fill that appreciation gap.

Purpose of performance reviews

Performance reviews may fulfil several purposes for partners, partner-leaders and partnerships, including:

- Gaining a shared understanding of contribution;
- Providing honest and constructive feedback to the partner;
- Recognizing, praising, and celebrating partner contribution;
- Identifying underperformance;
- Identifying and supporting partner learning needs;
- Aligning partner objectives to strategic firm objectives;
- Implementing partner career planning and succession planning;
- Supporting the application of the firm's remuneration policy;
- Providing clarity about remuneration outcomes; and
- Promoting partnership cohesion by enhancing the sense of fairness from reward determinations.[1]

Each firm will balance these purposes differently, yet several of these should be emphasized in any partner review design.

The debate – formal versus informal feedback

In a 2015 polemic, *Harvard Business Review* argued that firms should kill performance reviews.[2] The cover story described how Deloitte had moved away from annual performance reviews, ratings, and rankings. The authors of the article argued that traditional performance reviews were not fit for purpose. They were too rigid, too late, too focused on ratings, and needed to be replaced by regular check-ins that are flexible, agile, and feedback-focused.

While many high profile companies and professional firms experimented with these ideas, most have now settled on the view that having both formal and informal feedback is desirable. While formal reviews ensure structured, fair assessments, informal feedback fosters ongoing development and responsiveness. A hybrid model incorporating both can leverage the strengths of each type of feedback, ensuring comprehensive and continuous performance management.

Figure 1: Complementary role of reviews and check-ins

	Formal review	Regular check-ins
Primary focus	Compensation determination	Contribution management
Orientation	Reflective (mainly)	Forward looking (mainly)
Key objectives	Agreeing/aligning objectives Agreeing learning	Progressing objectives Progressing learning
Frequency	Annual	Weekly, monthly, quarterly
Process accountability	Managing partner, practice leader, remuneration committee	Managing partner (small firms), practice leader (medium and large firms)
Leader skill set	Decision making Aligning/agreeing objectives	Coaching
Structure	Heavily structured to support key decision-making criteria for compensation and clarifying targets/objectives for the coming year	Lightly structured for information capture to streamline check-in conversations, provide ongoing data points for leaders and to provide an ongoing record for later reference

Source: © 2022 Performance Leader and MHPR Advisors. All rights reserved.

A regular performance conversation cadence, as illustrated in Figure 2, ensures that partners receive timely feedback while still benefiting from the structure and thoroughness of formal reviews. It also acknowledges that managing underperformance needs to be addressed separately.

Figure 2: Partner performance conversation cadence

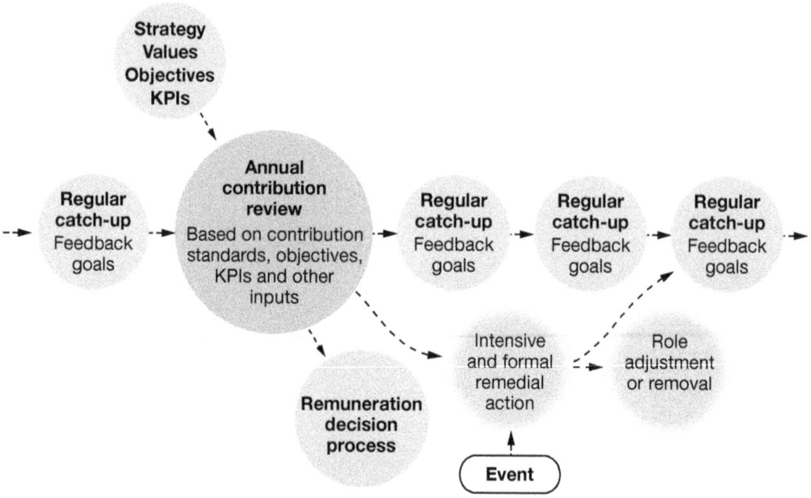

Source: © 2024 Performance Leader. All rights reserved.

Designing an effective and efficient review process

Effective review design will consider both effectiveness and efficiency. An effective process will incorporate relevant qualitative and quantitative inputs, self-evaluations, and peer and leader feedback. The process should balance reflection and planning, and be transparent, with clear guidelines on the assessment.

Process design should also consider efficiency. The complexity and detail of the approach taken by many firms to partner evaluation places a heavy burden on some stakeholders. Efficiency is often overlooked in favor of effectiveness. Yet there must be a point where inefficiency starts to impact effectiveness, and where tired decision makers struggle with discernment.

Key stakeholders and their interests

Table 1 shows the key stakeholders in this review process, and their associated needs and interests.

Table 1: Review stakeholder needs and interests

Stakeholders	Needs and interests from the review process
Board, executive	• Align partners to longer-term objectives • Track progress to the firm's long-term, strategic objectives • Balance long-term and short-term results • Align the firm's remuneration policy and formal review process • Align key messages to individual partners from the board, executive, remuneration committee, and partner-leaders • Promote partnership cohesion through fairness and transparency
Remuneration Committee	• Align the firm's remuneration policy and formal review process • Provide review data in a timely manner to support preparation • Ensure that review content can be easily analyzed (e.g., avoid wordy self-assessments, support cohort comparison, and provide data analytics tools for data visualization and text analysis) • Provide means for the committee to communicate to partner-leaders and partners, align feedback messages, and provide high-level guidance on objective-setting • In larger firms, streamline the presentation of review data to flag if high, medium, or low intensity decisions will be required from the committee
Partner-leaders	• Provide an efficient means for tracking review-related tasks and providing input (possibly in coordination with other leaders) • Identify success stories from review data to recognize and celebrate individual and collective achievements

continued on next page

Stakeholders	Needs and interests from the review process
Partner-leaders *continued*	• Ensure that difficult messages are delivered in a clear way to avoid any potential confusion • Align with remuneration committee feedback messages and guidance on objectives to support the partner and agree objectives and development priorities for the coming year
Partners	• Support the self-evaluation to be completed in a timely manner • Provide confidence that all inputs will be properly considered and that a fair assessment will be made • Give honest and constructive feedback to help the partner consolidate strengths and identify areas for development • Recognize and celebrate achievement • Provide clarity and support for objective-setting and development priorities for the coming year
Process managers (e.g. IT, HR, finance)	• Agree on timelines to produce external review data, such as financial metrics • Implement technology that supports compliance and enables effective and efficient conduct of reviews • Generate data for the remuneration committee that supports effective decision-making (e.g., preparation packs, tools for data visualization, and text analysis)

Review workflow elements

A typical review process includes several elements, which are outlined in Figure 3.[3]

Figure 3: Typical partner review workflow

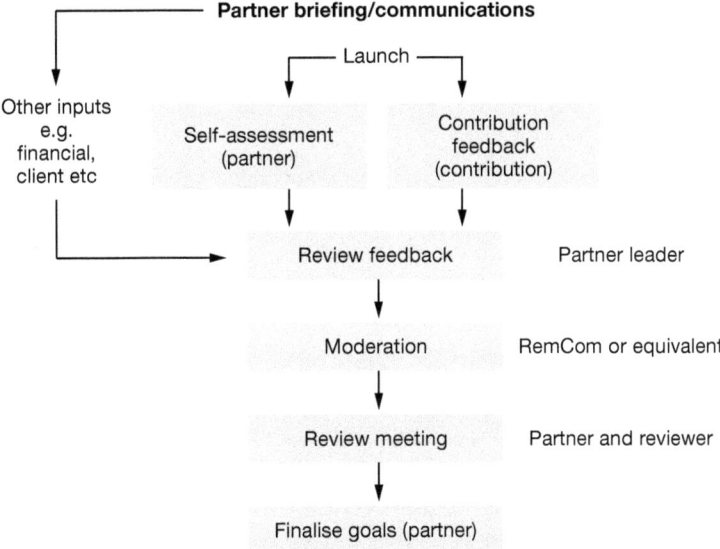

Partner briefings

Partner briefings involve informing partners about the review process, timelines, and support available. These briefings ensure that all partners understand the purpose and mechanics of the review process, which helps to build trust and transparency.

Self-evaluation

Self-evaluation allows partners to reflect on their performance and set objectives for the future, which is important for their self-efficacy. This step empowers partners to tell their performance story and take ownership of their performance outcomes. The self-evaluation also provides valuable insight into the partner's self-perception.

However, the self-evaluation process has its challenges. When the partner demonstrates a lack of self-awareness or intentionally seeks to anchor the discussion in their own favor (as a negotiation tactic), the job of the reviewer and remuneration committee becomes much harder. Both the reviewer and the remuneration committee must be steeled for this eventuality if they are to avoid favoring those who use these tactics and disadvantaging those who engage self-critically. The latter category typically includes traditionally marginalized groups who may experience imposter syndrome and be inherently more self-critical. To help overcome these risks, the need and rationale for honest self-assessments should form part of the partner briefing.

Contributor feedback

Through contributor feedback, partners and reviewers can gather insights from colleagues to provide a well-rounded view of performance. Peer feedback helps to capture different perspectives on a partner's contributions, which can highlight strengths and areas for improvement that may not be evident to the partner or their partner-leader. Contributor feedback inputs should be short and simple to minimize workload and keep the process moving. Contributor feedback, as described, should not be confused with traditional 360 degree feedback, which has development – not assessment – as its primary purpose.

Additional quantitative and qualitative inputs

It is useful to incorporate data from practice management systems, client feedback, and other relevant metrics. This data-driven approach ensures that assessments are based on objective measures, which reduces the risk of bias and enhances the credibility of the review process. Many firms struggle to produce quantitative inputs beyond production and origination metrics. In a dedicated chapter of *The Partner Remuneration Handbook*, there are several examples of metrics that go beyond traditional financial metrics,[4] including highly developed client, people, innovation, and collaboration inputs that leaders should consider, depending on the firm's reward philosophy.

Reviewer feedback

Reviewer feedback provides partners with written feedback based on the gathered data and evaluations. To help partners to understand their performance and how they can improve, this feedback should be constructive, specific, and actionable. The partner-leader will typically be someone with a group or team leadership role, who is close enough to the partner to be able to properly consider the self-evaluation, contributor feedback, and quantitative and qualitative inputs.

In larger firms, there may be two partner-leaders providing independent input. Firms can use these two perspectives to streamline the remuneration committee discussion. When both reviewers agree, the remuneration committee discussion is likely to be brief. If there is disagreement, the remuneration committee may need to undertake a more detailed review.

Moderation meetings
These meetings ensure consistency and fairness in the assessment process by facilitating discussions among firm leaders. These meetings help to align different perspectives and ensure that all partners are evaluated against the same standards.

Review meetings
In review meetings, partners and leaders have detailed discussions to agree on assessments and future objectives. These meetings provide an opportunity for open dialogue, which allows partners to ask questions, seek clarification, and collaborate on setting realistic and challenging goals. Suggestions for preparing for, and facilitating, an effective review meeting are detailed later in this chapter.

Follow up
Beyond the review, the focus for ongoing contribution management will be on how the partner is tracking against their objectives and key financial metrics. As mentioned, the cadence and nature of the ongoing dialogue should be agreed, and there should be accountability for both partners and partner-leaders to ensure this happens. On a practical note, if the review process is overengineered and burdensome, firms will find it harder to develop ongoing dialogue.

Assessment criteria
Assessment criteria are at the heart of the review process. Criteria cover both the subject matter that will be reviewed and the weighting of the criteria that applies when determining the overall review result.

The specific subject matter will depend on the firm's reward philosophy. In a financial meritocracy, financial data will be the primary focus. In a balanced meritocracy, the subject matter for the review will likely cover financial, client, leadership, knowledge contribution, and other factors. Where the firm operates a lockstep, the subject matter will reflect the strategy, culture, and operating environment of the firm.

Research consistently demonstrates that financial performance remains the most important factor when assessing partner performance.[5] It fits the business model, as most law firms are production-oriented. What's missing is a balance between these short-term inputs and strategic medium- and long-term priorities. Absent from many reviews is a meaningful assessment of people, client, collaboration, and innovation contributions. This is changing. Firm leaders are increasingly interested in how to draw strategic priorities, such as collaboration, into the measurement, assessment, and reward process.

Inevitably, as firms move beyond simple and simplistic financial inputs, the review process may become more complicated. Calibrating performance expectations, non-financial metrics, and objectives alongside financial metrics has the potential to overwhelm existing systems and processes. Good design can overcome this challenge. For example, some firms align contribution to strategic pillars and draw in performance expectations, objectives, and metrics under these pillars. When combined with fit-for-purpose technology (see chapter 19), a streamlined and simple process is achievable.

Preparing for and facilitating the review conversation

Training and preparation are the keys to effective performance review conversations. There are several ways partner-leaders and partners can prepare for and execute these conversations, as described in this section.

Synthesize and align messages

Reviewers should identify patterns in the partner's performance and prepare to discuss these themes comprehensively. Synthesizing feedback into a finite number of observations allows for an evidence base to be built using multiple inputs. It also allows for a finite number of objectives to be set. This makes ongoing conversations more focused and accountable for both the partner-leader and partner. Ideally, feedback messages will be aligned between the remuneration committee and reviewer.

Mitigate bias

Reviewers must be aware of unconscious biases that can affect their judgment, such as confirmation bias, recency bias, and empathy gaps. Biases can distort the review process and undermine its fairness and credibility. For example, confirmation bias may lead a reviewer to focus on information that confirms their existing beliefs about a partner's performance, while ignoring evidence to the contrary. When equity determination processes use the previous year as a starting point, confirmation bias is a real risk.

A well-designed review process with varying inputs and peer feedback will help mitigate bias. Reviewers should be conscious of their own assumptions and judgments. Regular unconscious bias training can be beneficial for raising awareness.

Train partners in conversation skills

The role of reviewer requires a range of conversation skills, from listening to facilitation to coaching. These skills should be developed across the whole partnership. Firms that are committed to an effective review process will build regular training into their review program. Some firms teach partners mindfulness techniques to deal with everyday practice challenges. These skills can be highly beneficial in review conversations where a calm and clear dialogue is required.

Manage difficult conversations

Difficult conversations should never be saved for review conversations. However, difficult issues may come up. The following four approaches may be useful when faced with a challenging conversation.

1. *Start with intentions.* When both participants outline their intentions regarding a difficult issue, they can first agree on common objectives before getting into the detail. This shared viewpoint – a broader, higher perspective – is a good place to start and may be a useful reference point as the discussion goes on.

2. *Be direct and offer support.* There is no value in obscuring direct feed-back. The so-called "feedback sandwich" is nonsense. Being direct can be difficult, but being indirect is worse. Mark Rigotti, former CEO of Herbert Smith Freehills, says "I've always found if you hold the bad news back... you're anxious. They know something's coming. It's better off going in hard with the bad news first and then empathizing."[6] Support is more readily accepted where there is a strong leader-partner relationship already in place, and the partner knows that the leader has their best interests at heart. Intentions can also be fallen back on at times.

3. *Manage emotion and volatility.* If the reviewee has an extreme reaction to the feedback, pause and take a break. The meeting can continue later. It is important to make sure things are not left hanging for too long. Group facilitation skills can help here, so have a clear agenda, let the partner talk, and be comfortable with silence because it might just be that resolution is around the corner. Reviewers should not become too emotional either. Rigotti suggests self-care – no more than one hard conversation per day, given how much it takes out of the leader.[7]

4. *Consider partner wellbeing.* Partner wellbeing is a paramount consideration in review conversations, especially difficult ones. The zero-sum gain nature of equity allocation means that reviews may cause anxiety for both the partner and reviewer. Ideally, for difficult conversations, the reviewer and reviewee are in the same room. That is not always possible in geographically dispersed firms. In these situations, it is preferable to have another partner or a trusted HR advisor in the room with the reviewee. Reviewers should refer the partner to resources or counselling services if required. Reviewers should also have someone they can talk to when things are becoming difficult. This person could be a managing partner, senior partner or external coach.

Taking a proactive approach to difficult conversations is recommended. Helping partners to understand their inherently self-critical nature (as high achievement-oriented professionals) can provide insight into why these difficult conversations are so challenging for all concerned.

Balance past and future

An important and sometimes overlooked component of the review process is objective-setting. While so many aspects of the review process are based on past activity and lag metrics, objectives provide a future focus.

There are many aspects to effective objective-setting, including the alignment of objectives to the firm's strategy and objective-setting methodologies, which are covered in a dedicated chapter of *The Partner Remuneration Handbook.*[8] In summary:

- Reviews should always include an objective-setting process, with objectives agreed between partner and partner-leader.
- Objectives should relate to both strategic business objectives and personal development objectives.

- Objectives should be an ongoing focus for regular check-ins between the partner and partner-leader.
- Reviews should assess the successful completion of objectives for the previous period.

Beyond the review

The review process should be complemented by regular check-ins through the year. These informal conversations are essential for accountability. Law firm strategy and leadership expert Gerry Riskin calls a commitment to frequent, ongoing conversations the "winning behavior" in the overall context of managing performance.[9]

The frequency and nature of these conversations will differ for each firm; however, at least quarterly check-ins are recommended. The main barrier to achieving a regular check-in culture remains time-poor partner-leaders. Ensuring the right governance structure and appropriate reward for partners in leadership roles goes a long way to addressing this challenge. Technology used to streamline this activity is also an enabler.

The agenda for these check-ins should cover some of or all the following subjects:

- *Progress against objectives.* Tracking progress against objectives ensures recognition for achievement and adjustments to be made or support to be offered where things are not tracking well.
- *Work reflections.* Check-ins should allow partners to reflect on their work, including recently completed matters, to identify what's working, what isn't, and what needs to change.
- *Learning and development.* Conversations should focus on the partner's learning needs, some which may have been articulated in the most recent performance review.
- *Wellbeing.* Partner wellbeing has become a more explicit focus for firms, with regular check-ins used to identify wellbeing issues.
- *Financial progress.* Key financial metrics should be reviewed using live dashboards. Check-ins build insight into the story behind the numbers.

Regular check-ins help ensure there are no surprises in formal annual reviews.

Conclusion

Complementary formal reviews and check-ins ensure a culture of continuous development, where issues are routinely identified and addressed. For the individual partner, there is both accountability and support. For the firm, there is a balanced focus between reward determination (dividing the pie) and setting objectives (growing it). Together, these elements build partnership confidence and cohesion in both contribution and compensation management.

References

1   Michael Roch and Ray D'Cruz, *The Partner Remuneration Handbook* (Globe Law and Business, 2022), p.191

2   Marcus Buckingham and Ashely Goodall, "Reinventing Performance Management", *Harvard Business Review* (April 2015) https://hbr.org/2015/04/reinventing-performance-management

3   Roch and D'Cruz (n1), p.194.

4   *Ibid*, p.

5   Nick Jarrett-Kerr and Jonathan Middleburgh, "Edge International 2024 Survey on the Management of Partner Performance", www.edge.ai/2024/06/partner-performance-management-survey-results-2024/. See also Michael Roch, Maria Georgakopoulos, Polina Pavlova and Ray D'Cruz, R. "Evolving Performance in the Professions" (Research Report, Performance Leader, 2016) https://info.performanceleader.com/evolving-performance-management-professions-2016, p. 6.

6   Ray D'Cruz, Performance Leaders podcast, "Mark Rigotti on leading dispersed, collaborative teams" (23 March 2021), www.performanceleader.com/resources/performance-leaders-podcast-s2-ep-5-mark-rigotti.

7   *Ibid.*

8   Roch and D'Cruz (n1), p.155.

9   Ray D'Cruz, Performance Leaders podcast, "Gerry Riskin on Leading High Performance Firms" (11 December 2020), www.performanceleader.com/resources/performance-leaders-podcast-s2-ep-2-gerry-riskin.

Chapter 12:
The role of partner compensation systems in managing partner performance

By Michael Roch, partnerships advisor and founder, MHPR Advisors, and head of partnership consulting, Performance Leader

Many professional services firms view their partner compensation system as the one-and-only tool to manage a partner's contribution, address "underperformance" and reward, and even incentivize "overperformance".

While the mechanisms of how partners share profits shapes accountability for behaviors, partners will not automatically do the right thing just because the remuneration system is "right". As other chapters explain, there are many more factors beyond compensation that influence how a partner "performs".

Yet a firm's partner remuneration system remains one of the most important management tools available to partner-leaders – as first among equals or otherwise – to influence how a partner contributes to the strategic and financial goals of the firm.

Managing "partner performance" or managing "partner contribution"?

Most management vernacular talks about "performance management". Yet most people equate "performance management" as something that is done to them just before getting fired. For this reason, I have long preferred "contribution management" as a more positive, constructive term to describe the more influence-based – rather than command-based – approach to leadership that is prevalent in most successful professional services firms (PSFs) today.

The term "contribution management" is apposite for another reason. The notion that partners are in business together as co-entrepreneurs in pursuit of common profit is partnership's most foundational element – with each partner contributing unique skills and money in exchange for some freedom of how to achieve success and for a share in partnership profit.

Being an equity partner is different from being a salaried or non-equity partner – being an equity partner is not a "job", and an equity partner does not "get paid". Instead, equity partners share in their firm's profits as a result of its success, which is best achieved jointly with other partners; equity partners receive their payout after everyone else has received theirs. Some partners no longer understand or no longer want to understand this.

Most partners thrive when they are invited to join the equity, and others struggle to make the shift. Firms scaling back co-entrepreneurship while scaling up managerial control have been surprised that partners feel less connected as co-entrepreneurs and start to behave more like highly paid senior managers. Firms seeking to invest have leveraged differences in profitability to pay a "market value" for equity partners, fueling the game of "lateral hire musical chairs" and reinforcing the notion that being an equity partner is just a highly-paid "job".

The best professional services firms today manage to strike a balance and continue to instill the value of "co-entrepreneurship" in their partners – along with the all-in commitment of money, energy, and sweat that the term implies. They don't just "manage partner performance" – they inspire their partners to contribute in the form of achieving great results together for the long-term financial benefit of the partnership.

The firm's system of how partners share profits influences the means of how this is done.

Locksteps, merit systems, and formulas – the seven archetypes of how partners share profits

Based on our work with dozens of international, regional, and independent partnerships across all professions and regions over the last 20 years, we know there are as many partner compensation systems as there are partnerships. This flexibility is healthy because each partnership delicately balances its structure to suit its unique strategic purpose, business model, culture, and organization.

In *The Partner Remuneration Handbook*,[1] my co-author and I introduced a typology for understanding how partners share profits. While there are many nuances, all partner reward systems fall within one of seven principal partner reward archetypes, as shown on The Partner Reward Disc™ (see Figure 1).

Figure 1. The Partner Reward Disc™

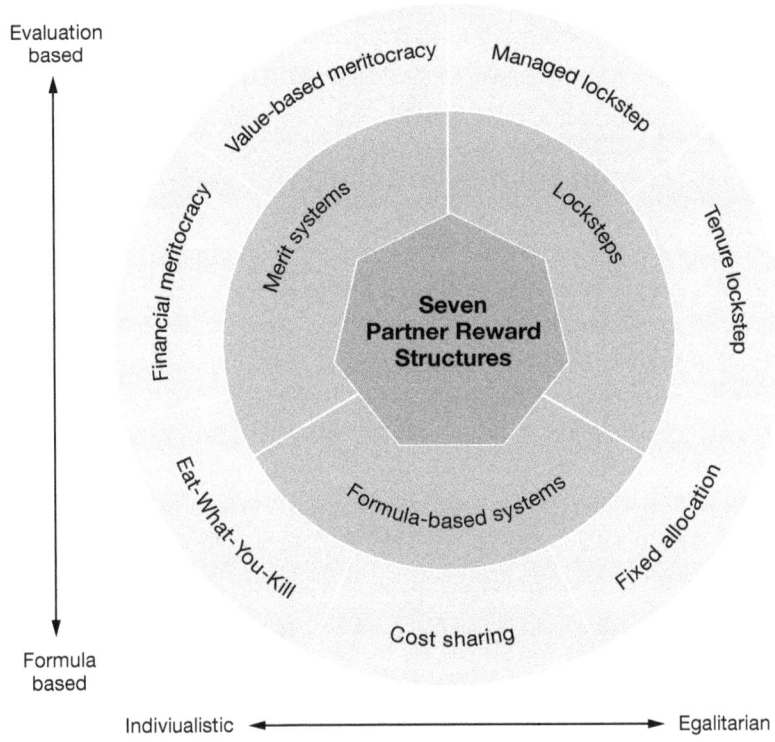

The Partner Reward Disc™ helps classify partner reward types across two continua:

1. The degree to which they are based on a formula or evaluation.
2. The degree to which they prioritize individual results or the results of the partnership as a collective.

As to the vertical dimension, some partner reward systems (Eat-what-you-kill, Cost sharing, Fixed allocation) operate in a rather hard-coded way. Human intervention in the form of leadership primarily occurs at a partner's entry or exit or to resolve fundamental problems that result in an adjustment to "the formula" for that partner or in that partner's exit.

Other systems (Value-based meritocracies and Managed locksteps) rely less on a formula and more on an evaluation. While the numbers continue to matter, a partner's contribution to the business is defined through a partner contribution framework, a "scorecard", or some other mechanism. In these systems, the "formula" is replaced by principles or rules guiding the firm's management, a partnership board, or a partner remuneration committee on how a partner's contributions to the firm should translate to a partner's reward outcomes.

The horizontal dimension explains how profit shares are influenced by outcomes achieved as an individual and by the outcomes achieved as a collective. Eat-what-you-kill systems and Financial meritocracies tend to place individual partner contribution at their core. Yet some systems (Fixed allocation systems and Tenure locksteps) care almost entirely about the results achieved by the collective. Yet because partners do contribute differently and often with widely different impacts on the business, nearly all Fixed allocation and Tenure lockstep systems operate with some kind of financial valve (typically in form of a bonus, a special profit pool or some other form of profit reallocation) that transfers profit share to partners who make exceptional contributions.

Value-based meritocracies and Managed locksteps rely on well-grounded partner evaluations and will have a balance between individualist and collective elements. Both systems care deeply about individual accountability and operate in very similar ways, with some important practical differences – when compared to Value-based meritocracies, Managed locksteps tend to:

- Have originated from Tenure locksteps and thus value collective success more than individual success;
- Produce fewer fluctuations in partner reward outcomes over time; and
- Produce less of a difference in reward outcome between the highest and the lowest profit share (top-to-bottom spread).

We do see a slow convergence of the two approaches, with Holistic, Value-based meritocracies leading the way in most highly evolved professional services firms today.

These seven fundamental partner reward structures, each with countless variants and crossovers, help express a firm's fundamental self-understanding of what "being in partnership" means day-to-day and provide a shorthand view of how partners share in profits. This view also informs how partners are expected to contribute, how their contributions are evaluated and assessed, how individual contributions affect a partner's profit share, and how the firm manages a partner's over- and under-contribution to the firm.

Managing partner contribution in Cost sharing and Eat-what-you-kill systems – and in Financial meritocracies

Cost sharing systems

Cost sharing arrangements are the simplest form of partnership – each "partner" is essentially treated as their own business. The partnership agrees an annual cost budget, and partners contribute to these costs *per capita* or based on some other formula.

Three types of firms tend to employ Cost sharing systems – very small practices (such as traditional English barristers' chambers), firms where partners don't need to collaborate much (such as where each partner just "works" their own client base), and partnerships of partnerships (such as some global networks and alliances of professional services firms).

As a key advantage, Cost sharing systems don't need a lot of partner management – partner-generated revenue is largely irrelevant. As long as they make the agreed periodic cost contributions, partners largely do as they please. The exception is where a partner causes reputational harm to the group, which – as in any partnership – will cause expulsion, the ultimate form of partner contribution management. Yet even here, because there is usually little cross-over of partner business, disengaging from a Cost sharing partnership – or from a partner – requires relatively little effort and has few organizational implications.

Therein lies the biggest disadvantage, too – Cost sharing systems almost never scale, precisely because relations among partners are mainly transactional; there is little else in the form of organizational purpose or unique culture. There is no impetus for partners to collaborate towards common business goals, and even much-needed investments often are stifled because no one wants to see an increase to their cost contribution ("muddling through" is deemed easier). Indeed, the most difficult conversations the business executive will have with partners is collecting their contributions, agreeing changes to the cost-allocation formula, or making investments requiring a special assessment.

Eat-what-you-kill systems

Eat-what-you-kill (EWYK) systems begin to socialize some profits among the partners. Each partner is still their own business, and their profit share is determined by the revenues or profits for which they are responsible. Often these systems distinguish between originated, managed, and worked revenues, with a pre-determined percentage being allocated to each type of revenue.

While the simplicity of EWYK can be great for some smaller firms, they share the same problem as Cost sharing systems in that they rarely scale (there is not a single large, market-leading, professional services firm deploying an EWYK profit sharing model). This is precisely because the relationship among partners is highly transactional. Partners must always tend to their short-term numbers (and haggle over credits) to maintain their share of profits; they tend not to grow clients beyond what they themselves can service; and investments in firm leadership or anything else that doesn't drive current-year numbers are stifled.

Similar to Cost sharing systems, EWYK systems don't need a lot of partner contribution management because financial outcomes self-adjust profit shares. For example, a partner generating GBP 2m in profit can happily co-exist next to a partner generating GBP 200k in profit because profit shares will be – more or less – relative to generated profits.

EWYK systems – other than their close relative, the Financial meritocracy – also have no tangible means of holding partners accountable for their commitments to the partnership – there are no valves enabling reward for valuable outcomes that go beyond the formula. This is one reason why EWYK firms tend to suffer from chronically underdeveloped firm management, the other being that even the managing partner always needs to maintain their own numbers.

Financial meritocracies

In Financial meritocracies, a partner's personal financial contribution (either revenue or profit) continues to dominate their profit share. Yet this model is no longer strictly formulaic and introduces other quantitative and qualitative contributions that "count" for purposes of allocating profit shares.

At its simplest, a Financial meritocracy is an EWYK system that accommodates additional, non-financial factors to impact profit share. The key differentiator is that now a modicum of evaluation and judgment is required by a decision-maker to arrive at a profit share allocation. This decision-maker is typically management, a partner remuneration committee, or both.

As the partnership grows, it is inevitable that ladders, tiers, bands, or a combination become convenient ways to manage a financial merit system. When designing a merit ladder, three main factors apply – the number of levels (tiers or bands) and sublevels, the increments chosen among and between levels and sublevels, and the value ascribed to each.

The main advantage of a Financial meritocracy over an EWYK system is that now firm management has a reward lever – albeit small – to hold partners accountable for results that further firm goals (see section on Value-based meritocracies below). The key disadvantages of EWYK systems remain.

Managing partner contribution in Tenure locksteps and Fixed allocation systems

Basics of Tenure locksteps and Fixed allocation systems

Tenure locksteps and Fixed allocation systems are also formulaic systems, yet their philosophy is the complete opposite to that of Cost-sharing or EWYK systems.

Fixed allocation systems are the original "true partnership". Partners agree and re-agree their equity interests in the partnership from time to time. This occurs typically when a new partner joins or a partner leaves – yet any change in the equity can occur only with a new agreement among the partners. In their most basic form, fixed share partnerships allocate their profits per capita, irrespective of individual performance of any kind. Because individual contribution or merit does not feature in partner reward, the hurdle to being admitted to equity partnership is very high.

Tenure locksteps are a variation of this theme and were the most common form of partnership model in the UK and some continental European firms until about 25 years ago. Tenure locksteps are based on a ladder that starts a newly admitted equity partner on a fraction of a full *per capita* share. The partner rises up the ladder automatically, improving their position each year (which is why some refer to these systems as "escalator locksteps").

Once a partner reaches the top of the lockstep (with full *per capita* share in the partnership), they remain there until they retire or are asked to leave the equity due to underperformance. As time served is the only "performance" required by a partner to receive a higher share of economic profits, a partner's performance is mainly "managed" by peer pressure as no one wants to be an "underperformer" relative to their profit share.

Collaboration, free-riding, and merit pools

Lockstep systems can be amazing collaboration enablers, and this is their single biggest advantage. When they operate at their best, there are no risks involved for partners working together to achieve great outcomes for the firm. This is because their own personal contribution does not affect their profit share as long as this contribution remains within the window of what the partnership accepts. For example, should a partner's personal revenues decline because they are developing a new service line, their personal share of profit would not be impacted in the short-term. Until recently, professional services firms with a Tenure lockstep, originating mainly from the UK, have dominated most markets with their collective approach to sharing profits.

Yet there are vulnerabilities. First, free-riding is well-documented – in Tenure locksteps at their worst, most partners cruise while few partners graft. Second, reward is not available as a tool to tie a partner's accountability to partnership goals. Third, a Tenure lockstep has no built-in means to financially reward a partner for contributions – financial or otherwise – that go far beyond the contributions of most partners. All in all, Tenure locksteps can ignore the practical reality that each partner contributes differently to the business and that all partners need to contribute broadly equally for a lockstep system to remain fair and competitive in the long-term.

As firms have grown in size, strict locksteps also have proven too inflexible to accommodate differences in profit potential among geographies or service lines (see discussion below), and this too can contribute to undermining partnership cohesion.

For these reasons, most firms have modified their Tenure lockstep by introducing some form of merit pool or by managing partners' position on the lockstep. By "merit pool" we mean a separate profit pool that allows firm management (or a remuneration committee) to allocate profit shares to those partners who clearly contribute more (financially or otherwise) than other partners at their level or whose geography or service line allows for higher levels of profitability.

"Underperformance" and improvement plans

Putting aside for a moment the question of whether a small merit pool can keep over-contributors happy, free-riding is fundamentally unfair – and this means "underperformance" needs to be "managed". The notion of being an "underperformer" causes severe psychological stress, both for the under-contributor but also for the firm leader having to address it. Merit firms by their nature are more self-adjusting – partners who contribute less simply receive a smaller share of profits, and there is less direct stigma of being an "underperformer" (at least until the difference in contribution is so significant that the partner is no longer tenable).

Managing underperformance in Tenure lockstep firms tends to involve agreeing a performance improvement plan with the partner in question with specific goals a partner needs to achieve to retain their profit share. Sanctions for continued underperformance involve a reduction in points or in ladder position, de-equitization or, ultimately, termination.

Performance improvement plans in locksteps often don't work as well as intended. First, most lockstep firms still don't have meaningful partner contribution frameworks in place that allow partners to self-regulate and that help managing partners to structure their contribution conversations with partners. In firms that do, partner contribution frameworks often are far too vague or don't articulate indicative measures to explain contribution expectations or to define how contributions are assessed.

Second, the problem often is that the partner has found their contribution level – and delivers broadly similar contributions year-on-year. Yet the firm and other partners on the same lockstep position have pulled beyond that contribution level and now are contributing – financially or otherwise – a multiple more. The partner hasn't slowed down, they just haven't kept up – and their practice in its current form doesn't deliver more even if the effort is there. Unless a partner can completely re-invent themselves, this partner will not be able to improve, with a profit share reduction – and the likely resulting voluntary departure – being inevitable.

Third, as one managing partner put it to me, "partners think that underperformance is catching". Instead of supporting their partner so their contribution can come back up to par, many partners will stop collaborating with that partner altogether for fear that their misfortune becomes contagious or to hedge their bets for who will service their clients. This "quiet" ostracism can of course further accelerate the affected partner's underperformance and ultimate departure.

Part of the solution could be in form of a partner improvement plan that not only involves the affected partner but those around them. This means coupling their success to the affected partner's success, much in how legacy partners are tied to the success of a lateral hire. Most firms don't do this because the partners around the underperformer resist – yet not doing so then becomes a political decision and not one due to lack of availability of an incentive that could be put in place to improve chances for success.

As the authors of other chapters point out, the best way of avoiding underperformance is to prevent it from happening in the first place. As I explain below, the best lockstep firms have in place a robust contribution dialogue that continuously aligns partners to what the firm is seeking to achieve.

Managing partner contribution in Managed locksteps and Value-based meritocracies

The convergence of two similar merit systems

Nearly all of the world's large, market leading, professional services firms use some type of merit system to determine how partners share profits. Yes, there are exceptions that prove the rule. And no, operating a merit system doesn't mean operating a snake pit. Today's merit systems in professional services firms come in two forms.

Managed locksteps are the modern incarnation of Tenure locksteps. Many partnerships have found Tenure locksteps don't easily address free-riding problems, and they lack a valve for accommodating different profitability among service lines and significant divergence in how partners contribute. While there remains a presumption of moving up the equity, firms increasingly recognize the value of flexibility in how they manage partners' lockstep positions based on meritocratic results (however defined).

Some firms manage their lockstep more actively, some more gently, and the options and variants are nearly endless. Gentle management might include review points (gates) on the way up when maintaining a dominant tenure (seniority) element alongside a – nearly inevitable – separate merit pool. Active management might include reducing the importance of tenure or requiring a periodic business case repositioning for all partners.

In the end, the overall objective is to determine reward outcomes that are commensurate with (a) ability to contribute, (b) commitments made, and (c) actual contributions made to the partnership, without either tenure or financials dominating the evaluation.

Value-based meritocracies (VBMs) share this objective, yet they start from the other end of the spectrum. Most VBMs that don't originate from Managed locksteps originate from Financial meritocracies. This means that instead of having to temper the effect of tenure, most VBMs must temper the outsized effect the financials have on partner profit shares.

Similar to Managed locksteps, VBMs seek to take a step back from the numbers and use the evaluation of a partner's complete long- and short-term, financial, and non-financial contribution to the business as the basis for allocating profit shares. As an example, where in a Financial meritocracy the numbers will count for at least two-thirds or more, in a Value-based meritocracy a partner's personal production will count for at most about one-third when it comes to allocating profit shares.

A firm's size, business model, and maturity will shape the exact design of Managed locksteps and Value-based meritocracies. For example, any internationally operating firm will need to take into account different levels of potential profitability in the design of their system, as both pricing and partner talent market can vary widely from country to country or from region to region. A firm operating a high-value, low-volume business model for some service lines and a low-value, high-volume model for others will be wise to consider how its reward philosophy integrates the two.

The same holds for how the profit-sharing model accommodates partners dedicating themselves to long-term strategic initiatives that take longer than a financial year or two to gestate (for example, starting a greenfield site). Here, the wrong compensation policy will be a limiting factor in both strategy design and its execution.

Making merit systems work

Beyond principles-based partner-led leadership, both Managed locksteps and Value-based meritocracies require five elements to align partners to a common purpose and to be successful in the long-term.

1. *Partner contribution frameworks (PCFs).* PCFs are a great way to explain how partners can contribute to the firm and how their contribution across different elements translates into reward. They are an integral part of the firm's partner remuneration policy. Most PCFs touch production, clients, people, and firm in some way, borrowing from Kaplan and Norton's famous Balanced Scorecard. Yet we only rarely see this model implemented in practice. When given a clean sheet of paper, our starting point is centered around intellectual capital management as this fits so well for knowledge firms operating in a digital world.[2] The model itself is much less important than that the partner contribution framework is developed uniquely for each partnership and is well-embedded in the partnership as the way to manage the firm. Only then can it become both an effective management tool for the firm's leadership, the partnership board, and the partnership at large – and an effective decision-making tool for the partner remuneration committee.

2. *Objectives and commitments.* Co-entrepreneurs make commitments to each other as partners. These commitments must be formulated in a dialogue between firm leadership and each partner alongside the philosophy and guidance given by the partner contribution framework.

3. *Measures and ongoing assessment.* Putting the technical difference between measures and KPIs aside for the moment, the best partner contribution frameworks explain the principles for how partner contribution is assessed and measured. Most merit systems break down because the metrics used in the daily business dialogue focus too much on production or numbers that come from the accounting systems. Often, measures are too focused on the individual and not sufficiently on group results. Partners believe what they see day-to-day more than what they see once a year. By implication, if you care about, for example, how many service lines your clients use, reducing unwanted talent turnover, revenue growth from new services, or widening the diversity in your firm, then you'll want to find ways to put relevant measures alongside the financial information partners see every day.

4. *Quality of contribution dialogue, processes, and infrastructure.* A good strategy needs committed partners for its execution. Partners who are set objectives once a year that are then forgotten about will do a lot of things, yet they won't be focused on delivering for the firm. Before reaching agreement on goals, a preceding high-quality, supportive dialogue as to how the firm can support a partner in reaching these goals will carry a much higher chance of success. Chances of success are further improved by light-touch processes and infrastructure, yet the quality of the dialogue with firm leadership is critical.

5. *Effective partner remuneration committees.* In large, mature, professional services firms, the partner remuneration committee's primary remit is to allocate profit shares to partners based on management's assessment of how partners have achieved their objectives and contributed to the firm's business. In smaller firms, the partner remuneration committee (PRC) may take on the assessment role. Either way, the PRC's decision-making needs to follow the philosophy of the firm's partner contribution framework. We have worked with many firms that on paper operate a Value-based meritocracy yet, in the last step of the chain, revert solely to financial production when allocating partner reward. This not only breeds partner cynicism, but also holds the firm back strategically. It's ok to operate a Financial meritocracy, but it pays to be transparent about that. Effective induction of partner remuneration committee members, effective committee chairing, and critical self-evaluations after partner reward rounds all play a critical role in ensuring PRC and management remain aligned.

Some readers will argue that a good culture can replace one or all of the above. It is true that the stronger the culture, the less formality is needed, yet the firm will struggle if it relies on its culture alone to support partner leaders in achieving sustained strategic, operational, and financial performance.

The importance of clarity and alignment

We created The Partner Reward Disc™ as an aid for analysis and design of partner compensation systems – nothing less and nothing more. It will be rare that any one system will fall neatly into one of these seven archetypes, and most systems are some form of hybrid, borrowing elements from one another to create the best fit for their partnership.

When designing a partner reward structure, it is important to understand the starting point. A Financial meritocracy and a tightly managed lockstep could conceivably end up producing the same reward results in the short-term; yet how the policy is articulated shapes the way that partners themselves frame their views on how they contribute to results, how they collaborate to achieve them, and the fairness of how profits and other results are shared.

Getting the detail right is fundamental to reaching and maintaining partner harmony. For example, we have seen firms where discord has caused the partnership to fall apart, usually because one group of partners is convinced that only originated revenues matter, while another group believes that mentoring should be a major factor when allocating profit shares. This lack of consensus quickly undermines cohesion.

Is there a recipe?

The pandemic has fundamentally changed people's relationship with their work. Nowhere is this more apparent than in professional services firms, and there is plenty of change ahead in how artificial intelligence will transform PSF business models.

The partner remuneration system is one of the most important building blocks for any professional services firm to compete. This is because the system for how partners share profits remains one of the most important management tools available for partner-leaders to influence how a partner contributes to the strategic and financial goals of the firm.

Most of today's most successful PSFs operate some form of meritocracy in which partners collaborate to achieve common aims. This is simply because high contributors are drawn to organizations that recognize them for what they contribute. Their flexibility will give well-designed, well-led, and well-managed Value-based meritocracies the edge as professional services firms navigate their futures and overcome the challenges to their business model.

Reward system aside, high performing firms will ask more of their equity partners than merely achieving short-term financial objectives. The best firms will take a long-term view of a partner's contribution to the firm, connect a partner's personal goals to the firm's strategic purposes, and embed a high-quality dialogue about how this partner can be successful at their firm. They will also ensure that each partner is a worthy partner (i.e., that true under-contributors are managed out) and that the firm's profitability produces meaningful profit shares that the firm earns in an ethical way.

References

1 Michael Roch and Ray D'Cruz, *The Partner Remuneration Handbook, A Guide to Compensation in Law and Other Professional Services Firms* (Globe Law and Business, 2022).

2 See, e.g. Ordonez de Pablos and Edvinsson, *Intellectual Capital in the digital economy* (2020) or Edvinsson, *Corporate longitude: What you need to know to navigate the knowledge economy* (2002).

Chapter 13:
When to cut your losses

By Jonathan Middleburgh, principal, Edge International

Few partnerships decide to move a partner out of the equity. Getting rid of a partner altogether is even rarer – truly an option of last resort. Most firms will prefer to try to find ways to deal with underperformance, falling well short of either of these two options.

This chapter tackles the following question – when should a firm cut its losses, removing a colleague from the partnership through de-equitization, voluntary or negotiated departure from the partnership, or in extreme cases by expulsion?

The chapter first explores how a firm should engage with an underperforming partner. Who should have the relevant conversation or conversations and how should those conversations be managed? Next, the chapter considers what options are available to a firm that wants to attempt to improve the performance of a failing partner. These range from coaching through formal performance improvement plan or similar through to offering the partner "intensive care" or other hands-on support. Third, the chapter reflects on the circumstances where it is appropriate for the firm to cut its losses, i.e. to decide that parting ways with the partner is, regrettably, necessary. Finally, the chapter looks at the various options for fundamentally changing or bringing the partner's relationship with his or her other partners to an end, ranging from de-equitizing the partner all the way through to expulsion from the partnership.

Engaging with the underperforming partner
Generally, it makes sense for the firm to engage constructively with the underperforming partner at the earliest appropriate opportunity. A partner who is performing badly or failing is more likely to get back on track with support. Ignoring the problem or not engaging constructively will not make the problem go away and is unlikely to improve the situation.

Who is the right person to engage with the underperforming partner? This is above all a question of context and organizational structure. In many firms (particularly smaller firms) it is likely to be the managing partner. In larger firms, the partner might have a line manager or someone to whom the partner effectively reports – and in most cases (s)he will be the appropriate person to engage with the underperforming partner. In some firms, someone in HR will be the right person; in other firms there will be someone specific who deals with partner performance issues.

Some firms don't tackle the issue of underperformance head on, consigning it to the box marked "Too difficult to handle". This is not a sensible management strategy and is mostly likely putting off a conversation that will have to happen at some stage. That only becomes more difficult the longer the underperformance is allowed to persist and fester without intervention.

In terms of timing, why wait for the annual performance review (if the firm has performance reviews or similar for partners)? Why not have the conversation at the earliest opportunity? Senior management in one firm I know had put off and put off what they perceived as potentially a highly difficult conversation with a failing partner. When they eventually, and with trepidation, had the conversation, the failing partner felt a burden had been lifted from her shoulders and she was finally able to get the support she needed. This was a good outcome both for the underperforming partner and for the firm.

How to conduct the conversation both in terms of approach and content depends on the context and seriousness of the situation. Sometimes firms use a sledgehammer to crack a small or medium-sized nut. In one situation I encountered a few years ago, HR had a very heavy-handed conversation with a partner who had not been performing particularly well (there were also allegations of intimidating and overexploiting juniors). The subsequent intervention, far from being nurturing, brought an already stressed and underperforming partner close to the point of emotional collapse. It would have been far better, in my view, to have had a softer conversation – or at the very least to have worked out in a more intelligent way what was intended to be achieved through the conversations that took place.

Generally, an underperforming partner knows that (s)he is failing or underperforming. The need to improve is not going to come as a surprise. The conversation can either be a productive one or an unproductive and potentially unpleasant one. The conversation is more likely to have a positive outcome if:

- There is clarity around the underperformance and what better / good looks like;
- The approach taken is supportive and non-punitive (so try to step into the underperforming partner's shoes and, knowing what you know of them, figure out what is most likely to help boost or turn around his or her performance); and
- There are clear goals and a shared understanding of the process by which you hope that the partner will improve his or her performance.

Options available to help the underperforming partner "turn it around"

There are various options available to help the underperforming partner. The range of available options will depend on the size of the firm and the extent of available internal and external resource. Most of the options referred to here will be unavailable to small firms – but even small firms can do a lot to support the underperforming partner.

Even in a very small firm there is often (usually) at least one partner who is good or very good at developing and supporting other partners. If a partner is failing or underperforming, help from another supportive partner can be transformative. Partners' performance can hit the buffers for a variety of reasons. The common-sense help of a fellow partner is sometimes all that is needed to turn things around.

Sometimes it will be necessary to institute a formal performance improvement plan (or similar). It may be necessary to do so to show that the firm has followed best practice in terms of process, if subsequently faced with a legal claim from the partner in question.

I would generally advise against having an overly formal process unless it is indeed necessary. An overly formal process does not create the conditions conducive to collegial conversations, and in practice is likely to produce an unproductive developmental environment.

Some firms have excellent internal coaches or mentors who can support the underperforming partner. External coaches can also provide support, although in my experience external coaching is often more effective when it is about "good to great" development rather than about the need to turn-around a bad situation. Remedial coaching can work, but it requires the buy in of the underperforming partner, and in practice such coaching sometimes fails. Several years ago, I was asked to coach an underperforming partner in a large international firm. It was clear from early in the coaching process that the partner had not really bought in to the coaching and had agreed to the coaching in an attempt – successful as it happened – to kick the can down the road. HR had failed to identify the partner's passive-aggressive approach to the coaching process, and management failed to call out the behavior once identified.

Whatever approach is used, key (in my experience) is to ensure that there is a supportive environment conducive to the partner's improvement. This does not mean, it should be emphasized, a soft environment. It is often necessary to be crystal clear about labelling and spelling out the underperformance. Indeed, the underperforming partner often lacks good insight into the reasons for his or her underperformance and sometimes these are clear to others. It makes no sense whatsoever, in those circumstances, to withhold clear feedback from the failing partner.

There are other options to help the underperforming partner. Where the partner is unwell (this can, and often does, include mental ill health) or burnt out, he or she might need some medical support or time out. Some firms adopt a system of "intensive care" whereby the partner is given intensive support.

Edge International (the global consultancy of which I am a principal) conducted a survey in 2024, aimed at exploring how different firms deal with the performance management of their partner populations. Around 100 firms participated in the survey, varying in size from very small firms (two to five partners) up to firms with over 100 partners. More information on this survey can be found in chapter 20. Seventy-four percent of respondents reported that their firm has used coaching, mentoring, and/or counselling to help an underperforming partner. 44 percent reported that their firm had provided financial or business development (BD) support to an underperforming partner, whilst 26 percent of respondents indicated that their firm had taken medical advice in order to support an underperforming partner. Eight percent said that their firm had adopted a system of intensive care to try to turn around partner underperformance.

How long is a reasonable time period to allow for a partner to meet agreed standards or to regenerate his or her practice? 15 percent of respondents to the 2024 Edge Survey expressed the view that six to 12 months is a reasonable time frame for a partner to turn it around. Just over 40 percent of respondents felt that 12-24 months is about right, whilst 17 percent would allow longer than that. 25 percent of respondents said that the period will vary depending on the compelling nature of the partner's business plan for revival.

When should your firm cut its losses and change its relationship with the underperforming partner?

At what point should your firm decide that enough is enough and that it is time to change the relationship between the firm and the underperforming partner?

This has to be a decision for the firm in question and cannot be answered simplistically in a few sentences. Some partnerships will be more tolerant of underperformance than others. In some firms there is significant history between the partners that means that the performing partners will be reluctant to de-equitize or to cut the underperforming partner loose from the partnership. Even where there is real history between the partners (and therefore an emotional nexus between the partners), a point will usually come where the performing partners decide that they cannot continue to (effectively) subsidize an underperforming partner, regardless of whether that partner is in the equity or not. Commercially it clearly makes no sense for performing partners to subsidize a loss-making colleague, regardless of history, compassion, or sentiment.

In the firms I have consulted to, there has always been an attempt to let the underperforming partner retrieve the situation. The performing partners are often extremely patient and reluctant to have the difficult conversation, still less to press the button marked "Cut your losses". However, if underperformance and loss-making persists, the performing partners (or the firm's senior leadership) will inevitably push that button at some point.

One significant factor is the extent to which the underperformance is skewing or impacting the dynamic between some, many, or most of the other partners in the firm. In a small firm, it can be highly undesirable to have one underperforming partner who is allowed to limp on. Other partners who are working harder and/or more effectively can resent the underperforming partner. They can also resent leadership for not dealing with the underperforming partner and allowing a situation to fester whereby the underperforming partner continues to draw on the firm's profits whilst not contributing (or indeed running at a loss). In larger firms, the effect of having an underperforming partner will be diluted by the size of the partnership, but the partner in question may well cause resentment or dysfunction within his or her team or department. Leadership should be keenly aware of the impact that the underperforming partner is having on his or her fellow partners, and indeed associates.

Options for parting ways with, or de-equitizing, the underperforming partner

What options are available once the decision has been made that enough is, indeed, enough?

Firms will often or usually try to find a solution that falls short of forcing the partner out of the firm. In the case of an underperforming equity partner, precisely what happens in detail will depend on the firm's remuneration structure. At a high level, what happens will be a partial or full de-equitization of the underperforming partner. One option is to reduce the partner's equity, for example by moving the underperforming partner down "the points" in firms that have a points-based equity structure and/or by restricting the underperforming partner's share of the pot or bonus in firms that do not have a points-based structure. Clearly, reducing the partner's equity will only work if the partner deserves a reduced slice of the cake. If the partner is persistently loss-making, the firm will want to remove the partner from the equity altogether – sometimes this will be done by moving the partner onto a consultancy type arrangement (e.g., an eat-what-you-kill arrangement) or moving the partner onto a salary (he or she might still be called "partner" but ceases to be an equity partner of the firm).

Another option is to negotiate the partner's exit from the firm altogether. Sometimes this will be preferable as it is unpalatable for the partner to relinquish his or her partner status and he or she prefers to leave the firm altogether. Sometimes it is the other partners / other senior leadership that wants the underperforming partner out of the firm – for example because he or she is a loose cannon, is giving bad advice to clients, or is in some other way an ongoing risk to the firm. A loose cannon partner poses financial, legal, and reputational risk and it is better to get that partner out of the firm.

It is obviously preferable to negotiate an agreed departure from the firm, with an orderly departure on agreed terms including as to what is to happen with clients. Sometimes, however, the breakdown of the relationship between underperforming partner and the other partners renders this impossible. Here the remaining partners will have to expel / remove the underperforming partner involuntarily, following processes laid down by the partnership agreement or deed. This assumes, of course, that there is a clear partnership deed and that it sets out a clear process. Sometimes that is not the case and lawyers can structure their own affairs in a way that they would criticize or berate their clients for doing. In situations where the partnership agreement is unclear (or there is no written partnership agreement), the performing partners are best advised to take legal advice from a lawyer / law firm who really understands the partnership law of the relevant jurisdiction.

The 2024 Edge Survey explored how departure occurs when it occurs. 49 percent of respondents reported that voluntary departure had occurred in their firm (this was the most common situation). 28 percent reported instances of negotiated departure; seven percent reported departure as a result of a formal resolution of the partnership; eight percent reported victory after a lengthy and time-consuming battle; and only one percent reported departure as a result of court proceedings.

The Survey also explored what percentage of *equity partners / members* had left the firm over the past five years, primarily as a result of underper-formance issues. 50 percent of respondents reported that no partners had left over the relevant period primarily as a result of underperformance issues; 30 percent reported that a small number (up to five percent of part-ners) had left for this reason; ten percent reported that as many as one in ten partners had left in circumstances of underperformance. The percentage of *non-equity partners* leaving primarily due to underperformance issues was somewhat higher – more than 50 percent of respondents reported attrition of up to ten percent of non-equity partners in their firms.

A further issue explored in the 2024 Edge Survey was the extent to which firms had (within the previous five years) altered their constitution or members' agreement / partnership agreement to facilitate the orderly depar-ture of an underperformer. Around 75 percent of respondents reported that this had not happened. Around 25 percent reported that it had. Around 20 percent of respondents said that their firm requires a 100 percent majority to achieve expulsion whilst around 50 percent said that their firm requires at least a 75 percent vote in favor of expulsion.

To give some further color, one respondent said that the power to expel, *"Sits within the executive although for a significant equity partner it is possible there would be some broader consultation amongst the board and / or equity group".* Another reported that, *"After a conversation with the Board, the partner in question has the right to dispute the expulsion by having a vote of the partnership. However, that has never happened – expelled partners have always agreed that they should leave without further voting."*

Facilitating partner moves

Sometimes, firms facilitate the move of a partner or partners. My co-editor, Nick Jarrett-Kerr spoke to several firms when he wrote an earlier book about partner performance management.[1] He was told by one firm, *"We have some-times talked to other firms that we know who are downstream of us and who could do with an improved skill set. This has enabled us to make an introduc-tion of a partner to another firm where they might prove to be happier"*. I haven't myself encountered this situation, but Nick has and the remainder of this sub-section borrows (with his permission) from his earlier work.

Some firms have also shed themselves of whole offices or practice groups by facilitating a management buy-out by the incumbent partners. A more devious (and often denied) tactic is to talk to head-hunters off the record about the possible availability of an unwanted partner in the hope that the head-hunter can introduce the partner to another firm. This is known as "reverse head-hunting" or "shunting".

It is also relatively common for a firm to tell an unwanted partner that there is no real future for him or her and to give that partner ample time (sometimes up to two years) to place themselves elsewhere, possibly with outplacement assistance. As one managing partner has said, *"Often, partners who are aware they are under performing "jump" before they enter any formal process"*.

Conclusion

Firms are understandably reluctant to part ways with an underperforming partner. Doing so is potentially destabilizing, especially in a small partner-ship. Some of the other "non-star" partners might feel insecure as a result, and morale can suffer. Chapter three on lateral hires analyses the costs asso-ciated with partner failure. There is a well-known psychological averseness to swallowing sunk costs and a tendency to plough on rather than to shoulder those losses – the so-called sunk cost fallacy.[2] Yet there are circum-stances where it is important for a firm to cut its losses and to break with an underperforming partner. Failure to do so can itself cause disaffection among some of the other partners on the basis that underperformance is not subject to proper sanction and that underperforming partners continue to take significant drawings from partnership profits. I have endeavored above to define the sorts of situations where it makes sense for the firm to cut its losses and exit the underperforming partner or partners.

References
1   See Jarrett-Kerr, Nick (2018), *Tackling Partner Underperformance* (2nd Edition), Ark Group p.171-172.
2   Arkes, H. R., and Blumer, C. (1985), *The psychology of sunk cost. Organizational behavior and human decision processes*, 35 (1), p.124-140.

Chapter 14:
Good leadership practice to avoid discrimination – or how to lead inclusively

By Stephan Lucks, BSc. MSc. C.Psychol, managing psychologist, Pearn Kandola LLP

The essay question for this chapter was "Good leadership practice to avoid discrimination". However, this chapter isn't going to focus on the employment legislation that you need to be aware of to avoid being taken to a tribunal. We're focusing on excellent leadership. We already know that good leaders lead in a way that avoids discrimination based on employees' protected characteristics, but excellent leaders lead in an inclusive manner. In short, by becoming a truly inclusive leader, you will avoid discriminating against people not only on their protected characteristics (which is illegal) but also on those not covered by the legislation.

One such example is weight. Our research has shown that, on average, 48 percent of obese people have experienced some form of discrimination based on their weight, whereas only 25 percent of their colleagues with a normal/healthy weight have experienced the same.[1]

The benefits of inclusion
Exclusion not only hurts the individual, but it also hurts the team and ultimately the firm. Here's how:
- At a physiological level, the moment a person experiences exclusion, there are increases in heart rate, blood pressure, and cortisol. This is the classic stress response and the same physiological response that you'd experience during the fight or flight response. In the longer term, these elevated physiological responses are associated with impacts on health such as increased risk of cardiovascular disease.
- Cognitively, working memory is impacted. The individual's focus shifts away from the task in hand and focuses instead on what they have experienced and why. The individual may become focused on figuring out what has happened and this uses up cognitive bandwidth, which can impact how effectively they read/write/do the thing they're

supposed to be doing. Over time, research[2] has shown that these psychosocial stressors (i.e., stress caused by social situations) impair our cognitive control processes (which enables us to keep our eye on the ball and shift focus between context and tasks). It also impacts our working memory and goal setting ability.

- At an emotional level, exclusion also impacts our self-belief. The knee-jerk reaction to exclusion is to take it personally – the individual internalizes it and assumes that they are being excluded because they lack something. Over time, this can lead to riskier coping strategies to numb the feelings of low self-esteem, such as poor eating habits, drinking more alcohol, or not exercising.

As can be seen from the above, the impacts on the individual are significant, but it goes beyond that to impact team and ultimately firm performance.

By implication, when a person's cognitive functioning is impacted it will also impact their job performance. Over time, role and job performance declines. People can disengage from work, which affects team and firm performance and impacts financial performance.

From a health perspective, the physiological impact of exclusion can result in increased sickness and absence rates. This has a direct financial implication for any employer.

Levels of innovation also decline. When an individual is excluded, feels less comfortable at work, and less safe (more on this later) they are less likely to speak up and share ideas and perspectives. This leads to a lack of creativity (a component of innovation) as well as less engagement in discussing and critiquing ideas that are on the table, meaning that fewer good suggestions are approved. The other component of innovation is the implementation of ideas. Where people do not feel included, they are also less likely to support others, which reduces the opportunities for great ideas to be implemented.

When one considers the cumulative impact of reduced individual performance, lower discretionary effort, high rates of sickness, and less innovation, one can see how this can result in poorer financial performance at an organizational level. Indeed, Bourke's[3] 2016 research showed that where organizations get diversity and inclusion right, they are two times as likely to achieve performance targets, three times more likely to have high performing teams, six times more likely to be agile in handling change, and eight times more likely to achieve better outcomes.

Lastly, there's reputational risk. Hitting the headlines or professional press for exclusion is one thing but being reported for discrimination and being taken to tribunal quite another, and both are not good for business. It impacts how the business and brand is perceived by clients, potential clients, and the talent pool the business is trying to attract. Crucially, 67 percent of job seekers consider D&I an important factor when considering employment.

Taking all the above into account, it's fair to say that exclusion doesn't just hurt the individual, it also hurts the organization. Better, therefore, to be inclusive.

Inclusion

Inclusion is about creating a culture where the differences that people bring to the workplace are recognized rather than eliminated, such that people flourish as individuals and as part of a high performing team.

The key words in the above are "differences", "recognized", "eliminated", and "flourish". The fact that people differ is undisputed. From a diversity perspective, differences in relation to ethnicity, gender, sexuality, and disability have long been understood, but diversity is more than that. Diversity is about all the ways in which people differ – both visible and non-visible. It includes working styles and preferences, thinking styles, personality, religion, political views, life experiences, parenthood, handedness, neuro diversity and so on. The list is endless. The key to inclusion, however, is that we recognize and accept those differences and create an environment in which people feel accepted despite those differences, and indeed have a sense of belonging. This will enable them to be themselves and be their best. It also creates opportunities to benefit from the strengths that those differences bring. However, as humans, we are not automatically inclusive.

Why humans aren't automatically inclusive

Earlier, we mentioned the fight or flight response. This is an autonomic nervous system response to situations that pose a threat to us. It's an involuntary and unconscious reaction triggered in our brain when it notices a change around us. Our brains have evolved to notice differences and changes in our surroundings. Think of difference or change = danger. As such, we are very quick to notice differences in people around us as, from an evolutionary perspective, these differences were a potential threat. We also have a clear preference for developing relationships with people who are like us – this is called homophily. We are therefore attracted to people we have something in common with, and are likely to feel less comfortable with people who are different to us. This can have some profound consequences for us:

- We tend to focus on the positive information about people we have something in common with.
- Conversely, we focus on and remember the negative information for people who are different to us.
- We put people into categories – broadly those like us and those different to us – and thus have an in group and an out group.
- Furthermore, given the human brain's capacity to develop and hold stereotypes, we only need a few examples of positive behavior (in the case of our in group) or negative behaviors (in the case of the out group) to develop positive and negative stereotypes for members of our in group and out group respectively.

So, what does this all mean? Three things are implicit in the above:

1. The stereotypes we hold can influence the decisions that we make about people.
2. We develop relationships differently with people based on whether they are similar or different to us.
3. The decisions we make and the relationships we have influence the culture that we establish at a team level.

In short, we treat people who are different to us differently, even if only marginally so, and from their perspective we may be less inclusive of them. In extreme cases this can express itself in prejudice towards people who are different (and potential discrimination) but in most cases it manifests in subtle behaviors that can make the person feel marginalized. They may, for example, not be given the same opportunities for stretch pieces of work, or we may just not show as much interest in how their weekend was compared to other people in our team. Over time, this is noticed and can result in people leaving, being less engaged and productive, or raising a complaint about unfair treatment.

By this stage, the reader should have developed a clear view:

- That inclusion is good for individuals and organizations.
- That leading inclusively is excellent leadership and avoids discrimination.
- What is meant by inclusion.
- Why we are not automatically inclusive.

What, then, do inclusive leaders do that is different to their less inclusive counterparts? Four key attributes are suggested:

1. They have a belief that inclusion is a good thing.
2. They make decisions about other people that are fair and do not exclude or marginalize others.
3. They have inclusive relationships.
4. They create a team culture in which people develop a sense of belonging and feel that they can contribute and add value.

Let's look at each of these in turn.

The inclusion mindset

Much of our behavior is shaped by our personality, our beliefs, and our attitudes. Exactly how much each of these contributes towards our behavior is debated, but let's focus on beliefs.

Inclusive leaders have an "inclusion mindset". In other words, they have a belief that inclusion is positive and will have a positive impact on people and the business. When that belief is held, they are more likely to behave in an inclusive manner, and when they behave in an inclusive manner, they will see the benefits that result. Seeing the benefits can reinforce the original belief. In effect, it's a positive feedback loop.

Positive beliefs about inclusion can be developed in several ways, for example by being informed about the benefits of inclusion, knowing about the negative consequences of exclusion, or simply taking a "risk" and acting inclusively.

Take Jack, for example. Jack is an associate who's just completed his training contract. In group settings, Jack is always very quiet and when discussing matters with the group of associates involved in the work he rarely if ever ventures an opinion. When the group is asked for a view, other, more vocal, team members always jump in with their views. Over time, the partner develops a view that Jack has no opinions and possibly concludes that he's not up to the work. Over lunch one day, the partner complains to a peer about Jack's lack of engagement and contribution. The peer says, "Have you ever asked him directly?". The partner responds in the negative, but at the next meeting, he makes a point of asking Jack for his view. Jack is at first surprised but shares a well-informed opinion. The partner starts thinking that perhaps he needs to ask Jack directly more often.

Whilst the above example might appear to be over simplified, it illustrates how a small change in behavior on the partner's part can bring about a different outcome and sow the seed in a change of belief about Jack.

Inclusive decisions

Inclusive leaders make decisions that do not unfairly exclude or marginalize others, or in any way disadvantage them. Furthermore, inclusive leaders are open and flexible in their thinking, such that they are prepared to consider new and (to them) unusual options. Finally, they are self-aware, and understand that they, just like everybody else, are biased, and they know what their biases are.

First of all, however, let's look at some UK data from the legal sector. In December 2023, the UK's Solicitors Regulation Authority (SRA) reported the following:[4]

- Representation of women is up from 52 percent in 2022 to 53 percent in 2023, although the gap between women at partner vs solicitor level remains significant. Women made up 37 percent of partners.
- 19 percent of lawyers working across firms were of Black, Asian, or minority ethic (BAME) origin (an increase from 18 percent in 2021). Overall, 17 percent of partners were from BAME backgrounds, but there was a higher proportion of partners working in one partner firms (36 percent) than for any other size of firm. Only eight percent of partners were BAME in the largest firms of 50+ partners.
- Attendance at fee-paying school was 21 percent in 2023, compared to 7.5 percent nationally.

Meanwhile, in Australia, women accounted for 35 percent in the second half Law Partnership Survey,[5] whilst in the US,[6] women made up 50 percent of associates in 2023, but only 28 percent of all partners. Although these numbers are an improvement, and in the case of associates a real success, the data shows there is still some way to go. For associates and partners of color, the figures are 30 percent and 12 percent respectively, and again, represent an improvement, although there is still some way to go.

Although decision making cannot be held solely responsible for these statistics, it will clearly be a contributory factor, especially when looking at, for example, the decrease in proportions of minority groups towards more senior levels. Something is happening in terms of either people's experiences or opportunities to progress that is resulting in lower proportions at more senior levels.

There are more than 180 different cognitive biases that affect how humans process information, far more than can be addressed in this chapter. We will focus on two key ones – stereotypes and homophily.

Stereotypes

Stereotypes are commonly known, but for the avoidance of doubt, they are "a widely held but fixed and oversimplified image or idea of a particular type of person or thing".[7] As soon as we hear the word "the" or "those" in front of a group of people, we are likely to hear a stereotype.

There are two different types of stereotypes – descriptive and prescriptive. Descriptive stereotypes describe behaviors or characteristics that are held by a particular group of people. Prescriptive stereotypes describe the behaviors and characteristics that are expected of a group of people. Thus, for example, we have stereotypes of men that describe them as being analytical, calm, and rational, and women as being caring and emotional. These descriptive stereotypes become prescriptive when we expect members of the group to behave in ways that conform with the descriptive stereotype, and when people do not conform to the stereotype, it can count against them. For example, comments such as "he needs to toughen up" might be said about a man who does not live up to the stereotype of men being "confident, assertive, bold, and brave", whilst a woman who is assertive and confident might be described as aggressive, or bossy.

Given that many job roles are described in masculine ways, i.e. drawing on male stereotypes of management roles, for example, the application of stereotypes is particularly damaging for women. Where they conform to their stereotype, they are not right for the role, and where they do not conform, it counts against them as they break the female prescriptive stereotype. You can see how stereotypes are not helpful and can result in exclusion and even discrimination.

Furthermore, the effects of what is known as stereotype threat are potentially very damaging. Stereotype threat occurs when people feel at risk of conforming to the stereotype that is held about their group. In this situation, individuals can become anxious about their performance and this anxiety reduces their performance on the task. What this can mean in practice is that even in situations where others do not hold the stereotype, it is the mere existence and anticipation of being stereotyped that can negatively impact performance.

Finally, we may be prone to what is known as benevolent sexism. Take, for example, the tricky and complicated matter of a client who is in a vastly different time zone. Not only will hours be long, but they may also be very unsociable. If, even for the best of intentions, a partner was to decide not to give the work to a female associate because she is expecting, then they're demonstrating benevolent sexism. Its roots lie in stereotypes (pregnant women can't/won't do the hours). The effect is that a female lawyer is being excluded and denied a chance to shine.

So, what do inclusive leaders do?

1. Check your own stereotypes. What stereotypes do you hold? Seek feedback from others, and where this is not possible, raise awareness of your own stereotypes by using tools such as the Implicit Association Tests (IAT) hosted by Project Implicit at Harvard University.[8]

2. Treat people as individuals and consider them on their own merits, rather than as a member of a group.

3. Challenge others when you hear them apply stereotypes. The only way to reduce the impact of stereotype threat is to create an environment where others (members of minority groups) feel safe that stereotypes are not being applied.

4. Consider involving the person in the decision rather than assuming on their behalf what they would/would not be prepared to do.

5. Ensure that you create the right conditions when making key decisions about other people:
   - Allow for sufficient time for discussion/consideration, and give structure to the discussion.
   - Make use of clear decision-making criteria and apply them rigorously.
   - When discussing with others, allow for open discussion and be prepared to question and challenge others' views as well as for yours to be questioned and challenged.
   - Question your own and others' "gut feel" or "instinct". It may be based on stereotypes or any of the other many biases that we have.

Homophily

As already discussed, homophily is where we are drawn to people with whom we have something in common. Where homophilous relationships exist, we are more likely to think of people that are close to us and in our network, and less likely to think about others. When we have that urgent piece of work for our most important client, we are more likely to think of and pass it onto someone in our closer network than to think about other people. We may, therefore, not involve the best person, and at worst be seen to exclude other people. We'll discuss what to do about homophilous relationships below.

Our decisions can result in other people being excluded and treated differently to others. This is inherently unfair and the effects of exclusion on them can be profound, as already described at the beginning of this chapter. Partners may need to ensure that systems and processes are monitored to ensure that some groups of people are not more adversely affected than others (adverse impact). Key processes to look at would include hiring, promotion, access to development opportunities, program nominations, remuneration, and bonus allocation, as well as resourcing of work. Lastly, I leave the reader with two key risks to consider when consistently excluding others in our decision making:

- They are not given an opportunity to prove themselves, and thus the view/stereotype that is held is never challenged.
- The consistent exclusion of others amounts to discrimination.

Inclusive relationships

We've already explored that as humans we are not naturally inclusive, and that it requires conscious effort to be inclusive. So, we need to be conscious about how we develop relationships at work.

Networks are a fact of life and all organizations rely on them. They can be inclusive or exclusive, however, and the way that a leader networks has an impact on more junior people. Firstly, as a role model, where a leader has an inclusive network, they act as an effective role model to others. Secondly, the membership of a leader's network is also likely to influence more junior people's networks because of the relationships that are extended to them through the more senior person's network.

The networks that exist in organizations typically serve two purposes. People use them to access knowledge, information, and resources (we call this instrumental support) as well as emotional support. It's the access to instrumental support that supports career progression as that is where they get the help that allows them to succeed.

At the same time, we need to consider the impact of "social capital", which is the potential to access resources, favors, or information. In other words, there is social capital in being part of the networks where one can gain instrumental support. It is therefore good to be a part of and to be seen to be a part of a network where there is instrumental support. The level of instrumental support available tends to increase with seniority, such that partners in a law firm hold the most instrumental support and therefore social capital. It's therefore important that partners develop relationships and networks that are inclusive and treat people equally in terms of their relationships. Being seen to have an inner and outer circle amongst employees, or possibly even showing favoritism, is very damaging. Favoritism can have profound consequences for a team as it can lead to toxicity and decrease the entire team's morale. Moreover, favoritism is linked to lower productivity and higher staff turnover.

What, therefore, sets inclusive leaders apart from their less inclusive counterparts in terms of their relationships?

- At a personal level, they foster inclusive relationships by investing time in getting to know all members of a team.
- They do not show favoritism in their relationships and are transparent in the decisions they make about people when delegating work, for example.
- They establish diverse networks, get to know a range of people, and seek to limit the extent to which homophily influences the development of their relationships.
- They challenge out group behavior, such as cliquey behavior and disparaging comments or stereotypes about other groups.
- They help members of the team overcome disagreements between each other.

Inclusive culture

The last area that inclusive leaders are good at is creating a culture (at team or practice group level) that allows people to be themselves and to be their best. The two critical ingredients to this are psychological safety[9] and psychological standing.[10] Let's look at each of these in turn.

Psychological safety

Inclusive leaders are able to create working environments in which others feel safe. What does this mean in practice? To understand better, let's look at work cultures that are psychologically safe. They are usually associated with:

- Continuous learning;
- High levels of engagement;
- Higher levels of innovation;
- Higher levels of employee satisfaction; and
- Open sharing of information.

Clearly, all of the above can be seen as benefits of creating a psychologically safe working environment, and the leader is instrumental in creating this.

For team members to feel safe and therefore be able to do the above, they need to experience behaviors that support psychological safety from others around them, and not be exposed to behaviors that undermine psychological safety. The leader's role is to role model those behaviors as well as address situations where others do not show those behaviors.

People learn when they are able to openly discuss and share ideas, views, and opinions with each other. They also learn from experience and – critically – mistakes. To support continuous learning, therefore, the inclusive leader makes it clear that no topic is off limits (within reason) so that ideas, thoughts, views, and opinions can be openly discussed, without fear of discussion being closed down, or disparaging remarks being made. The leader encourages debate.

The leader also encourages a degree of "experimentation" and avoids blame when things go wrong, focusing on the learning instead. Clearly, the level of experimentation possible needs to be discussed and agreed upon. A psychologically safe environment also does not mean that all ideas are good ideas, or that all behavior goes unchallenged. Quite the opposite. Ideas are discussed and the merits and downsides brought into the open, and behaviors that undermine this are challenged appropriately.

Once people feel that it is safe to contribute, to show initiative, and know that behaviors that undermine this are going to be challenged, they will feel more engaged and more likely to contribute openly. This in turn supports higher levels of innovation – colleagues are likely to more easily share diverse views and opinions, which underpin innovation and decrease group think. Ultimately, the inclusive leader is showing trust in individuals and the team as a whole, and by appropriately challenging behavior that undermines this, showing care and concern for team members.

So, leaders that create psychologically safe working cultures:
- Encourage debate;
- Ask others for their views;
- Avoid apportioning blame;
- Identify the learning points when mistakes are made; and
- Challenge behavior in others that do not role model or undermine the above, such as disparaging remarks, not listening, interrupting, excessive criticism, and the application of stereotypes.

Psychological safety can go a long way towards encouraging the active participation and contribution of colleagues; however, a team also needs psychological standing, because without this some people may still not feel able to give of their best self.

Psychological standing

Fundamentally, psychological standing is about making others feel that they matter and are seen as valuable and adding value to the team. Research has shown that groups that are in the minority start at a lower place in terms of psychological standing than the majority group. For example, the latest addition to the team (being new and in the minority) is likely to not yet have a sense of psychological standing and may therefore be less active in contributing to debate, volunteering for work, or showing initiative. People that do have a sense of psychological standing feel valued and entitled to speak up and act. Inclusive leaders are able to instill a sense of psychological standing by:

- Encouraging quieter members of the group to contribute, by for example directly asking for their views.
- Not allowing more vocal members of the group to interrupt or talk over quieter people when they do speak.
- Recognizing individual achievements and talking about those. This can help to raise awareness of value being added, and ultimately contributes to that individual's social capital.
- Reward success in words and actions.
- Build on the contributions of others, rather than setting them aside.
- Explicitly value differences, be these in terms of thinking style, perspective, opinions, life experiences, etc.

The reader may have noticed a degree of overlap between psychological safety and psychological standing, and indeed there is insofar as some of the behaviors that support one, also support the other. What seems to be clear is that psychological standing follows from psychological safety, and that, without the former, the latter is less likely to develop.

Psychological standing can further be enhanced by recognizing and accommodating individual needs. From the employee's perspective, this speak volumes as to how they matter. In practice, this means using relationships to better know and understand people's needs and seeking to find ways to accommodate these. This is because the systems and processes that exist are typically designed to meet the needs of the majority and in so doing overlook the needs of the minority, for example those with childcare responsibilities who may benefit from a different working pattern. For example, the gender parity in firms in the US shown above has been put down to being more flexible about working from home.

Summary

This chapter has explored the three key concepts that make up inclusive leadership and posited that, instead of taking a defensive approach to avoiding discrimination, i.e., focusing on compliance with local employment legislation, excellent leadership is inherently inclusive, and that by being inclusive, discrimination is avoided. It has further described the downsides of exclusion for the individual and the organization, and highlighted the benefits that can be achieved when leaders act inclusively. Where relevant, it has described the actions/behaviors that inclusive leaders demonstrate, in contrast to their less inclusive counterparts.

Table 1: The features of inclusive leadership.

Decision making	Relationship	Culture
Are aware of and know their biases.	Have diverse networks.	Encourage debate.
Focus on making fair decisions.	Do not show favoritism.	Invite quieter members into discussion.
Create the right conditions for decision making.	Invest time in getting to know their team, and encourage others to do the same.	Ask for views and opinions.
Avoid stereotyping and treat people as individuals.	Challenge out group behaviors.	Avoid giving blame.
Challenge stereotypes in others.	Help team members overcome disagreements.	Support learning from mistakes.
Ensure process are monitored for adverse impact.		Openly recognize achievements.
		Reward success.
		Challenge behavior that undermines inclusion.
		Build on the contributions of others.
		Value the differences that team members have.
		Show interest in individual needs.

References

1   Pearn Kandola research (2023). "Weight discrimination at work". https://pearnkandola.com/research/weight-discrimination-at-work-report-2023/

2   Taylor, J. (2020). The effects of discrimination. In B. Kandola (Ed.), *Free to Soar: Race and Well-being in Organisations*. Oxford: Pearn Kandola Publishing; Haslam, C., Jetten, J., Cruwys, T., Dingle, G., & Haslam, S. (2018). *The new psychology of health: unlocking the social cure*. Routledge: Abingdon.

3   Bourke, J. 2016. *Which Two Heads Are Better Than One?*

4   www.sra.org.uk/sra/news/press/2023-press-releases/2023-firm-diversity-data-pay-gaps/

5   www.afr.com/companies/professional-services/two-law-firms-hit-gender-parity-and-credit-wfh-20231204-p5eoqz

6   www.americanbar.org/groups/journal/articles/2024/for-the-first-time-women-make-up-a-majority-of-law-firm-associates-nalp-report-says/

7   From Oxford Languages.

8   https://implicit.harvard.edu/implicit/takeatest.html

9   *Psychological Safety: The History, Renaissance, and Future of an Interpersonal Construct*. Amy C. Edmondson and Zhike Lei

10   Morrison, K. R. (2011). A license to speak up: Outgroup minorities and opinion expression. *Journal of Experimental Social Psychology*, 47(4), 756–766.

Chapter 15:
The importance of clear purpose and strategy

By Nick Jarrett-Kerr, principal, Edge Consulting

Introduction

There is a spectrum of transparent management in law firms. At one extreme, there are firms where even the partners are tightly controlled and closely managed by a leadership group operating though codified regulations and a comprehensive performance management system. In some such firms, operations are conducted in a black box of secrecy and lack of open communication – the axiom often seems to be "knowledge is power". At the other extreme, there are firms that manage the partners with such a light touch that partners seem entirely free to practice and express themselves with large amounts of autonomy. At this extreme, there are few secrets and partners are brutally aware that their every shortcoming is known to all. Partners in such firms often feel that, as partners, no rules apply.

Most firms operate somewhere between the two extremes, in the knowledge that the result in the worst cases can either be unpleasant martial law or hopeless anarchy without accountability.

Whatever might be the chosen or default style of each law firm between these two extremes, it is important that performance issues are clearly understood and communicated.

Incidents of underperformance create substantial communication difficulties for a managing or senior partner and the firm's top management team. In general, the partners want to be kept up to date with all material issues with which the management team is dealing, but at the same time, individual discussions have to be kept entirely confidential. The issue of trust is important. In order to be able to deal with underperformers without partner interference or inquisitiveness, the management team needs to acquire the credibility of being perceived as safe hands capable of dealing with any crisis. In the case of planned departures, the management team also needs the authority of the partnership to negotiate and agree terms. The first and most important communications' prerequisite is to agree a set of standards and to communicate them to all partners.

Communicating performance issues

There are three important rules when communicating with partners on performance issues, particularly when issues of underperformance have to be confronted.

Rule 1: Honesty and openness in one-to-one dealings

All managing partners and law firm leaders to whom I have spoken over the years have stressed the importance of confronting the brutal truth honestly and openly on a one-to-one basis. As was once observed by Oscar Wilde (who probably got it from someone else), "Whenever one has anything unpleasant to say, one should always be quite candid". It is clear that such conversations will always involve more than the mere facts and will include feelings that are potentially painful or damaging. However, dealing with underperformers requires assertiveness and not confrontation, and rigor, not ruthlessness. As Jim Collins observes:

> *"To let people languish in uncertainty for months or years, stealing precious time in their lives that they could use to move on to something else, when in the end they aren't going to make it anyway – that would be ruthless. To deal with it right up front and let people get on with their lives – that is rigorous".*[1]

Conversations with individual partners should therefore confront facts and data, unfulfilled personal objectives, promises that have been broken, and excuses that have been made. In extreme cases, the managing partner should ask underperforming partners to consider whether they might not be happier in a different role. Furthermore, partners who perceive (or indeed are bluntly told) that there is no future for them at the firm, will very often leave. As one law firm partner told us, "Often partners who are aware they are underperforming 'jump' before they enter any formal process".

Rule 2: Harnessing the power of listening and asking questions

The reason that most underperformers leave firms before they are forced out is because a period of self-reflection has caused them to think carefully about their future. Partners who underperform usually are aware that they are not meeting standards. Accordingly, the most dignified (and indeed a very powerful) way of getting such partners to acknowledge the issues is to get them to talk openly about their performance as well as their strengths and weaknesses and to put the past behind them. It is not easy to shift the

focus from the historical baggage of the past to an appreciative and constructive view of the future. One option is to harness the power of active listening,
allied with asking the right questions.

All involved in law firm management and leadership know that active
listening is one of the most basic of skills and is utilized in almost every
learning situation. The outcome of active listening on a one-to-one basis can
include reassuring the partner, particularly when they express sensitive feelings. Indeed, I have often found that encouraging others to verbalize their
feelings can clear the air and allows constructive discussions to resume.
Active listening also promotes a sense of rapport and trust between
managing partner and the other partner. The experience of being heard and
understood is a catalyst to developing the bond of trust.

I have always found it important to ask meaningful questions when
dealing with performance issues and to encourage the partner to continue
dialogue. Seeking clarification in vague areas not only prevents misunder-
standings but shows the partner that you're interested in them as
individuals.

Rule 3: Communicating past accomplishments linked to needed change

All good books stress the merits of giving positive feedback where you can.
It can be seen as highly artificial to start a difficult conversation with praise
and positive feedback when both parties know that the meeting has been
fixed to discuss difficulties and underperformance. It is, however, sometimes
useful to work, as a starting point, from the partner's strengths. This
approach is grounded in the theory that the mind cannot develop a negative
image or picture and that "the power of the positive images shared and
studies will move participants toward thoughts and behaviors that make
them successful".[2] Hence, identifying moments of excellence can be built on
to provide feedback and insights as to what should be done in the future to
move towards improved outcomes.

As Hal Plotkin advises:

*"Look for areas where the employee has been successful and point out how
the traits that led to those successes can be applied to areas that need
improvement. Don't just offer exhortations; build an employee's confidence
by letting him know exactly why you think he will be able to handle whatever tasks are at issue. Explain how current workplace requirements are
related to his previous accomplishments."*[3]

Communications within the firm about performance issues

Communications within the firm are notoriously difficult while a partner is in "intensive care" or during a period of discussions and negotiations over a possible departure or adjustment in partnership status. Even in firms that prefer an atmosphere of complete transparency, confidentiality has to be preserved in the case of sensitive discussions. The leadership challenge is to build management confidence in the leadership team from the partnership group so that the issues can be tackled without interference. It helps greatly if the partners trust their leaders, both in terms of grasping issues of under-performance and in the handling of negotiations and discussions. Conversely, partner interference in issues of underperformance can be extremely detrimental, not least because many underperforming partners will remain at the firm in a different capacity. Even where departure negoti-ations are underway, the aim should be both to maintain the employability of the departing partner and to part ways as friends and not enemies.

Practical suggestions for internal communications therefore include the following guidelines:

- Make sure that the firm has clearly established and communicated a rigorous and uncompromising set of standards, which partners under-stand and agree.
- Establish responsibility for communications on any issue of underper-formance – a single person needs to have a dedicated communications role.
- Address communication issues on a confidential and one-to-one basis to group or department heads and those who need to know within the affected partner's team.
- Be extremely wary of what is said in emails or in writing – this is not just an issue of whether such discussions count as privileged (or not) but that in the wrong hands an unwise email can undermine discus-sions.
- Think carefully about the timing and coordination of any internal announcements.
- Gain the agreement of the affected partner to a communication amongst partners that – for example – negotiations are underway.
- Where partners are in "intensive care", it helps to agree with that partner a restricted list of those who need to be made aware that his or her position is under review and being monitored.
- Ensure that those who are carrying on discussions or negotiations have

the authority to conclude any agreement to save the constant need to communicate changes in positions.

- When the issue is ready to be opened up, both to the whole group of partners and elsewhere in the firm, make sure that an agreed "song-sheet" is drawn up and that everyone sticks to the message.
- Update the partnership or membership agreement to ensure that departing partners are under a continuing obligation for confidentiality.

Client succession issues

Client succession issues often form part of the negotiations with any partner who is leaving the firm. Whilst clearly it would be misguided to communicate departure news too early with any client, there can be no objections to ensuring that other partners use every opportunity to meet and interact with important clients – indeed, ensuring more than one partner is involved with every key client relationship is now common practice in many firms. Equally, it is leaving it too late to communicate with the client after a partner has left. As with all communications, timing is everything. It is essential to agree the wording of the communications agreed with the outgoing client and to be able to spell out the arrangements that the firm plans to put in place, subject to the client's agreement. Clients may also need to be reassured that they will not be charged for reading-in time. In some cases, it is appropriate to allow the departing partner to continue to represent a portfolio of selected clients, subject to their wishes. Where the firm has agreed to allow a departing partner to take clients with him or her, it is also vital to agree and communicate the necessary handover arrangements, both for transferring files and for settling any sums owing to the firm.

External publicity and communications

Fortunately, the legal press has become used to the regularity of partner moves, but it is nonetheless important to have an agreed strategy for all external communications. This strategy does not need to be complicated or wordy but should address the following.

- *The overall message.* Think about how this ties into the firm's high level strategic intent – its identity as a firm, its purpose, and its vision.
- *Whether the firm needs to communicate at all.* Internal problems that are unlikely to pose little impact on the firm may not need to be made the subject of media attention. Silence can be a communications strategy.

- *The kind of story the firm wants to portray.* Many firms have been involved in significant restructuring over the last few years in order to reshape the cost base of the firm for the future. Firms that are prepared to take decisive action in order to adopt a more efficient business model can often build a strong and compelling story around such restructuring.
- *The weight of response the firm wants to make.* Too heavy a response can create its own crisis. However, an inadequate response may add to an already complicated situation.
- *The level of proactivity or reactivity needed in communicating the message.* After all, the press is often quick to portray an orchestrated departure from one firm as a clever acquisition by another firm.
- *How the reputation of the firm can be preserved.* Here it is important both to play down the importance of the departures and to avoid being drawn on any personality or performance difficulties.
- *Communications priorities.* Some 20 years ago, media specialist Sue Stapely[4] gave the example of an entire tax team defecting from a law firm and commented:

  > *"The main audience for the messages should be the existing clients of the departing tax team, and other existing and potential clients of the firm. The secondary audiences will be other partners and staff within the firm, and those who make referrals to the firm or supply it with assorted services. The primary media focus should be the publications it is thought the key clients will be reading, not just those read by rivals, although preserving the firm's reputation in the legal marketplace via the legal trade media will be important."*

Supervising and monitoring partners by means of a performance management system

The framework for a successful performance management system should meet a number of objectives that embrace all aspects of partner performance. The main thrust of any performance management system should be to encourage and support behavior and performance that contributes towards the profitable development of the firm towards its strategic goals. The objectives of a successful performance management system should therefore include (or be judged against) the following principles and objectives.

Strategic

The performance management system should identify the areas where the firm must perform as a whole in order to achieve its strategic and economic objectives, which can then be drilled down into "critical areas of performance" or a balanced scorecard, as discussed in chapter one. It should also ensure that financial rewards match contributions to strategic objectives of the firm, as well as the maintenance of cultural values. As a further objective, the performance management system should recognize and reward long-term growth towards strategic objectives rather than just short-term results. It should encourage partners to support new ventures and develop new services in line with objectives. It should furthermore encourage, motivate, value, and reward high achievers who are critical to the firm's strategic success and who contribute to an exceptional level. Finally, it should set the foundations for the firm to manage and develop performance in the broadest sense in all of the critical areas of performance or the balanced scorecard, and in so doing it should quickly identify partners who are failing to contribute to the firm's strategic goals or are underperforming against agreed standards.

Teamwork

Properly used, the performance management system can sustain concepts of teamwork between partners with greater collective responsibility for the performance of practice groups and departments. It can also help to encourage and reward the most capable partners to lead the firm and practice groups as effectively as possible. It should also identify partners and others who are behaving in a way that is antithetical to teamwork. Firms of individualists are not necessarily unhappy as such, but (apart from being in many cases commercially inefficient) can breed an atmosphere in which firm members are not encouraged or forced to build close ties with fellow members. Instead, people stay in their offices with their heads down and keep to their individual routines. I have noticed that, in such an environment, people can often wear a mask or outer shell to hide their inner feelings of isolation, boredom, and lack of career fulfilment. A culture can then easily grow in which everyone's mask or shell condemns others to live the same pretense and keep their dissatisfaction a secret.

There are of course many ways in which teamwork can be built – such as weekly team meetings, firm retreats, and frequent face-to-face interactions. In short, the performance management system firms use should encourage and not detract from efforts towards a "one-firm firm". The principle of good teamwork has been thrown into sharp relief by virtual working, working from home, and by the growth of dispersed law firms. Dispersed firms (such as FisherBroyles and Rimon in the US, and Keystone and gunnercooke in the UK) rely on virtual teams, which can make collaboration and communication more complex. Lawyers may be in different time zones or have varying work schedules, affecting real-time interactions. For any firm where virtual working is a strong element, effective communication depends on technology tools like video conferencing, messaging apps, and project management software. Technical glitches or connectivity issues can hinder collaboration.

Culture, values, and behaviors

The performance management system must reflect the values of the partnership and cohesion of the firm.

It is also vital to value performance that contributes to the sustained growth of the firm and to a one-firm approach. The performance management system should embrace a firm-wide approach to enable partners in different practice areas to be rewarded on a consistent basis and should discourage maverick, bullying or insulting behavior.

It is important for firms to take a balanced view of the expected work ethic. I was told by a young lawyer recently. "My family and friends think I'm mad!". Fairly new out of law school after the attaining of two degrees, he leaves home for the office at 5.30am to miss the traffic and is in the office until at least 9pm each night. He also works most weekends. In his firm, the expectation is for hard work and long hours. By contrast, at another large firm, one can often nearly be knocked off one's feet in the rush for the door at about 6pm, where moderate productivity has recently resulted in mediocre results.

My good friend and colleague, the late Ed Wesemann, was fond of looking at the mediocre utilization statistics in average-performing firms and posing the question, "So what do these people do in the second half of the month?" At the same time, we all know about the stresses and strains of working in high performing firms.

What is not often done is to look at the work balance position from the point of view of the client. From a host of in-depth client interviews, I have drawn five rather generic insights into issues that touch upon time and effort commitments on the part of their lawyers.

- First, clients increasingly demand more for less from their lawyers, and match high expectations for work quality with sustained pressure on fee levels. Sophisticated clients justify their fee pressures by pointing to the need for systems, processes, and efficiencies to avoid wheels being reinvented at their expense.

- Second, clients do want their lawyers to provide value for their fees by dedicating themselves responsibly to their matters. They also want lawyers to be both responsive and accessible, sometimes at unreasonable hours of the day and night.
- Third, and in contrast, they want their lawyers to be fresh and attentive and not exhausted and distracted. A client would never want a lawyer to produce slipshod work or to be too tired to think straight.
- Fourth, clients expect their lawyers to delegate responsibly and effectively so that work can be done at the right level, but are always reluctant to pay for the internal conferences and engagement strategy sessions that will enable appropriate discussions of client objectives. In the same vein, I have recently heard in-house lawyers complain that an external law firm was over-delegating work to junior lawyers with the result that work fell short of the mark and had to be re-done.
- Finally, clients do not want to see their matters over-lawyered and resist over-academic approaches that result in long and tedious recitations of the law. In short, they want their lawyers to do work that they consider worth paying for.

The work ethic challenge is not confined just to lawyers. In the past few years, I have spoken to a considerable number of young professionals outside the law who are at the start of their careers. In this most difficult of centuries, I find many of them working no fewer than ten-hour days. Added to this, I have had the great honor to work with a number of law firms in emerging jurisdictions in Asia and Africa, all of whom put most European lawyers to shame in their dedication and commitment to their careers. It is true that nothing comes for nothing. There are many ingredients to the successful (and profitable) law firm, but a hard but hopefully balanced work ethic seems to be a necessary prerequisite to a positive culture.

Human capital development
The performance management system can help to clarify the differing roles of partners as working lawyers, producers, managers, and owners. Its aim should be to enable the firm to attract and retain partners of the highest

caliber and to introduce partners from other firms. The PMS should therefore be linked to internal training and review processes that support partners' development and improvement in performance. However, every firm should play to the strengths of different partners and the PMS should therefore recognize that partners have different qualities and should be encouraged to focus on areas where they have strengths whilst contributing in all areas. Here it can link with the firm's career development structures for its professionals.

Performance expectations

One of the main purposes of the performance management system will continue to be the management of performance. The performance management system should aim to achieve clarity in the processes for reviewing / appraising partners and setting objectives, and part of the written documentation must be definitions of the requirements and appropriate performance levels for partners at each stage of progression on the firm's lockstep ladder or partner career structure, both qualitatively and quantitatively. It should also set out the methodology, processes, and frequency by and through which partner performance will be monitored and evaluated.

It should identify the data and evidence that will be collected and used to measure performance. Finally, the performance management system should provide a clear methodology for dealing with underperformers.

Partners' personal plans

A key question that partners constantly ask, sometimes implicitly and sometimes very explicitly, is, "What have I got to do to succeed around here?" At all levels within a law firm, lawyers want to know what they have to accomplish in order to gain promotion and financial advantage. Partners in particular want (or should want) to be able to make a valuable contribution to their firm. To achieve this, they need to be clear about what the firm expects of them.

Law firm strategies are often highly conceptual. However, if all partners are to carry out daily and weekly work to support and contribute to the firm's overall needs and objectives, then they need to know exactly what actions they need to perform in order to be perceived as dynamic performers and in order to achieve all that is expected of them and more.

A well-drafted personal plan helps to set practical and detailed goals. Plans identify where partners need assistance and support to enable them to achieve their goals and help partners to concentrate on areas where development is needed. Consideration of personal development highlights resources that will help. For more than 25 years, Malcolm Shelton-Agar has been variously managing partner, managing director, chief operating officer, and chief executive officer of a number of firms. Malcolm's thoughts are included in more detail in chapter 20, Views from the profession. He highly recommends the practice of persuading partners to agree objectives. In his last firm in Australia, every partner would fill out an annual business plan, which would then be peer reviewed by two partners, then approved by the board and published for all to see. These business plans would all have deliverable objectives by which the partners would be judged. They would be asked how they were doing against their objectives and whether they think that they have achieved equity of contribution. Reviews became conversations about plans going forward. Overall performance was looked at over a two- or three-year period. It worked because the firm was small with 30 partners in one building, and he felt it only really does work when there is collegiality in the corridor and consensus of approach in the firm.

There are, therefore, three compelling reasons in favor of partners being encouraged to complete a personal business plan or personal contribution plan.

Written goals improve performance

First, the existence of written goals and objectives has been shown to improve performance. Well verified statistics on this topic are hard to find though it has often been said – probably anecdotally – that only about three percent of the population in the western world has written objectives in place and only a small percentage regularly review those objectives. It is widely accepted that professionals who take time to consider their ambitions and to crystallize their plans into written objectives perform better than those who have no written goals. Whilst goals and objectives can arise from appraisal discussions, rather than a written plan, many professionals have found that their objectives can often be more personal, pragmatic, and measurable if included in a career plan that they have taken time to consider and write. In the case of the firm's poorer performers, the setting of written goals can often kickstart a process of rehabilitation and career rebuilding. But in cases where partners end up failing to meet written goals to which they have previously freely and willingly committed, the writing may start to be on the wall. A report by Smith and Bititci[5] in a paper on the interplay between performance measurement and management on the one hand and how that relates to employee engagement and performance on the other found that targets do not have a negative effect on partner engagement as such but that engagement "seems to be impacted by the way these measures and targets are used", particularly when they lead to a command-and-control environment.

Linking with the firm's strategy

Second, by requiring partners to think about how they are going to contribute to the success of the firm, it is possible to link their personal contributions and goals to the overall strategy and goals of their practice group and the firm. In addition, it can help force partners to think about their strengths, their skills, and their development needs as collaborative team members and in the light of the firm's overall direction and business recipe. Great care has to be taken, however, to ensure that the personal plans complement the plans of other partners in the same practice group and fit in generally with the plans of the firm as a whole. For this reason, it is best practice for all plans to be agreed with the relevant line partner (head of team, group, or department, or the managing partner) and should become part of the suite of documents that will be considered when partners are evaluated.

Measurable objectives across all critical areas of performance

Third, a well written plan should include some measurable objectives across all critical areas of performance, which are SMARTE (Specific, Measurable, Agreed, Aspirational and Advantageous, Realistic, Time scaled, and Evidence Based). The writing of a plan should help partners to reflect on their past accomplishments and successes, and how to build on those in both the short- and long-term. Once SMARTE objectives are drafted and agreed it then becomes somewhat easier to gauge success. The achievement of worthwhile personal objectives forms a vital part of the progression and rewards equation.

Underperformance procedures – the four phases

We have identified four suggested phased for dealing with an underperforming partner or indeed any partner where issues of performance or behavior arise.

Phase 1: Formal or informal identification of an area for improvement

The process starts with a one-to-one discussion with the partner of specific areas of a partner's performance that need to be clarified and addressed. In some instances, the discussion may result in the managing partner and the partner agreeing that there is nothing further to be done at the present time but that the situation will be monitored and discussed again. Where the identified concerns need some action, the managing partner should agree with the underperforming partner what specific action is needed to address the shortcomings.

The partner will then usually be expected to progress the action points and to keep the managing partner appraised of progress towards achieving the SMARTE objectives, in accordance with an agreed timetable. This will then be followed by a further meeting once the action plan has run its course with a view to agreeing the outcome and, in the majority of instances, concluding the review process.

Phase 2: Intensive care

The failure of informal attempts to improve performance should usually move the procedure onto the second phase of the scheme for a period of formal remedial action. It is important here to discuss and agree with the underperforming partner why the previous action points had not been achieved and the parties should agree a more drastic and final action plan and review process. At this phase, it should be made abundantly clear to the underperforming partner that he or she is "drinking in the last chance saloon".

Once the timetable contemplated by the second action plan has run its course (no more than one year) then there should be a review meeting and an agreement reached between the managing partner and the underperforming partner as to the outcome of the phase two period, which in some firms is known as "intensive care".

This will hopefully lead to agreement that the area of concern has now been addressed with the help of coaching, counselling, and training.

Equally, it may be clear by now that there are aspects of the partner's contribution or behavior that are still not acceptable to the firm.

Phase 3: Redeployment or de-equitization

In some cases, it is clear that the underperformance is due to factors outside the partner's concern. The most common reason is where the area of law in which the partner has traditionally practiced is not sufficiently busy to keep him or her fully productive. In such cases, it may be possible to consider redeployment of the underperforming partner to another area of the firm.

Redeployment of a partner whose only problem is under-productivity can be an attractive option for firms because it is both humane (in comparison to firing partners or demotion on the lockstep ladder) and in some cases has a good chance of success.

De-equitization or reduction in equity share has also proved to be a favored route for firms where equity partners are underperforming. It has to be recognized that most de-equitizations usually result in the partner ultimately leaving the firm. It rarely seems to work as a permanent solution.

Phase 4: Leaving the firm

If (and only if) the first three phases have been concluded without significant success, it is probable that the underperforming partner should be asked to leave the partnership. At this stage, the morale of other partners should be considered. The firm should be prepared to be generous, as it is easy to desta-bilize the other partners if leadership is seen as excessively ruthless. At the other extreme, firms that ignore or fail to grasp issues of underperformance in a timely and sensible manner also run the risk of demotivating partners who are performing well.

References
1   Collins J. (2001), *Good to Great*, Random House, p.53.
2   Preskill H. and Catsambas T.T. (2006), *Reframing Evaluation Through Appreciative Inquiry*, Sage Publications, p.77.
3   Von Hoffman and Others (2005), *Dealing with Difficult People*, HBS, p.136.
4   Stapely S. (2003), *Media Relations for Lawyers*, Law Society Publications, p.247.
5   Smith M. and Bititci U.S. (2017), "Interplay between Performance Measurement and Management, Employee Engagement and Performance", *International Journal of Operations and Production Management*, Vol 37, Issue 9, pp1207-1228.

Chapter 16:

Conflict resolution and team dynamics

By Jonathan Middleburgh, principal, Edge International

The focus of this chapter is the interplay between teams and partner performance, the impact (positive and negative) of team dynamics on partner performance, and how interpersonal conflicts within a team can negatively impact partner performance.

Anyone who has worked in any organization – law firm or otherwise – knows that a great team can achieve wonders, and that correspondingly a dysfunctional team can be a painful environment in which to work, which impacts both on team morale, individual morale, and productivity.

This chapter covers the following topics:

- What constitutes a high functioning team, presenting the well-known Belbin "team roles" model and discussing the formation and development of teams into high-functioning teams.
- How a good leader can foster a healthy team – and the impact this will have on team members, including partners.
- What to do when a team is riven with conflict – is there a way to improve things, short of disbanding the team or expelling / moving on poor team players?

A new team "forms"

Picture the all-too-common scenario. A lateral partner joins your firm from one of your competitors. A well-known player in the sector, the lateral is bringing a couple of more junior partners and a bunch of associates. Everyone is very excited – the lateral has a big book of business, and he has been charming in the rounds of conversations that have preceded the announcement of his joining. Senior management have pushed a narrative that is overwhelmingly positive and that has spoken of a reboot of the practice area in question. The mood music is sweet. What could possibly go wrong?

What indeed?

Within weeks, it is clear that the book of business wasn't quite as extensive as promised. There is a clash of egos between the joining lateral and one of the established partners in the practice area. Tempers start to fray between some of the associates and soon it's an all-out turf war.

What went wrong?

An initial observation is that senior management / leadership in many law firms are prone to gravely underestimate the difficulties of melding a new team into the existing organization and getting it to moderate levels of performance, still less to the status of high functioning, productive, and happy team. Senior leaders often put limited effort into building the "new" team – they are too busy with business as usual, new business development, and a basket of other priorities.

Yet the reality is that every time someone new joins a team, the team dynamic inevitably shifts.

A team is a complex thing. Two people have one relationship. Three people have a triangle of relationships. As you get to five, six, seven, and more team members, the complexity of the web of relationships multiplies (to say nothing of the relationship between the "team" and other teams / groupings in the firm). How much time is typically devoted to building and consolidating the new team? In many firms, next to none.

A second observation is that there are typical stages in the development of a new team. A useful model to understand that development is the relatively well-known Tuckman model of team development[1] – the "storming – norming – performing" model. This model, based on empirical research, asserts that teams will first *form*, and that this period of formation will be followed by a period of *storming*, characterized by team members experiencing friction, tension, bits of "acting out" and so on. Some teams remain stuck at the storming stage of their development. They never get to the third stage of *norming*, a stage characterized by the team figuring out shared rules of conduct and behavior. If all goes well at this stage, the team will *perform*, either as a functioning or ideally high-functioning team.

All too often, in my experience, teams in law firms are stuck somewhere between the storming and norming stages of development. Insufficient time is devoted to figuring out how to get the team to steady-state "performing". The next section of this chapter examines the importance of clear team roles and how to foster better functioning teams.

Team roles and better functioning teams

A high functioning team axiomatically achieves better performance than a moderately performing or a low performing team. A high functioning team is also likely to optimize individual partner performance, together with the individual performances of team members. It will not always be the case, but a team that is high functioning will elevate the performance of the individuals in the team and the sum of the parts will achieve more than the individuals acting as solo players. We have all experienced this when we've been a member of a great team or indeed when we studied in a class that was shaped by an outstanding teacher into something resembling a team.

A question that I am often asked is the extent to which "groups" in law firms truly operate as teams – or whether they need to do so.

One response is that "teams" in law firms are indeed somewhat different to teams in other organizations. This requires some explanation and analysis.

The paradigm team in many organizations is widely understood to need a variety of well-defined roles and responsibilities.

The well-known Belbin model[2] posits that the "ideal" team will have team members who cover the following roles:

- *The Team Worker.* This person helps the team to gel, is cooperative, perceptive, and diplomatic, and listens, builds, and averts friction.
- *The Plant.* This person is creative, imaginative, and unorthodox and solves difficult problems.
- *The Resource Investigator.* An extrovert, enthusiastic, and communicative, (s)he explores opportunities and develops the team's network of contacts.
- *The Coordinator.* Mature, confident, and a good Chair, the Coordinator clarifies goals, promotes decision-making, and delegates well.
- *The Shaper.* Challenging, dynamic, and thriving on pressure, this individual has the drive and courage to overcome obstacles.
- *The Monitor Evaluator.* This person is sober, strategic, and discerning, and sees the range of options and evaluates with judgement.
- *The Implementer.* Disciplined, reliable, conservative, and efficient, this person turns ideas into practical actions.
- *The Completer.* This individual is painstaking and conscientious, searches out errors and omissions, and ensures "on time" delivery (often carrying the anxiety needed to complete).
- *The Specialist.* This individual provides the knowledge and skills that can be in scarce supply. He or she is single-minded, self-starting, and dedicated.

The orthodox view of team performance is that, to achieve optimal performance, a team also has to have a clearly defined mission and purpose, in addition to clearly defined team roles and responsibilities.

Turning to law firms specifically, there are a variety of teams in law firms and not all of them are amenable to being analyzed through the lens of the Belbin model – or indeed require the full range of team roles posited by the model. Some teams would, however, benefit from having clearer roles and responsibilities, and all would benefit from understanding how high-performing teams function optimally and achieve stellar results.

Within the context of the law firm (and professional services firms generally) I would draw a distinction between work teams and management teams – even if the distinction isn't always entirely clean, clear, and watertight.

The archetypal management team in a law firm is the management committee (ManCo) or Executive Committee (ExCo). What exactly the ManCo or ExCo looks like will often vary according to the size of the firm and the governance structure imposed by the partnership agreement or other agreement between the relevant partners. The largest firms will have a senior leadership structure that looks similar to that of some of the larger corporates – a "top" board setting the firm's strategy and a ManCo executing on that strategy. Smaller to mid-sized firms typically just have a ManCo, often chaired by the managing partner. The composition of the ManCo will vary from firm to firm, according to what has been agreed between the partners. In less mature firms there will not be highly clear rules of governance.

The purpose of these paragraphs is not to examine the range of governance structures operated by different firms – rather to focus on what will make these management teams perform better.

In my experience, few management teams will have nine individuals of any kind, let alone the nine individual roles summarized above that constitute the ideal team.

The important thing in my experience is that the relevant management team has a diversity of leadership talent, such that the members of the team can fulfil the majority of the roles suggested by Belbin as requiring fulfilment. It is not, for example, ideal if all members of the management team have very similar, "convergent" thinking and decision-making styles. This will inevitably increase the risk of groupthink.[3]

Often, management teams consist of a mix of elected and appointed team members. Whoever is responsible for appointing team members should reflect on achieving diversity on the team. This includes:

- Diversity of thinking styles.
- Diversity of decision-making styles.
- Diversity of personality types.

The empirical evidence is that gender diversity (and other diversity, including diversity of cultural, socio-economic, and other backgrounds) enhances decision-making.[4] This makes sense as diverse perspectives will inevitably weigh diverse factors in their decision-making. In any event, non-diverse management teams will be unrepresentative of the "clients" they serve. For example, in many law firms, more than 50 percent of younger lawyers are female, so having an exclusively or predominantly male management committee clearly runs the risk that decisions will be made that do not reflect the range of needs of the majority of those younger lawyers.

When it comes to management team roles it is fanciful, in my view, to expect firms to assign Belbin roles to team members – but a good leader will think about whether the team has, for example, someone who is more of a creative thinker, as well as someone who is highly grounded and who thinks through the realities of implementation and operationalization of decisions made by the team.

A good leader will also:

- Get the team to reflect on and be clear about its core purpose – or themselves set the core purpose for the team.
- Ensure that team meetings are run efficiently and effectively (e.g., ensuring there is always a clear agenda, ensuring there is adequate space for appropriate discussion but that discussions don't ramble and that unfocused discussions are appropriately shut down, ensuring that there are good notes of the meeting, and that such notes are action-oriented etc.). One might think that none of this requires restatement, but having sat in on many team meetings, it really does.
- Get the team to do some work on its own development – for example, working through any dysfunctional team dynamics / dealing with any intra-team conflict (see more below).

A good team leader will also navigate the usual road bumps of running a team, typically using their own common sense, skills, and experience. Good leaders will generally have built up experience over many years, often through informal leadership roles (e.g., captaining sports teams, leadership roles at school / university; trustee / leadership roles in voluntary organizations). They will also typically have spent some time working on themselves (this includes reflecting on mistakes they've made and learning from them, attending to formal and informal feedback from others etc.).

Good leaders often read extensively (and nowadays listen to podcasts on leadership, watch videos online etc. – there is a plethora of free material that can help leaders to become better at what they do). Leaders at more mature firms often have the benefit of focused executive leadership development. Sometimes, law firm leaders complain that the executive leadership development they have experienced was too generic – this can indeed be the case, but it is better to experience some generic leadership development training than no training at all. The 70:20:10 rule is apposite here – i.e., the notion that the ideal mix of development is 70 percent "on the job" experience, 20 percent through colleagues and friend, and ten percent through formal learning interventions.

Team members also need to take responsibility for their roles and their own management and leadership development. Many partners in law firms, in my experience, take a passive approach to their leadership roles and devote very little time to building up their skills. They would never adopt such a cavalier approach to their technical lawyering skills – yet for some reason they see their leadership roles as not requiring active skills development, relying excessively on a belief that this stuff is all pretty straightforward. It clearly isn't.

Thus far in this section I have focused on leadership teams / management teams. These are clearly only one of the various types of teams that exist in most law firms. In reality, ad hoc work teams pop up all the time in law firms, every time more than one person works on a client matter. These teams also need to function well to produce optimal performance. Many firms devote insufficient time to training their lawyers (and support staff) so that they become better at working together effectively and productively as ad hoc teams. This includes aspects of team working as basic as ensuring:

- That the team is properly briefed at its inception – i.e., ensuring that the person who received the instruction from the client properly explains the instructions to other team members and gives them the full context needed to do the work properly.
- That team members understand some of the dos and don'ts of email communication / excessive reliance on email communication. Email communication can be very efficient and effective, but tone is important and it is easy to misinterpret emails. If in doubt, team members

    should be encouraged to pick up the phone, hop on a video call, or – dare one suggest – meet face to face. Don't forget that email communication is often one-way communication – it doesn't replicate the to and fro of verbal communication.

- That there are periodic check-ins to ensure the work is progressing at the right pace and to iron out any problems.
- That (with more complex pieces of work) there is a project plan and some basic project management.
- That there is some sort of mechanism for feedback (the so-called "feedback loop") so team members learn from their mistakes (and their successes).
- That there is some sort of project review and lessons learnt at the end of the work.

None of the above needs to be over-engineered. Often what causes suboptimal performance are really basic failures – e.g., an inadequate initial briefing of more junior team members, failure to discuss a basic work plan, failure to monitor the work adequately, and so on. Getting the basics right is often all that is needed to ensure good performance.

Dysfunction and resolving conflict

As mentioned above, teams often get stuck at the "storming" stage of their development. Others cycle between "storming" and "performing". Some teams never fully "norm" – in other words, they don't really develop a shared understanding of whatever their task or purpose is. Each of these situations are examples of dysfunctional team performance – and the performance of the team (and its individual members – including partners) will almost inevitably be less effective as a result.

    Team performance can be sub-optimal for several reasons, some of which have already been identified above. Some of the key causes of sub-optimal team performance are summarized in the following table, together with suggested "solutions" or "fixes" to get performance back on track. The balance of this section of the chapter will focus on item five in the table, i.e., dysfunctional team dynamics.

Table 1: Key causes of sub-optimal team performance and suggested fixes.

Reason for sub-optimal team performance	(Possible) consequence(s)	Solution / fix
1. Lack of clear initial briefing	Poor execution of task. Wasted time and resources. Time spent needs to be written off / full fees irrecoverable. Damage to reputation / failure to be reinstructed.	Better initial briefing.
2. Lack of proper project plan / project management.	As above.	Better project plan; better implementation / execution of project plan. Better project management.
3. Lack of clear allocation of roles and responsibilities.	As above. Plus possible friction between team members.	Clearer initial allocation of roles and responsibilities. Periodic check in to ensure everyone understands their role and responsibilities.
4. Lack of team leadership.	As above. Team members potentially directionless.	Improve leadership – this may require upskilling.
5. Dysfunctional team dynamics.	As above. Plus likely friction between team members.	Intervention to improve team dynamics. Removing one or more team members from the team if all else fails.
6. Under-performing team member(s).	As above. Plus possible friction between members.	Intervention to improve performance of underperforming team member(s). Removing the relevant team member(s) if all else fails.

What should a leader or a team member do in the event of a dysfunctional team dynamic?

It is well beyond the scope of this chapter to provide an extensive guide to conflict resolution.[5] What I aim to do here is to provide some hopefully helpful pointers and tips that might assist in resolving a dysfunctional team dynamic in some circumstances. If the dynamic is really stuck, it might be necessary to bring in a third party (e.g., consultant) to try to help shift the dynamic – and ultimately it might be necessary to disband the team, form a new team, or even exit an individual or individuals from the firm. These options are discussed more fully below.

Here's what I'd suggest when a team leader or team member encounters a dysfunctional team dynamic.

1. Try to analyze the reason for the dysfunctional team dynamic. In other words, try to imagine that you are a third party consultant who is parachuted in to work with the team. The first thing such a consultant would do would be some data-gathering, coupled with an analysis, producing a working hypothesis or a diagnosis / view as to what is going wrong.

2. It may or may not be appropriate to speak to members of the team to elicit their views as to what is going on. Do so with caution in case you make things worse by approaching the discussion in the wrong way. A good rule of thumb is always the imperative: "Do no harm".

3. If it's not appropriate to talk to members of the team, reflect on what you've experienced in the team – and if necessary, spend a bit longer observing the team in action, with a measure of detachment (always difficult if you are yourself a member of the team – remember that the team is a "system" and you are yourself part of that system).

4. Having done your data-gathering (whatever exactly that consists of), spend some time analysing the data and producing your working hypothesis or diagnosis.

5. Common causes of the dysfunction will be:
   a. One team member who is skewing the dynamic – this can be someone who has an unhelpful agenda, who isn't a good team player, or who has (at an extreme) a mild or more serious personality disorder. This list is not an exhaustive one.
   b. Two or more team members who have a personality clash. The more you can unpack and understand the personality clash, the more likely you are to figure out a work around. Sometimes it isn't easy to understand what is going on.

   c. Poor team leadership – the leader (sometimes you!) hasn't set the team up properly. The team's purpose, for example, isn't clear. There has been an inadequate allocation of roles and responsibilities so that team members are tripping over each other. You know the kind of thing, and you've probably experienced it – maybe, being honest with yourself, you've even been responsible for it.

6. Once you've developed your working hypothesis or established a diagnosis, develop an action plan for making things better. Possible actions might include:

   a. Intervening with one or more team members in an attempt to improve the situation. This may be as simple as chatting one-on-one with the relevant team member(s). Sometimes a simple conversation will surface the cause of the dysfunction and resolve it. Sometimes several conversations will be needed. Sometimes, no matter how much conversation takes place, things won't get better.

   b. Getting some training or coaching for one or more of the team members (including yourself). In my experience, no one ever has "too much" understanding of human behavior or "too much" training. But clearly it is a question of time and available resource as to how much training and/or coaching is practical.

   c. Bringing in an internal "third party" to try to improve the situation. HR, for example, might be able to make things better through some sort of formal or informal intervention. Some larger firms have internal OD (organizational development) professionals.

   d. Bringing in an external "third party" to try to improve the situation. An external consultant (with expertise and experience in conflict resolution and team dynamics) might be a further available resource – and often a last ditch measure prior to more radical action.

   e. Exiting one or more team members from the team or indeed from the firm. This will clearly be an action of last resort and any potential exit from the firm is highly likely to involve internal consultation and will need to follow local HR best practice (and legal requirements).

   f. Disbanding the team and potentially forming a new team. Again, this is an action of last resort. Clearly it is preferable to try to fix whatever is going wrong rather than pressing the nuclear button and disbanding the team. But sometimes the dynamic is so dysfunctional that this needs to happen.

Conflict resolution is sometimes time-consuming and tortuous. It requires considerable patience and a tool kit of interpersonal skills and techniques. Two key elements are focused active listening and empathy. Active listening means just that – listening intently and without presupposition or prejudgment, and attending both to the verbal and the non-verbal content of what is being said. Often body language can help one to understand that something is going on beneath the surface and gentle open questioning (and non-open questioning) can help surface what is going on. Empathy requires you to step into the shoes of whoever you are talking to, to try to understand what is going on from their perspective. A common error is to come to the conversation with a pre-formed view as to what is going on and to look unconsciously for evidence that supports that view. Often this will derail attempts at conflict resolution as the proposed or attempted resolution will be an imposed solution rather than one that emerges from a rounded understanding of what is actually going on.

Conclusion

I have endeavored in this chapter to cover a series of topics, each of which would merit a chapter (or several chapters) in their own right. Issues of conflict resolution are particularly complex and fraught with potential difficulty. A deep understanding of team dynamics is a lifetime's work for those who work extensively with teams and groups. That said, in most firms, senior leaders and managers have to adopt a pragmatic approach to the running of teams and to issues of team dysfunction. Hopefully this chapter will have provided readers with some helpful practical pointers if they work in a law firm and interact on a regular basis with leadership teams, management teams, or work teams.

References

1 Tuckman, B. W. (1965). Developmental sequence in small groups. *Psychological Bulletin*, 63(6), 384–399.
2 Belbin, R. Meredith (1993). *Team Roles at Work* (Elsevier).
3 Janis, I. L. (1997). Groupthink. In R. P. Vecchio (Ed.), *Leadership: Understanding the dynamics of power and influence in organizations* (pp. 163–176). University of Notre Dame Press. (Reprinted from "Psychology Today," Nov 1971, pp. 43, 44, 46, 74–76).
4 See e.g. research summarised at www.cloverpop.com (White Paper on diversity and decision making).
5 I have written elsewhere about conflict resolution in the context of law firms – see articles on the Edge International website at www.edge.ai

Chapter 17:
Training and development

By Martin Hill, Okano Consulting

The business case

Beyond legal and market updates, training and personal/professional development for most lawyers can stop on election to partnership. Given a typical career lasts around ten years as an associate and another 20 years as a partner, this leaves the most significant part of a lawyer's career without much in the way of formal development.

Compared to the accountancy and consultancy firms, the legal industry has historically underinvested in its most important assets. This is changing and firms are investing more in partner development, so this chapter aims to make the case for why partner development is necessary, and what firms should consider if they are approaching this topic for the first time. The chapter is written from a "big law" perspective so assumes a certain size and scale of partnership (and budget). However, many of the practical points – particularly around reflective learning – will apply to firms of all sizes.

Whilst associates are managed and supported, partners are left to their own devices to build a successful business from the day they join the partnership, with or without much guidance or support. Firms extend this leave-be attitude to partner development – few firms have the time or resources to devote to it and not many partners want to put up their hand and ask. Often, the partners who volunteer to attend training are the ones that don't need it – they have an interest in the topic and prioritize their own development. Others may feel they are too busy, believe they should already know everything, or see asking for training as a sign of weakness. Consequently, if partners don't request training, firms are unlikely to provide it on a large scale.

This approach carries risks. The workplace is rapidly changing, with younger generations having different career expectations, new technology transforming service delivery, and clients demanding more speed and efficiency. Partners must stay updated on changes to remain relevant. The habits and approaches learned early in their careers may no longer be effective decades later. To maintain a successful practice, partners need to continually update their leadership and management skills and stay informed about current trends and technologies – and adjust to an ever-increasing pace of change.

Firms often underinvest in their leadership team – it is not uncommon to find partners running multimillion-dollar businesses (sometimes 100s of millions) with no formal management or financial training, or even necessarily with that much leadership experience. Whilst most large companies appoint CEOs with formal backgrounds in business/accounting or years of experience running increasingly larger businesses, law firms promote leaders on different criteria such as their book of business, their personal standing in the partnership, or because they wanted the job when others did not. Many firms and leaders are still successful but could be even more effective with better support.

Although the learning curve may not be as steep as at the beginning of their careers, most partners want to continue evolving professionally. Whether this involves taking on leadership roles, developing new practice areas, focusing on core client relationships, or other firm responsibilities, few partners want to do the same job every day for 20 years.

This chapter explores the professional development of partners and the tools and processes to support them. It does not cover training in black letter law or updates in market practice, as these are fundamental to maintaining competence and meeting bar requirements. Any firm neglecting these basics has bigger problems than partner skills development.

It is also important to point out that partner development is hard – its success depends on organizational culture and systems more than the effectiveness of any particular course. For example, does the remuneration system support or penalize time spent on personal development? Is there a learning culture open to experimentation and change? Firms looking to invest in development should be aware of the wider firm culture and context and be realistic about what can be achieved and not assume it is an extension of associate training at a higher price point.

Two simple approaches to partner development

As a simple model, there is what the firm needs and what the partners want. The former is the traditional organizational/L&D approach – define expectations, identify gaps, and solve with training. This implicitly assumes a minimum standard, e.g. partners need to be better managers, so introduce management training for this cohort regardless of their personal strengths or interests.

The other approach is to ask partners if and how they want to develop in their careers and practice and then personalize the support. Partners are producer-manager-leaders and have different interests and aptitudes around each of these roles. If someone wants to enhance their business development skills and has the potential to be a rainmaker, support their strengths. If their management skills are poor, as long as they are not problematic, let that be. Aim for high performance and encourage partners to be authentic. This can be as simple as providing each partner with a personal development budget to spend on whatever supports their practice or career aspirations, be it coaching, executive education, or otherwise. Encourage them to take ownership of their own development.

The two approaches can be combined, and the intersection between what the firm needs and what partners want provides easy wins for partner development.

The partner-centric approach is fairly simple to adopt – allocate a budget, set up governance around how it can be accessed, and then leadership and partners can have quality conversations around what training they want to do. Given the comparative simplicity of this approach, the following looks at the more traditional organization-focused approach.

Defining the role – performance models

A recommended starting point is the simple TAG approach:

- *Target:* what does the business or individual need to achieve? ("What does good look like?")
- *Actual:* where are people now against this target?
- *Gap:* what is the gap and what is the best way to address it?

Start by defining the partnerial role(s) and relevant expectations (the Target). Skills and behaviors expected from newly promoted partners differ from those of senior rainmakers, partners in formal leadership positions, line partners, or partners nearing the end of their careers. Clarifying these expectations at each stage helps identify performance gaps.

The approach depends on the firm's size and managerial processes. Smaller partnerships might use a partner charter – separate from the formal partnership agreement – to outline expected contributions in revenue, practice development, interactions, and behavior standards relevant to the whole partnership. Larger, more complex firms benefit from a more structured approach, mapping out required skills and expectations for various roles, from line partners to managing partners. Many firms have competency frameworks for associates, so the concept is familiar. The partner version is not a linear extension of the associate one – different partners take on different roles at different stages, so more flexibility is required.

Whilst all partners must demonstrate certain common skills and behaviors, as they progress in their career and take on different roles within the business, additional skills are required, and development support should reflect this. For example:

- *Newly elected partners.* Focus is on building a practice, establishing a market reputation, managing matters profitably, managing the internal transition (being recognized as a partner by associates and having one's voice heard by more senior partners). Training might cover business development, fee negotiation, personal branding, giving feedback, and coaching including around imposter syndrome.
- *Established partners.* Individual focus will vary but will include expanding the practice and feeding other parts of the business. Specific individuals may wish to enhance their market reputation, develop new product lines, take on firm or client leadership roles, evaluate the next stage of their career – or any combination of these. Training could focus on client leadership, influencing skills, leadership styles, personal values, and finding new meaning in work.
- *Leaders/succession planning.* Focus is on leading peers within the partnership, making investment decisions, and managing internal politics. Leaders approaching end of tenure will be thinking about what next. Development support could include setting and evaluating strategy, leading leaders, negotiating and influencing, and coaching around career paths.

Creating this framework requires time, effort, and collaboration within the partnership. The firm's central team typically delivers it to align with firmwide requirements and establish objective standards for all partners.

Once established, the framework can guide a curriculum of training to support partners throughout their careers and help identify individual training needs.

Identifying needs and addressing the gap

The *Actual* skill levels of both the organization and individuals can be determined once the requirements for each level of seniority/role are defined.

Performance reviews can offer insights into individuals' development needs. However, since they are often of inconsistent detail and quality across the partnership it can be hard to obtain a comprehensive view for the firm. For a thorough analysis, a 360 approach is recommended.

- *Leadership insights.* Leaders will be aware of gaps from their own observations and experiences of partner challenges, crises, and behaviors. Their understanding of partners' needs at different stages of their career is invaluable, and they should recognize when their colleagues are struggling or succeeding.
- *Partner insights.* What are the partners themselves concerned about? What challenges are they facing and what support do they want?
- *Associate and support staff perspectives.* What do they want from their leaders? Who do they respect and why? What behaviors destroy trust? What will encourage them to go the extra mile versus looking for reasons to work for someone else or leave?
- *Client insights.* What do they look for from the firm's partners and are the partners delivering this?

Combining these insights will give a comprehensive view of the learning opportunities needed at various points in a partner's career. This framework should include a mix of structured training for cohorts (for example, new partner orientation programs, leadership development courses) and personalized support such as coaching and mentoring.

Leadership can then have career conversations with partners and identify the most relevant learning opportunities for each individual. These conversations form part of regular interactions with partners and can be integrated into annual performance reviews or personal business planning processes.

After establishing the broad framework, the next step is to identify the details to fill the Gap. The rest of this chapter suggests high level guiding design principles, some common methodologies, and explores options for working with external providers.

What makes a good learning experience?

For any training program to be perceived as valuable by partners it needs to be credible, relevant, and practical – in that order. This is more important than having the most cutting-edge or well-researched content. Leadership can mandate attendance, but partners will still be working on something else unless the person running the session can capture their attention. If the audience would rather be doing something else or if the content is not immediately applicable, its academic brilliance is irrelevant.

- *Credible.* Participants will wonder, "Why should I listen to you?". The trainer must understand professional service firms, ideally law firms, which are different in structure, mindset, and pressure to other organizations. As well as the speaker's credentials, their examples and war stories need to be relatable and relevant, so they are perceived as having something useful to add. Partners are at the top of their field and want to work with top experts.
- *Relevant.* "Will this solve my specific problem?" If not, then it is hard to get people into the room. Even if leadership think the topic is important, partners will not attend if they do not see the value.
- *Practical.* "Can I do something with this as soon as I get back to my desk?" Thought-provoking is good, but only if it results in something actionable. Theory, models, and academic research are less useful if they cannot be applied. The wider organizational context also has bearing on practicality – partners can return from training inspired to change the world but then encounter the demands of their day job and organizational inertia.

For most lawyers the ideal "trainer" is a reputable expert who presents well, is interesting, and has first-hand experience of what works and what does not. Simple and practical wins out every time – it is how clients want their advice; it is how lawyers want their training.

Some options for training and their relative merits

Given partners are already experts in the practice of law, they do not need instruction in these areas so learning focuses on reflection and improvements.

In areas where partners have not had formal training – such as leadership – there are opportunities to learn new ideas and approaches through more standard classroom-type training. The biggest challenge with partner training is the "knowing/doing gap" – they grasp the theory immediately but can struggle with effective implementation.

Informal and reflective learning

Informal learning, where partners gather outside a classroom setting to discuss business or practice challenges, market updates, and general knowledge sharing, should not be underestimated. The challenge that action-oriented partners have with reflective learning is finding the time to pause when they are running many matters simultaneously, so the art is persuading them of the value.

End of matter reviews

End of matter reviews, where the team discusses what worked and what could be improved, are rarely implemented despite a grudging acceptance that they should be done regularly. They can be made to work and work well.

The benefits of the reviews are numerous – they can be cathartic, junior and senior lawyers learn from each other's reflections, and process improvement/best practices can be identified.

Three elements are recommended – psychological safety, defined areas for review, and capturing and embedding the learning.

Psychological safety is essential if there is to be honesty, which in most cases means the partners should be absent from review meetings. It may be "safe" for the partner to attend if the review topics are neutral and do not review partner performance – but in general, associates are more comfortable to speak up when no partner is present. Questions such as "What worked well?" are useful but risk being too broad. A narrower focus on, for example, communication or client interaction, will lead to something more thoughtful, particularly if flagged to the team in advance.

Capturing and embedding the learning can take different forms. Sometimes the output is little more than a "note to self" for the individuals involved, whilst other times it can be a practice note or a training session run for the wider team. As long as the team is looking for incremental improvements, both the team and individuals will be able to gain from this exercise.

As an introduction to these reviews, ask HR, practice support lawyers, or another third party to lead the process and synthesize the comments to reduce partner time, and allow for feedback to be collected anonymously. The partner and rapporteur agree the scope of review, there is a team meeting (with or without the partner present) with follow up one-to-ones if needed, and the partner is debriefed on the result. This approach is thorough but not scalable across all partners' matters, but will demonstrate the value of the review and is worth the investment for most significant projects. In an ideal world, a streamlined version of this process would take place both during matters (so that teams can adjust in the moment) as well as at the end. There are less resource-intensive ways to capture lessons at the end of matters using technology or stripped-down processes and firms should experiment to see what works and then make it part of the usual ways of working.

Should clients provide input? If possible, yes. Partners benefit from hearing directly what clients think of their service, and clients appreciate being asked. They are paying for an expensive service and anything that improves the experience and provides getting better value is going to be welcomed, as is anything that makes them feel personally valued.

Partner roundtables

Done well, these forums can be a powerful opportunity for sharing and learning from experts – for junior partners to learn from more senior partners, for problems within the business to be resolved, and for new approaches or lessons learned to be discussed. A keynote speaker (internal or external) who is a genuine expert can be useful to frame a specific conversation or to provide a new perspective – but really the value is in the discussion.

Done badly, there is a risk of partner politics playing out with particular individuals dominating, partners griping about the issues of the day without reaching solutions, group think, and echo chambers. Strong chairing and external perspectives can help prevent this, as can pulling in partners from different parts of the business who do not usually work together.

Action learning

Action learning has seen mixed success in partnerships, but it is worth considering due to its potential effectiveness when done well. There are variations but, at its core, action learning involves a team working to solve a business problem, reflecting on the experience to draw lessons, and then iterating in a "plan, do, reflect, learn, repeat" process. This method encourages creativity and flexibility in problem-solving, delivering beneficial outcomes for both the organization and individuals.

The projects should be identified by the partners in the group rather than by central management, as partners are more likely to commit to issues they feel personally invested in. Examples of valuable action learning projects include addressing talent or culture problems, such as retaining specific demographics of staff, or improving internal processes like billing or client onboarding.

The reflection process should be held in a meeting where partners are fully present and committed, not distracted by other tasks. A facilitator is recommended to capture thoughts and reflections, especially for partners new to this approach. Using whiteboards and flip charts can help visualize ideas and reflections.

The learning varies from project to project but typically includes a deeper understanding of the business, improved knowledge of client or internal pain points, and increased awareness of how to achieve results and one's own impact. As solutions are tested and refined, participants learn what works and what doesn't.

When taken further, this team can become a learning circle where individuals bring personal challenges for group discussion and peer coaching. This approach can generate new ideas, drive better business outcomes, and provide a broader network for support. It works well for large transformation projects or new partners forming peer support groups.

The main challenge with this approach is that partners are busy and may not have the capacity for new projects. There is also a temptation to focus on the action and not the learning, leading to quick delegation to HR or Finance, which defeats the purpose. Success is more likely when:

- Partners identify issues they are passionate about.
- There is a laser-like focus from an influential partner to "encourage" participation.
- Projects are timebound and not allowed to drift.
- Partners commit to being fully present and engaged.
- Review meetings are effectively facilitated to focus on solutions and discussions rather than just running the meeting.

Working with retired partners

Another source of expertise that is often underutilized is retiring/retired partners. Once a partner leaves the building for the final time, years of knowledge and experience are lost to the firm. For partners who are leaving the firm on good terms but would still like to add value, consider whether they can still have a role either training associates or mentoring new partners for at least a few years after leaving. These partners, who have had years navigating partnership politics, dealt with challenging client and peer relationships, and weathered multiple economic cycles – all of which can be daunting to new partners – can have a lot to offer. They can provide advice, and since they are no longer part of the firm, junior partners may find it safer to have conversations with people who know the firm, the personalities, and the challenges – but who will no longer impact their career.

This will be of interest to only some retiring partners, and not all of those partners may be appropriate for this, but it is worth exploring.

Formal learning

Firms have a range of formal training options at different price points, from business school programs to external L&D boutiques and trainers, self-paced digital learning, coaching, and mentoring. Coaching and mentoring are covered in more detail in chapter ten so some of the other options are covered here.

For the purpose of this chapter, business schools and L&D boutiques are being treated separately, but increasingly there is overlap in some parts of the market with business schools willing to offer a wider range of training methodologies and individual trainers affiliating with business schools.

Business school programs

Business schools can provide a premium brand, networking opportunities, and some useful perspectives. However, they are expensive, lean towards theory, which may or may not work in the law firm context, and – depending on the school or program – may not meet the day-to-day demands of front-line legal practice.

Some schools have developed programs specifically for professional services or law firms, making them more relevant to partners than general courses, and there are some specific instances when a general program will be the right solution.

These programs provide theories and approaches to leadership, business, and strategy that are typically new to most partners. They also offer perspectives from other industries, helping to shift partners' thinking. Good programs update their content to follow trends affecting businesses, such as technology, economy, and politics, and how these trends impact law firms and their clients. Modules, usually delivered by academics, can be theory- and research-heavy, and not always relevant to professional services firms. Better programs provide space for participants to discuss how to apply these theories to their own firms.

Three common ways of using business schools are:

1. *Open.* Sending individual partners to a public program with participants from other businesses. Firms need to be thoughtful about
   sending partners to open programs. The key consideration should be
   whether the nominated partner will learn something that they will be
   able to apply in their own firm or practice. (There can be internal politics about nominations, resulting in people being sent for the wrong
   reasons.) Partners can return motivated and inspired, and then find
   that organizational inertia / the day job prevents application of the
   learning. If the system is not geared up to support learning and change
   then the investment is wasted. One potential advantage of open
   programs is networking and learning from peers. If considering a
   law/professional service program, what type of firms will be represented? Peer firms with similar challenges that create learning
   opportunities, or firms of a different size and structure where there is
   less in common? Counter-intuitively, sending rainmakers / senior leadership to a general program may be an excellent approach. Attending
   with senior leaders in other industries offers fresh perspectives, as well
   as potential client networking opportunities.
2. *In-house.* Running the school's standard open program in-house for a
   cohort of partners. While the considerations around relevance and
   practicality continue to apply, this approach can provide economies
   of scale and a less politicized nomination approach. Partners can meet
   peers from across the business, and with enough partners going
   through the program there may be critical mass to embed and reinforce learning and change.
3. *Bespoke.* Developing a bespoke course for a cohort of partners based
   on the firm's specific needs (and potentially supplemented with wider
   consultancy). Some but not all business schools will design a program
   based on the firm's needs. They will work with the firm to identify relevant content, which can include skills training as well as more
   traditional business school type learning, and select the modules from
   their existing catalogue. Each module will be an individual academic's
   off-the-shelf offering rather than created specifically for a given firm.
   Bespoke programs give firms more control over content, but are also
   the most expensive, given the design work involved. Subject matter
   experts may not know the law firm context – which may or may not
   matter depending on the topic. The best speakers will help partners
   make the connections with their content, will be thought-provoking,

and stimulate new insights – but also will be practical enough for partners to take something away that they can apply at their desks.

Specialist L&D boutiques and trainers

Specialist L&D boutiques and trainers that focus on professional services or law firms – as opposed to the large generalist training companies – provide the best balance of credibility, relevance, and practicality. These will be coaches, facilitators, and trainers who have had careers in professional services, often as fee earners, and who understand the challenges, pressures, and nuances of the industry.

The best boutiques take a research-based approach to their content. Some do their own professional services industry research to develop their own models and thought leadership. Others will be using models and theories from academia or the commercial world, which have been tried and tested in business and are themselves research-based and known to be effective.

Boutiques are highly collaborative and aim to work with a firm to solve specific issues rather than offer general open programs. Even if providing a standardized course or offering, trainers will want to understand how the content can be adjusted to provide the best value or refreshed to stay relevant. Either way, they will bring examples from similar organizations, which will resonate with partners. They will say what has worked for others before and why, and what pitfalls need to be avoided.

Within this niche market are people who have further specialization around individual skills such as leadership, business development, and fee negotiation, lawyers-turned-actors who can roleplay clients or associates for conversations that matter, and people who can consult or lead workshops to develop firm capabilities such as culture change or law firm strategy, and then roll this out across the partnership. This latter organizational development work is just as much consultancy as it is training. For example, working with a firm to identify a culture best aligned to deliver the firm's strategy and then embedding that within the wider partnership and firm goes beyond pure training.

When working with a boutique provider, check the cultural fit and credibility for your audience. In addition to evaluating their subject matter expertise, test their understanding of the industry and identify how they can add value and how they will work with you and your partnership – just as you would expect your clients to evaluate your firm.

A brief word on digital and blended learning

Digital learning is becoming more popular in law firms, so it is worth mentioning it in the context of partner development.

Briefly, digital courses are technology-based standalone training programs, whilst blended learning combines these with traditional face-to-face learning (for example as pre- or post-course work, or a specific module within a wider program).

Firms use digital as it is available on demand, is scalable, cost-effective, and can cover off content that has not been covered elsewhere. Content can be pushed out to staff and attendance and completion rates can be tracked. In-house development teams can produce firm-specific content, such as mandatory compliance training, or legal content designed by partners for clients or junior lawyers.

This format works well for business services colleagues who may otherwise not have many development opportunities, and for junior lawyers who are happy to cover the basics in a range of (non-legal) subjects or are more used to consuming learning in digital forms.

The group who engages the least with digital learning is partners, and invariably they have the lowest completion rates of mandatory training. Digital training is a passive medium suited to transferring information rather than practicing skills, and there is no human interaction, networking, or opportunities for discussion. Partners need to complete the training in their own time and there is always something more pressing.

If you are considering a purely digital model for partner training, the evidence suggests there are better alternatives.

Measuring the impact of training

Measuring the impact of training in professional services firms is challenging, but firms will want to understand whether the investment is delivering returns.

There are two ways of looking at this – the effectiveness of a specific intervention, and the impact of professional development on a partnership over time. Neither are easy to evaluate.

Some interventions have measurable objectives, e.g. sustained behavioral change in a coachee based on stakeholder feedback – assuming there is follow up to get the feedback, or a percentage uplift in fees over a number of matters for a fee negotiation program. If the firm can measure these outcomes, it should – it is easier for budget holders to justify spend if there are tangible results.

Outcomes of other programs are more subjective. For example, results of transition programs designed to prepare new partners for partnership cannot be measured other than by asking participants whether they feel better prepared for partnership than before.

Ultimately, the question that needs answering for all interventions is, "How will this intervention help your career?" As long as the partner can give a convincing answer to this, the program has delivered value.

The second question looks at the impact on culture over time, and again this cannot be measured in a dollar value. Put simply, do partners feel that the firm invests in them or not? The answer may not lead to higher or lower partner engagement or turnover, but it will affect how they speak about the firm to their peers and clients.

Conclusion

Partner development involves more than enhancing previously learned skills. The increasing rate of change in the workplace requires partners to be agile and adaptable. They need to evolve their practice management, leadership, and team motivation to stay successful. As partners' career aspirations change, firms must provide support to keep them engaged and productive.

However, partner development is not simple – the culture needs to support it, and there is no one-size-fits-all or one right answer. Instead, firms need to pull on a range of approaches to meet specific needs and situations and be willing to experiment, accepting that measuring ROI is not always easy.

Chapter 18:
Accountability and consequences

By Jonathan Watmough, award-winning ex-City law firm managing partner and founder of HelpingLawyersTHRIVE

I look back sometimes on my time as a fee-earning partner and wonder how I did it. Building a career as a commercial lawyer in private practice is hard enough, but becoming and remaining a successful partner is the ultimate multi-tasking challenge in our world, and it is getting harder. On the other hand, it is a huge privilege to be in that position and an opportunity that must not be wasted.

But I also look back on my subsequent time as a managing partner and wonder if I was too hard on my partners and demanded too much. Partners are just human beings, trying to look after clients whilst also operating a business – they are not machines. On the other hand, it was my job to drive partner performance, there is a lot at stake, competition is fierce, and there is usually someone else ready and willing to perform in their place. Much as there was someone ready and willing to take my place if I did not improve collective performance.

Finding the right balance between the wants and needs of the individual partner and the wants and needs of the wider partnership and firm is very difficult. Each side is accountable to the other for delivering on their side of the bargain. Partnership is a two-way street. But finding that balance for every partner is almost impossible and most partnerships witness considerable politics as a result – because politics represents difficult choices between what, and who, is most important, and some things and some people are more important than others.

This is why professional partnerships are so difficult to lead and are so often misunderstood by outsiders. And yet the concept of partnership (even if it might be packaged within various different legal forms) remains the default choice for somehow coalescing free-thinking and reasonably individualistic professionals with personal trust-based client relationships together in business.

This makes "accountability" a difficult animal to describe in the context of partnership and an even harder animal to control.

"Accountability" connotes being responsible for your actions and answerable to others for results. Clearly, therefore, accountability goes to the heart of partner performance. It is in the nature of partnership that we each hold our own and play our part in some form of wider collective endeavor. It is the primary input that law firms depend on to be able to compete in the war for talent at all levels, and the war for talent is what ultimately matters in deciding which law firms win out. So, we have to address accountability head-on and we have to make the best of it. And like most things in life, sticking to a few fundamentals will ease our way in doing that successfully.

The four steps of accountability

- First, delivery expectations (both ways) must be clear and agreed (preferably set out in writing as far as possible). Neither side can be held accountable unless there is something to be held accountable for.
- Second, expectations (again, both ways) must be clear and understood (usually not to the extent of being "agreed" and hardly ever set out in writing) as to the potential consequences of delivery expectations either being met, exceeded, or fallen short of.
- Third, both sides have to regularly review progress against expectations, and be prepared to realign expectations as necessary and adjust activities and behavior to improve performance.
- Lastly, those leaders who are tasked with holding partners to account for performance need the courage, flexibility, skills, and backing to enable them to do their job.

This is a complex and sequential package that is not at all easy to deliver on, and few firms are able to pull off all four steps. Those firms that are able to pull off all of these steps even reasonably well will have a significant competitive advantage in the war for talent over those who do not.

Aligning expectations around delivery

Very few, if any, firms are such binary "eat-what-you-kill" environments that individual performance can be measured against expectations of delivery of simple financial metrics. Most partnerships have to work together in intangible, unmeasurable ways – for example, in reasonable harmony by sharing clients and resources. At the very least, the partners shouldn't be competing with each other externally.

Nearly all firms, therefore, have a range of expectations of partners, from delivery of financial metrics on one end to firmwide contribution on the other. But every firm's expectations of partners are different because every firm's culture is different – some firms are more focused on individual performance, some on collective performance, and most on some blend of the two. And every partnership organizes itself differently in terms of hierarchy, ranking, and seniority, and some may be partners in name only. So, what is expected of what type of partner, at what stage, and in which type of business will differ firm by firm.

A few firms are "one-firm" where the alignment between the businesses, the cohesion in the characteristics of the people, and the trust in a wide range of common cultural markers of "how things are done around here" are so uniform that expectations of partners are clear to everyone and rarely written down.

But most firms are not "one-firm" – instead, there will be greater divergence between the firm's businesses, greater variability in the quality and qualities of the people they have, and inconsistency in how they interact with each other and their markets. Many firms have multiple offices, often in multiple jurisdictions, which might pay lip service to the mother ship but often have their own peculiar approaches. Some firms are the products of mergers that never truly integrated, and so multiple cultural approaches to expectations may lurk beneath the surface. And lots of firms force growth through lateral hiring, which can quickly and unwittingly change partnership expectations around what is valued and why.

Setting expectations, therefore, in most firms around what "partner performance" means is difficult on a collective level and requires significant amounts of senior attention to make possible on an individual level. And yet it is arguably the single most important leadership challenge within a law firm environment.

Commercial lawyers at all levels in private practice tend to share reasonably common characteristics:

- We are driven by a dominant need for achievement – to meet high standards, to master skills and reach goals.
- We seek out challenges and autonomy in meeting those challenges.
- We like to plan and so we like clearly defined goals.
- We require feedback and recognition to verify whether we have

achieved the set goals. Achievement is more important than material or financial reward and, therefore, confirmation of achievement is a crucial motivator.

- We tend to avoid difficult conversations, especially around our performance and the performance of others.

This is why hierarchical advancement through the ranks up to the level of partner is very structured in many firms. In order to recruit, retain, and motivate large volumes of the above type of person in order to drive leverage, firms need to provide a defined pathway to enable people like us to "keep trading up to a better class of problem".

Clear expectations are set out, therefore, of what good performance looks like for associates on multiple dimensions – both in terms of activities to be done and behaviors to be demonstrated. This is typically written down in some form of associate career / competency framework, and the quality and openness of the feedback conversations both ways are carefully monitored centrally. HR teams will typically put a lot of effort into structuring, formulating, and implementing such a framework, with the help of management and behavioral science. Some of these frameworks will be better than others, but the general approach is a well-understood and well-trodden path because a career / competency framework is one of the fundamental tools required to be able to compete in the war for lawyer talent.

But in many firms this careful structuring of career advancement starts to fall down, or even stops altogether, once partnership is attained. Few firms' career / competency frameworks extend into the partnership, let alone to the top, even though in many ways the easier part is making partner, and the toughest learning and personal development journey is only then beginning.

Making partner is difficult in most firms, and very difficult to make a real success of when reached, because it is not only a complex and demanding role, but is a world away from being an employed associate. The step up to partner is usually manageable for most good lawyers in terms of their legal, client, and people management skills. But partnership in most firms requires two additional attributes – building and becoming a business, and providing leadership. And neither is natural for most lawyers.

Not many people become commercial lawyers in private practice to build and run a business – probably hardly any. The motivations to become a commercial lawyer will be many and various, but becoming a small, let alone a big, business in their own right will not register on the list for many. Most lawyers go into private practice to do the work because they are naturally suited to the legal role.

Leadership is a rare attribute generally – not just amongst lawyers, but a particularly rare commodity in law. Lawyers tend to prefer to focus on their work and their clients because it is what they enjoy most, and a complex web of factors within law firm partnerships, such as governance checks and balances, as well as reward structures, tend to mitigate against undue leadership emerging.

So, most lawyers (including many successful partners) are well out of their comfort zones as partners. They have to force themselves to do a lot of the difficult, entirely non-legal, things that partners have to do to become and remain a partner. And many do that because partnership continues to represent the defining achievement for those who are motivated to last the course – it is their Everest.

And yet in many firms, "partner development" tends to be learned "on-the-job" or is left to internal learning and development (L&D) teams to "train" and to some extent might be supplemented by external coaching. But precisely what is expected of whom and in what way is rarely written down. If it is written down, little attention is paid to it much beyond the junior partner ranks and virtually no attention is ever paid to it by lateral hires.

This is deliberate on the part of many law firm leaders because it is time consuming, expensive, perceived as a distraction, hard to develop partner alignment around, and takes both leadership and courage to implement a partner career / competency framework consistently.

Most firms will tend instead towards "wooliness" of partner expectations and "smoke and mirrors". They will expect partners to be able to work most of it out for themselves and be able to read the cultural mood music of what is expected and how. In some firms there will also be an almost Darwinistic approach that the law of the jungle applies, and it is survival of the fittest. That becoming a partner is just the beginning, and the big test is whether you can navigate your own way upwards. That a degree of chaos and competition is the best way to sort the sheep from the goats.

Most firms are also driven by short-termism and an annual profit and loss account, and therefore revenue and growth in partner profits are prioritized over long-term investment. Some law firm leaders will secretly prefer the flexibility that the lack of clarity around partner performance expectations gives them to be able to bend with the external commercial and internal political breezes as necessary and not be unduly tied down.

But in motivational terms, for all except a small number of outright competitive animals, this lack of goal clarity is corrosive for law firm partners. Without clear goals, there is ambiguity about what we're striving for and how we will measure our success in doing so. This in itself is demotivating, but our dominant achievement motivator is typically so strong that it can override this. But the consequence is that most law firm partners "overachieve" and at significant cost to themselves and those around them, such that in reality this represents "under-performance" because it is destructive to individual and collective wellbeing and relationships, and is ultimately unsustainable. It is sustainable performance that matters, not unsustainable overachievement.

It also encourages individualism over collectivism, which mitigates against many of the reasons why senior lawyers congregate in partnership and the benefits of doing so.

But even if individualism is what a firm is encouraging, objectives and expectations still have to be agreed – preferably collectively and always individually. This "contract" is the only way each party can hold the other accountable and responsible for delivery, and without that there can be no accountability either way. And without accountability there can be no "performance", because there is nothing to judge success or otherwise against, regardless of how sustainable that "performance" might be.

So, regardless of approach, every firm must make the effort to write it down!

First, we must write down on a collective level what activities and skills are expected of partners at which level of the partnership, what is required to progress to the next level, and which common behaviors are expected of all partners. This is difficult at a collective level and requires a good degree of soul-searching and often some difficult conversations. But it is well worth it – partners need that direction and clarity as much as associates, if not more. The obvious receptacle for this is that rare bottom to top career / competency framework for all levels of lawyer, but it could be separated from an associate framework if necessary if for unfathomable reasons what is expected of the partners has to be seen to be hidden behind a private veil. But not having some form of clear framework setting out what partners can expect of each other at what level is not an option in the vast majority of firms.

Second, and arguably more importantly, we must write down on a partner-by-partner basis what is expected of that particular partner in terms of the role they are being asked to play, how they will be judged, and the support they can reasonably expect from their partners and the firm in trying to deliver on that. Moreover, this must be co-created and agreed with the partner and their relevant group / team / department leader on the ground. This is where the specific balance between the individual partner's efforts and collective responsibility can be agreed, and billing and other financial targets, business development focus, personal development focus, group / team / department contribution and firmwide contribution can all be set out. This is very time consuming and would typically be refreshed and revisited annually as part of a review process, but it is crucial. It is typically shirked, however, or a perfunctory effort is made, because it involves open, honest, and sometimes difficult conversations around performance, longer-term strategic thinking, and not just short-term tactics, and a focus on how the partner (and other partners) fit into a wider team. Every partner is different and so every partner must be treated as an individual. Collective partner performance is simply the expression of multiple individual partner performances.

But two final warnings in aligning and defining expectations about what performance looks like – be careful what you measure and be careful what you wish for.

There is a saying that "What gets measured gets managed" and this is especially relevant to law firm partners. If personal chargeable time is heavily emphasized, partners will retain more chargeable work for themselves, delegate less to juniors, and will have less time available for longer-term development activity. If personal billings are emphasized, partners will share less work and contacts with other partners, and cross-selling will suffer. If recovery rates are emphasized, partners will charge what is on the clock regardless of the potential client relationship consequences. And so on. Broadly speaking, an emphasis on short-term individual financial measures will create a partner focus on individual behaviors in order to deliver an annual P&L, but this will be at the direct expense of wider firm-wide contribution and building a long-term balance sheet. There has to be personal responsibility for financial hygiene, but unless the aim is to create an individual-focused "eat-what-you-kill" environment, it is generally advisable to share financial responsibilities amongst a wider team of partners and balance this with goals around longer-term contributions.

But we must also be careful about the wider, and potentially unintended, consequences of dramatic shifts in emphasis in expectations, individually and collectively. Most lawyers don't like change, and the rather vulgar but devastatingly striking metaphor of "boiling frogs" is wise to bear in mind (that is, if you drop frogs into a pan of boiling water they will leap out, hence the need to raise the temperature only gradually). Positive cultural change tends to be evolutionary, not revolutionary, especially in a professional services context, and so it is always advisable to promote smaller and more gradual incremental changes over a longer period of time. Even in the context of a concerted push towards quite different high-performance behaviors, there will almost certainly be some key cultural anchors a firm will wish to hold firm to, and it is important that those cultural babies are not thrown out with the partner performance improvement bathwater.

Aligning expectations around the consequences of delivering or not delivering

The benefits of aligning partner performance expectations are clarity, ownership, and responsibility, both ways. The downside is that the firm's leadership has to follow through on the consequences of either the individual partner or the firm delivering, or not delivering.

Aligning expectations in this way is part of driving individual and collective partner performance, but it is also the surest way of destroying hard-earned trust if it is not followed through on. It will be perceived as a binding contract, even if it is more of the psychological than legal variety.

The difficulty is that it is impossible to write down the consequences of delivering or not delivering in any coherent way. The number of permutations of outcomes, plus and minus, are too great to be exhaustive and in seeking to even write down some guiding principles around "what happens if…" firms will likely tie themselves in knots. There will always need to be flexibility and wiggle room for the firm's leadership.

In the event that expectations have been met on both sides, or exceeded, the consequence will inevitably be some combination of increased reward (probably both financial and non-financial, for example additional benefits such as access to increased personal development) and recognition (typically in the form of career progression and/or increased status within the partnership).

Part of the judgment and expectation behind this will be driven by objective, external factors in terms of what the normal package for a partner of that standing might be in the market. However, the majority of what both the individual partner and the firm will be considering will be entirely subjective to the norms within the firm itself and relativity to other reasonably comparable partners within the partnership. For the firm, judgments on both reward and recognition for success will be constrained by what's reasonably practicable (and politically advisable) within the confines of the partnership and profit-sharing structures – the pie is only ever so big. If the individual partner has delivered on their side of the bargain, they will expect the firm to deliver on its side – but how the firm does that will likely be judged in terms of relativity of the individual partner to their peers – that is, their dominant "achievement" motivator in terms of meeting their internal partnership goal will have been satisfied by relative reward and elevation within the partnership, and explicit recognition of that.

These types of positive judgments are business-as-usual for law firm leaders and nice problems to have. The more difficult, and far more subjective and sensitive, judgments will typically arise where expectations have not been met on one side or the other – where the partner has "underperformed" – and potentially this is partly because the firm has "under-delivered" on its side of the deal. The potential consequences might range from doing nothing and giving things further time to come good on one end, to exit on the other end and many permutations in between, based on some combination of adjustment of business focus, leadership, support, training, reward, and status.

There is no right or wrong way of doing this – the approach depends on the way the partnership deal is formulated and the firm's cultural norms. But law firm partnerships are not hedge funds where you might be out on your ear simply because you missed one investment performance metric due to market fluctuations. Partners in law firms are the assets of the business and so the performance management of those assets has to be much more subtle and more by way of carrot than stick.

Whatever the individual approach, where there has been disappointment, the watchwords in most partnerships will likely be fairness and consistency. Fairness in the sense that the consequence is proportionate to the degree of, and reasons for, the underperformance as well as its longevity, and consistency in the sense that those principles of fairness are applied to all partners top to bottom and year-on-year. In most partnerships, those principles of fairness might manifest themselves in an approach something like this:

- Anything where the problem is unexpected and outside the control of the individual might well be supported for as long as it reasonably takes to find a mutual solution. Examples might include getting ill (an issue with role fit), regulatory change destroying a key part of their practice, or a key client departing through no fault of their own (both being issues with business fit). This may lead to a departure in time, but only after a lot of time and effort has been expended trying to reach a resolution, potentially involving agreed redeployment in a new role with different expectations. Remember, others will be thinking it could have been them.

- Anything within the individual's control that materially breaks the seal of mutual trust (an issue with people fit) between them and the partnership might well be fatal. For example, doing something materially outside cultural norms or repeatedly disregarding cultural norms. This can be very challenging territory, especially in a "rogue elephant"-type situation involving a senior person. But no one is bigger than the team. If the breach is deliberate or reckless and either material or repeated, there might be no going back, no matter the level of seniority. The debate in the mind of the firm's leadership will likely move on to how a departure might best be handled. These are decisions that most firms shirk, however, and the consequence is nearly always that the cultural ethos is thereby branded by others as worthless. Rogue elephants, left unaddressed, will destroy a partnership ethos.

- The more complex, nuanced, and typical situation is where the individual and/or their business / practice area just goes off the boil over time. Probably not deliberately, and probably not because of lack of effort, but because of natural changes in the individual, their abilities, their circumstances, and priorities and probably coupled with the market or the business focus of the team, gradually moving away from them. This is nature and evolution in action, and it comes to everyone at some point, and especially over a long career. It's to be expected but has to be managed by the firm's leadership with the individual openly and gradually over time, rather than by way of some form of surprise tap on the shoulder one day. The role of the leader is to pick these things up early and actively manage them to a mutually satisfactory solution, sometimes incrementally and over a reasonably long period. The individual partner will know that things are changing, where they are likely heading, and that it's in everyone's mutual best interests to surface the issues and find ways to address them within the confines of what's best for the partnership. This openness and honesty is the benefit of being part of a team. This might include reducing pressure, exposure, and expectations through a change of role, status, and/or reward, or they might prefer to maintain their existing standing and try their luck elsewhere. The firm's leadership's approach will depend on who the individual is, their history with the partnership, how iconic they might be, and how valuable they remain in relative terms. The firm will probably want (and the partnership will expect the firm's leadership) to go much further to accommodate someone who has a long history of performing well, is well-liked and respected, and still serves a valuable purpose.

- In nearly every case, and regardless of the reasons for the underperformance, the individual partner and their career must be shown respect, matters should be dealt with in private, and time should be allowed to reach a satisfactory negotiated outcome. It will generally be important to the partnership to be seen to be doing the right thing.

Reviewing progress and adjusting expectations

There has been a concerted trend in HR best practice over the last ten or so years away from simple set-piece annual reviews for associates and towards more regular formal and informal catch-ups, and that has to be right for both sides. In theory, this should apply at a partnership level too. In practice, however, it tends not to work out like that, and for good reason:

- The role of a partner is different, and the roles of some partners are very different, to servicing work that is fed to others as employees. Partners are typically businesses in their own right rather than resources that support a business. But performance is rarely a straight line for any partner or business – our world is reactively driven by client demand and the short-term pressures of what is in front of us, and quarterly financial results reflect only a small selection of the short-term outputs. Beyond immediate fee-generation, a huge amount of what partners do is with an eye on long-term credibility, profile, and relationship building.
- An organized catch-up every quarter between, say, the individual partner and at the very least their group leader and perhaps in some smaller firms the managing partner, is an admirable concept but difficult in practice to make work. Availability of time alone for those in the frontline of client work, whilst also building and running a business, is difficult to find – let alone the time and the inclination to do it properly.

These two factors alone beg the question how valuable anything approaching regular partner performance reviews can be and whether very many will actually take place in practice. They are hard enough to organize and develop focus on at an annual level.

My experience is that the most valuable regular conversations at individual partner level happen in two different contexts.

First, conversations at a team / group / department level between the individual partner, their fellow partners, and above all the partner responsible for leadership at that level. Most genuine teams of partners will have a formal weekly meeting to review progress and to surface and solve problems, as well as more occasional analytical and strategic reviews at quarterly or half-yearly intervals. Most genuine leaders of teams of partners will ensure that these group sessions not only happen but that they are in very regular dialogue with every partner at an individual level as to how they are personally and professionally, how things are going businesswise, and how performance at both an individual and collective level can be improved. These conversations are the foundation of partner performance, accountability for partner performance, and resolving in real time most issues around partner performance. And so, partner performance and accountability become chaotic and random, and uncontrolled and unexpected outcomes occur where there is an absence of leadership at a local level. No amount of centralized L&D or coaching support for individual partners will materially improve that. The primary challenge for any firmwide leader in inculcating improved partner performance, therefore, is to first instill strong, positive, and consistent partner leadership at a local level.

Second, the firmwide leader has to keep in reasonably regular contact with individual partners during the year. On a high level, they can do this by proxy through monthly conversations with the local team / group / department leader. But as far as possible, occasional personal catch-ups with individual partners should happen too, even in the largest firms, especially with the key people and those who might be struggling or might otherwise need greater personal attention. Everyone is different – some will want to be, and can be, left to their own devices whereas others will deserve, or need, more help or attention.

My experience is also that no amount of regular catch-ups and reviews is any substitute for everyone taking the time and making the effort to sit down on an annual basis and objectively look back on the rights and the wrongs of the last year and to adjust, plan, and set objectives both ways going forward in the context of that – both short-term (the coming year) and medium-term (perhaps up to the next three years). We cannot get away from the fact that nearly every law firm plans, measures success, and shares out the spoils of success on an annual cycle, and so partners think and act likewise. It's a fact of law firm life, and it is dangerous to pretend otherwise.

This makes an annual partner review, typically in the month or six weeks after the financial year-end, the most important period in the partnership calendar, whether law firm leaders either like it or care to admit it. It is when individual partners perceive they are being judged in relative terms against each other, and for most partners that is the judgment that counts most.

But it is a period that everyone – leaders and individual partners – typically hates. It takes up enormous amounts of time and energy at precisely the wrong time of year, requires a lot of information gathering, a lot of detective work to get to the truth, and ultimately the courage to have a lot of potentially difficult, open, and honest conversations that may have been bottled up for too long. And so too many partners and too many firms shirk it to some degree or other, and with two important adverse consequences:

- First, individual partners become demotivated because they are not receiving both the feedback and the recognition they need to satisfy their dominant achievement motivator in relation to the year just finished.
- Second, specific, measurable, achievable, relevant, and time-bound (SMART) individual goals are not being set going forward for the current year, so they cannot plan, they cannot be held to account, and they cannot be recognized for their achievements.

Instead, a vicious circle of individual partner overachievement but underperformance reasserts itself.

Although it is imperfect, painful, frustrating, and expensive, a formal and detailed annual partner review is the crucial underpinning of partner accountability and, therefore, performance.

The necessary people and tools to hold partners to account

Commercial law firms are just collections of individual commercial lawyers, so the collective law firm beast has the same fundamental characteristics as the individual lawyer beast.

A combination of the insecure nature of the work, the typical lawyer's preferences for free-thinking, incremental change, avoidance of conflict, and the need for professional achievement and growth generate certain typical behavioral tendencies. They encourage a laser-like focus on the work, a strong work ethic, and the need for regular feedback and recognition by way of proof of achievement. Inevitably, firms will tend to reflect very similar behavioral characteristics:

- A strong tendency to think and act short-term in order to give its lawyers what they need to perform the day job and the consequent recognition they need by way of profit share.
- A natural inclination to perpetuate business-as-usual, and to force growth in business-as-usual areas and ways.

This results in perpetual short-term collective pressure for firms to keep growing and moving forward and upward to renew and replace the work and access more and better opportunities, whilst making as little change as possible to the existing lawyers and the existing business model.

Breaking that tractor-beam-like pull towards doing what comes naturally and perpetuating the inconsistency inherent with business-as-usual takes both strong leadership as well as a reasonably strong stimulus to change. And yet leadership is in short supply in most firms. The profit-sharing systems in law firms also tend to promote individual short-term rainmaking over broader contribution to the long-term health and wellbeing of the firm. The strong leaders that firms do have tend to focus their efforts instead on their clients, their practices, their immediate team, and, potentially, their practice group because that is where their long-term value, internally and externally, lies. Few are inclined to be distracted from that by a broader leadership role (which is typically time-limited anyway), especially in their best years. Even though someone, or some group of people, has to do that if a firm and its future are going to be bound together in any coherent way.

Partnerships also seek to harness strong leadership through constitutional checks and balances – various elected committees of partners will typically exist to supervise, or in the case of profit-sharing even control, decisions of the executive. "Power" is typically distributed much more widely anyway amongst those who control significant client relationships. Law firm leaders tend not to have, therefore, that many explicit levers they can pull on in order to drive individual partner performance.

And so strong leadership from individuals is unusual within law firms, and committees of partners (that are typically elected to "represent" often quite varied and sometimes disparate bodies of opinion within the partnership) will frequently tend to either fudge difficult decisions or exercise unwitting bias. The result is that the honesty and clarity required both ways in any partner performance review is often lost.

This is a difficult cycle to break, but unless and until it is broken, no amount of virtuous adherence to implementation of the above will drive concerted improvement of partner performance. In fact, implementation of the above will likely transpire to be a very expensive waste of time. I suspect that, in the ultimate reckoning, this is the reason why most firms pay lip service to partner performance evaluation and goal setting – because the leadership either isn't there or isn't equipped to provide the honesty and clarity to make it work properly.

Those firms, therefore, that do have the leadership to make it work properly, and have the backing of those within the partnership who truly hold the power to make it work properly, have a significant competitive advantage.

But there is one final ingredient, which in my experience is the fundamental tool that anyone who is tasked with driving partner performance requires, and that of course is a combination of flexibility to adjust both financial reward and status.

Whilst money and status are some way down the list of the primary motivations of most partners, neither can be a problem and, above all, in relative terms within their peer group, they are very much a marker of achievement. They are, therefore, crucial aspects of the feedback and recognition that every partner (and the partnership collectively) requires. Moreover, within most partnerships, financial reward and status are taken to be a straightforward proxy for relative value and, therefore, success. Within a partnership, meritocratic adjustment of relative financial reward and relative status, plus or minus, are the proverbial pictures that are worth a thousand words and the consequence is typically behavioral change of a range of partners and not just that of the individual in question. It is a statement to the partnership as a whole of what is valued and rewarded, and vice versa, and widespread careful note is typically taken.

It is impossible, however, to implement this in either a pure lockstep system or a profit-sharing system where the individual outcomes are strictly confidential.

A pure lockstep system, where elevation of financial reward and status is automatic by reference to time served, can only ever work effectively in a one-firm firm that operates an up-or-out system – where the consequence of not performing to widely understood expectations is exit. Such a system requires close alignment and integration of the partnership's business, cohesion in the quality and qualities of the people, and trust in the cultural approach of how people are expected to behave. This is rare and, therefore, pure lockstep profit-sharing systems are similarly rare nowadays.

At the other end of the law firm spectrum, entirely closed and confidential profit-sharing systems tend to exist only in firms that lean towards an eat-what-you-kill approach, where animalistic individualistic tendencies tend to be valued above a partnership approach – where honesty around relative value between partners would be seen as divisive and destructive.

Nearly all firms today have graduated towards some sort of partner financial reward and status recognition system that is somewhere between these two extremes, with reasonable flexibility to adjust both on merit. Meritocratic adjustment to financial reward might typically comprise some form of retrospective upwards adjustment for the year just ended by virtue of allocation from some form of bonus pool and perhaps some form of either upwards or downwards adjustment for the new year going forward. Meritocratic adjustment to status recognition might typically comprise going through some form of gateway going forward in terms of seniority or category of partnership – for example, from salaried partner to fixed share partner to junior equity partner to full equity partner – which in turn might itself involve wholesale change to how financial reward is calculated and the consequences of that (such as contribution of capital). Or, typically by agreement, it might involve a reduction in status.

Every firm has its own system, for better or worse, but the important common denominator in all of them must be that those responsible for driving partner performance have some reasonable degree of flexibility within the system to be able to reflect short- and long-term improvements or declines in individual partner performance through meritocratic adjustment to reward and, if necessary, status. Without those two levers resting in the hands of those who are both courageous enough to use them and are backed by the partnership and its culture to use them, partner accountability for both performance improvement and decline is substantially toothless.

Closing thoughts
In my opinion, a lot of rubbish is talked about law firm strategy.

The core of every law firm's strategy is people, and one could argue that the only strategy a law firm ever really needs is how to develop a competitive advantage in the war for talent in their chosen markets. Because the clients and the people always follow the talent, and a firm's brand is the external manifestation of their talent. That talent is ultimately defined by the quality, qualities, and behaviors of a firm's partners.

But nearly all partner talent requires leadership to get the best out of itself. Few are "born" partners – most are nurtured and made through the efforts of others. Like every human being, all partners (even high-performance partners) require direction, support, encouragement, and occasionally a talking to, and some partners, especially those on the way up, might require a lot of leadership.

The common thread that runs through all four sequential steps towards partner accountability that I describe in this chapter is the need for leadership, and at multiple levels. Only through strong leadership is it possible to align clear expectations about collective and individual partner delivery, align clear expectations about the consequences of delivering or not delivering, have the courage to have open and honest conversations about partner performance, and vest the trust in the right people with the right tools to be able to reflect the consequences of partner performance in terms of reward and status.

Firms that are concerned about partner performance, and accountability for partner performance, are well advised to verify first whether the wider underlying issue is one of lack of leadership. No amount of clever performance management techniques will remedy a misfiring partner or partnership unless and until strong leadership is first able to create the clarity and alignment that every partner and every partnership needs in order to perform at their best. Partner performance, and accountability for that performance, tends to be a natural consequence of strong leadership.

Chapter 19:
Utilizing technology for partner performance management

By Ray D'Cruz, CEO and co-founder, Performance Leader

Technology in partner performance management

Technology is a key part of the partner performance management toolkit. Its role is to drive efficiencies, produce evidenced-based insights, track progress against objectives, and facilitate better quality performance management conversations and ongoing feedback.

For most large firms, technology is an indispensable factor in improving the efficiency, effectiveness, and fairness of the partner performance management process. For many others, the use of technology in partner performance management and the move to a real-time feedback culture remain ambitions.

Capturing the benefits of partner performance management technology

Efficiency benefits

One of the most obvious advantages is that technology can drive efficiencies in the partner performance management process, which can be notoriously time-intensive and challenging to execute. Technology solutions can streamline the review process, and save time for leaders, partners, remuneration committees, and administration staff. Time savings can be achieved by:

- Flowing data from the previous year's review into the current year (so partners don't have to locate and print manual forms);
- Automating feedback gathering (for example, peer feedback);
- Integrating financial performance data from firm systems;
- Incorporating nudge tools to keep the process moving efficiently;
- Providing partner-leaders with summary progress dashboards;
- Using AI to generate review summaries and objective-setting suggestions; and
- Going paperless (which also creates environmental benefits).

Effectiveness benefits

Partner performance management technology can also create a wide range of "effectiveness" benefits, including:

- Collecting and visualizing data to support better quality decision-making;
- Ensuring consistent preparation for quality performance conversations;
- Balancing formal reviews and regular check-ins; and
- Setting and tracking progress against objectives.

Importantly, the right technology solutions improve the user performance review experience for leaders and partners, which reduces dissatisfaction and disengagement with the process.

Technology can be used to help leaders and partners talk more regularly about work, objectives, and career development. For example, technology-prompted regular conversations help reviewers proactively identify issues that affect morale, wellbeing, and productivity. By developing and maintaining alignment of purpose through regular connection between partners and their partner-leaders, partners' engagement levels and discretionary efforts regularly increase, and retention follows.

Technology solutions can also underpin a more transparent approach to planning, which allows partners to identify potential collaborators and work towards shared objectives together. It can then be used to guide collaboration through shared objectives on the platform, as well as agree responsibilities, map progress, and celebrate wins. Importantly, by using technology to facilitate collaboration, it's also easier to ensure all contributing partners are appropriately recognized and rewarded for this behavior.

Overcoming technology uptake barriers

Despite the benefits of partner performance management technology, levels of its uptake are surprisingly low. The 2024 Edge International survey[1] found 73 percent of 100 firm respondents from around the world did not currently use a technology solution in managing partner performance. Of those, 11 percent were considering using partner performance management technology but had not yet introduced it to the firm. There are a few reasons for this low level of uptake.

There is a correlation between the size of the firm and the perceived value of this partner performance management technology. Firm leaders from medium and large firms are more likely to see this technology as important or essential.[2] This may indicate that firm leaders think of software as an efficiency tool, more than as an effectiveness tool. Used well, it is both.

Building a business case

As part of a simple value equation, business cases for technology solutions should assess efficiency and effectiveness, and costs.

The costs are easy to quantify as they involve the technology development and licensing costs (either outsourced or insourced), as well as resourcing for implementing and maintaining the system.

Robust benefit analysis should consider both efficiency and effectiveness benefits highlighted earlier in this chapter. Benefits can also be framed by broader talent and business propositions, such as engagement, retention, and collaboration, as shown in Figure 1 on the next page.

In most business cases, efficiency benefits alone justify technology investment. Time saved locating past forms, gathering feedback from peers, and using AI summary tools will amount to over one partner hour saved per review. The annual licensing and development costs of most technology platforms will cost less than an hour of partner billable time per year. With efficiency benefits alone creating the return on investment, effectiveness benefits are a further upside, with substantial gains to be captured depending on the firm's strategic focus.

Addressing resistance to change

Change resistance is another significant barrier to adopting partner performance management technology.

In smaller firms, resistance is commonly fueled by concerns about upfront costs. In larger firms, resistance comes from the perceived workload from changing well-established practices to the potential for political fallout from a failed implementation. Resistance from "once-bitten" firms is a common phenomenon. Often these firms have previously tried to do too much with technology and increased the workload on their partners. What followed was partner disengagement, task avoidance, and project failure.

In implementing the technology, it's important to recognize that – while not everything can be achieved at once – building initial trust and ongoing momentum is important. That is why it's critical to succeed slowly, rather than fail fast. Successful implementations occur when there is a reasonable timetable, adequate skills, effective change management, and partner

Figure 1: Business case for partner performance technology

COLLABORATION AND INNOVATION Together find better ways of working

An effective platform will clarify and align objectives via shared plans, allowing partners to collaborate on solving business and client problems. By using technology to both review performance and debrief work, the firm can identify better ways of working, and how to increase client value while capturing a fair share of that value. These are innovative and collaborative firms, enabled by software.

ENGAGEMENT Commit to the firm's vision

An effective platform provides regular touch points for feedback conversations. By creating opportunities for a more vibrant feedback culture, we help partner-leaders and partners to engage regularly about objectives, focus and career, increasing engagement and discretionary effort.

RETENTION Retain leadership and partner talent

An effective platform supports retention through better reward decision-making, a culture of recognition within the partnership. The flow on benefits from partner retention are client loyalty, team cohesion and saved recruitment and onboarding costs.

EFFICIENCY Save resources

Automation (and tools such as AI) streamline the process, saving partner-leader and RemCom time, improving compliance, and creating an efficient flow of data between performance periods and systems.

INVESTMENT

Costs include software licensing or development, resourcing project implementation and ongoing platform management.

Source: © 2024 Performance Leader. All rights reserved.

engagement. One of the best approaches is to start modestly, solve pain points, find quick wins, and build from there.

User engagement is the most important element of successfully implementing any new system. If partners find the system to be time-consuming or confusing, they are unlikely to engage with it. That is why it's critical to build partner confidence in the system by clearly communicating the benefits of the solution to them, their team and the firm, focusing on positive user experiences, and ensuring system predictability.

Other key change management factors include short- and medium-term technical and inherent skill development. In the short-term, for example, effective change management will be supported by running short technical training sessions, producing succinct user guides, and offering immediate support from HR and IT if needed. In the longer term, enhancing partner willingness to experiment and engage with partner performance management technology, and improving their inherent communication, capacity for difficult conversations, analytical thinking, and collaboration skills are likely to lead to significant competitive advantage.

Selecting a software solution

To take advantage of the value of partner performance management technology, it's critical to choose the right software solution. This decision should include an assessment of the firm's short-, medium- and long-term requirements, which is why any preferred solution must be flexible and capable of evolving.

Selection team

There's a depth of expertise in every firm that leaders should harness when selecting software. A partner performance management technology selection team will always benefit from the insights of HR, IT, Finance, and partner representatives. While some partnerships prefer HR to be excluded from the partner contribution aspects of partner performance management, the inclusion of a trusted HR leader is one of the most reliable predictors of a technology solution's success.

The selection team has a clear remit – identify what is important, what can wait, and what is unimportant. Too many procurement processes involve extensive stakeholder consultations that result in a long list of non-prioritized features and fail to crystallize the problems to be solved. At its heart, the partner performance management process seeks to address a discreet set of issues. If the obvious and pressing problems are solved first, the level of goodwill from partners to move on to other goals will be evident.

Platform options

When including technology in partner performance management, a fundamental decision to make is what type of platform to use. For many years, the debate has been whether to use a best-of-breed platform or an all-in-one enterprise platform. While both options have pros and cons, a third option – a hybrid solution – is increasingly being chosen as the preferred model.

A best-of-breed solution refers to the leading applications, systems, or software in a category. Firms that choose best-in-breed solutions to build their technology stack select tools that serve specific purposes. Responding to the nuances of a firm's contribution and compensation management system will often require a best-of-breed solution.

An all-in-one solution refers to a suite of integrated products from the one vendor. The upside of integrated solutions is that fewer individual applications need to be managed within the firm's technology stack as the systems should be interoperable. Gartner summarizes the problem with this approach:

"Although enterprise resource planning (ERP) vendors offer numerous enterprise applications and claim that their integrated system is a superior solution, all modules in an ERP system are rarely best-of-breed."[3]

A hybrid solution is a technology stack comprised of best-of-breed solutions and a base all-in-one solution. It offers the more compelling benefits of best-of-breed technology, which are a key factor in assessing the value of any partner performance management solution. The hybrid solution also leverages an all-in-one solution's ability to solve simple, functional problems. This helps keep cost down – which is the other key factor in the value equation.

Hybrid solutions rely on interoperability to make harmonization possible, which requires both best-of-breed and all-in-one providers to work together in the interests of their shared client. Generally, best-of-breed providers offer an application programming interface or bespoke approach to hybrid implementations.

In partner performance management, each firm's requirements are unique and will change over time. It's important to find a technology partner that aligns with the firm's objectives for the project, offers flexible solutions that can evolve with the firm's approach, and understands the partnership model as well as the nuances and sensitivities of partner contribution and compensation management.

Design and ease of use

Partners are time-poor. Any platform that is confusing or takes too much time to learn will be rejected. All the best laid multi-year plans will be redundant simply because partners don't engage fully. It sounds brutal, but that story is told time and time again. Poor user experience is sometimes cited as the reason a firm has abandoned its partner performance technology and returned to a paper-based approach.

While all technology vendors will claim their product is simple to use and saves time, the selection team needs to validate the pitch. The best way to do this is by speaking to managing partners and HR directors of like-minded firms that have implemented these solutions. These peers can attest independently on issues such as ease and speed of implementation, and ease of use.

Security and data protection

One of the most important factors in any selection process is security. As targeted and random cyberattacks increase, cloud-based vendors and third-party hosts need to have a strong security framework in place. The nature of the data being processed also demands compliance with all relevant data protection regimes. Ideally, vendors will be independently certified to the relevant information security standard (ISO27001:2013).

Implementing a technology solution

Once a technology solution has been selected, it's useful to create an implementation success plan that addresses the elements depicted in Figure 2 on the next page.

Using this approach, the software implementation success plan will consider:

- *Project objectives.* Short (one-year), medium (two-year) and long-term (three-year) project objectives ensure that planning encapsulates short-term pain points together with longer-term aspirational objectives.
- *Market context.* Developing shared insight into what is happening in

Figure 2: Elements of a partner performance management technology implementation plan

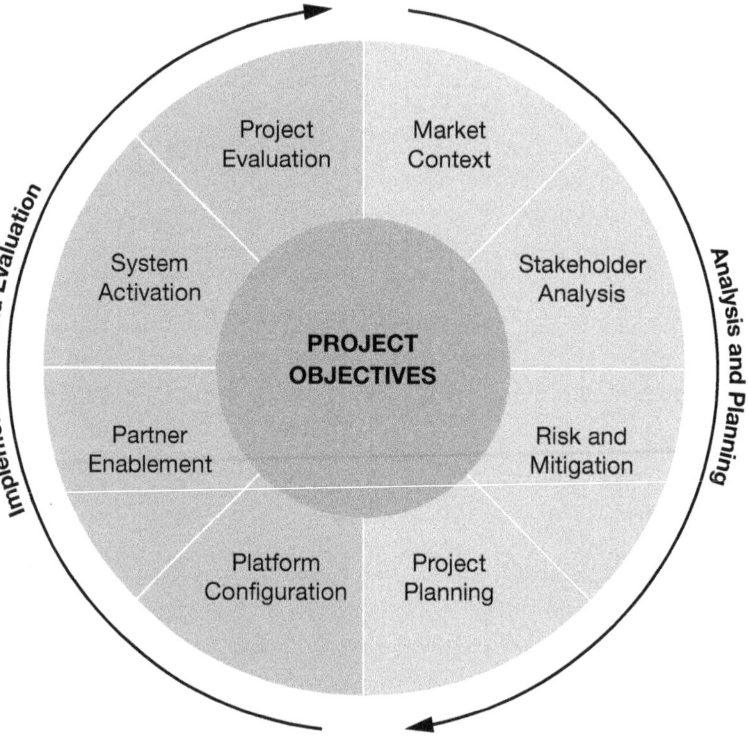

Source: © 2024 Performance Leader. All rights reserved.

the market for partner performance and development will support the firm to respond. For example, at the time of publication, there is a discernible interest from firms in recognizing and rewarding non-financial contribution. Clarifying how a new platform or process might support this interest would be helpful at the outset.

- *Stakeholder analysis.* Identifying the needs (both outcomes and experiences) of key groups connected to partner performance, including partner-leaders, partners, the renumeration committee, HR, and finance.
- *Risks and mitigation.* Anticipating potential risks from adopting new

technology will allow for mitigation strategies to be put in place. These responses may relate to system configuration, communication and training, timing, and clarification of roles and responsibilities. It's useful to reflect on recent technology rollouts at the firm to consider what works and doesn't work for key stakeholders.

- *Project planning.* Establishing a project plan will help keep the project on track. Dedicated project managers from IT are often deployed on these projects to support the HR team. In relative terms to mission-critical billing or document management systems, a performance platform should be simpler to roll out.

- *Platform configuration.* Systems that are built for partner performance should be more flexible and faster to configure. Configuration will usually involve setting up formal performance review and check-in cycles, uploading data (e.g., user data, capability data, financial data) and aligning the objective-setting process to the firm's strategy.

- *Partner enablement.* Providing partners with clarity about the process and how to engage with the platform should be part of a communications plan. Yet the barriers to the effective use of platforms are often more human-centered. This can be mitigated by improving feedback skills, handling difficult conversations, and establishing the authority to hold peers accountable in a partnership. These issues are best addressed in group development and individual coaching environments.

- *System activation.* User acceptance testing will be formalized in most software license agreements, and firms should take this process seriously. Detailed testing scripts and end-user involvement will help to ensure that the platform is fit for purpose, easy to use, and ready for rollout.

- *Project evaluation.* A debrief with key stakeholders will establish the success of the project, and how the platform can continue to evolve.

Using analytics for evidence-based decisions

Once successfully implemented, performance management technology enables firms to identify, capture, and analyze a wide range of qualitative and quantitative data that can be used to produce meaningful, evidenced-based insights about people and performance. Partner performance data is likely to include financial and non-financial metrics, as well as qualitative feedback from self-assessments, managers, peers and clients.

Through partner analytics, firms can improve partner talent and reward decisions by:

- Identifying or confirming performance issues or improvement opportunities at an individual, group, or firm level;
- Informing talent decisions ranging from promotions to de-equitization;
- Recognizing and rewarding behavior that contributes to firm success;
- Identifying predictive indicators for successful lateral hires;
- Mitigating risk by identifying partners who are at risk of leaving or at risk of burnout or stress; and
- Challenging the status quo and illuminating blind spots.

The engagement, retention, and recruitment benefits of a well-deployed analytics program can be significant. For example, IBM's former CEO, Ginni Rometty, stated that the company saved nearly $300 million by using people analytics to identify the people most at risk of leaving and prescribing actions.[4]

Despite its potential, research[5] shows a minority of professional services firms use people analytics, and only medium-sized and larger firms regard partner performance analytics as valuable. Part of this low uptake relates to the dominance of traditional financial metrics, and the reluctance of firms to move beyond these.

Some firm leaders also consider people analytics to be the domain of large corporations like IBM and see it as a subset of "big data". With a few hundred partners (or employees), the qualitative feedback text from a typical review process will be over a million words. That's over a million words of carefully scripted performance analysis by the firm's owners, leaders, and producers, who write well for a living. This data, when collectively analyzed using text analytics or sentiment analysis tools, can yield powerful insights. It is in many ways the most vital annual snapshot into the firm, and it should be treated as a valuable piece of research.

Having access to the data is one thing. Harnessing it to create valuable, evidence-based insights is another. There are many ways to achieve this, with the best processes sometimes being the most creative and experimental.

Most firms have access to in-house analytic capabilities, which is critical in ensuring any analysis includes an overlaid understanding of the firm, industry, and the relevant applications. Most medium-sized and larger firms have data analysts who understand statistics and spreadsheets. Smaller firms are usually able to draw on analytical capabilities within their finance team. In most firms, partner-leaders will easily be able to test these data-driven insights against their own experience.

The rise of AI tools

As with many technology solutions, the use of artificial intelligence (AI) in partner performance management solutions is becoming increasingly prevalent.

AI offers the potential to further streamline many time-consuming aspects of the partner performance management process. AI tools, such as Microsoft Azure Chat GPT, are being used to summarize feedback text and provide sentiment analysis. This reduces the time reviewers need to spend sifting through self-reflections, and peer or 360-degree feedback, to inform their own observations. With a click, AI tools provide a first cut of the collated feedback that the reviewer can then work with.

AI is also being used in the process of setting objectives that create strategic alignment across the firm. Good objectives are increasingly important for firms – but they can take time to create. AI assistants help partners strengthen their objectives or create new objectives based on the feedback they have received.

AI can also be used to sift through qualitative data sets to provide performance-related insights. For example, a large professional services firm recently used AI to analyze successful collaboration. The AI examined the narratives associated with a collaboration metric to identify the eight attributes of the best collaborators in the firm. This level of insight was previously difficult to achieve. These broader and deeper insights can then be fed back into partner expectations frameworks, suggested objectives, and development programs to properly close a performance-learning loop.

Communicating data-driven insights

To inform evidence-based decisions, it's important to engage firm leaders and reviewers in considering performance theories and data-driven insights. This process can be enhanced by using simple and compelling data visualization tools to help tell the performance story.

In many firms, HR leaders are the narrators of this story. Unfortunately, many of them report being fearful of this process due to their perceived risk of being strongly challenged or sidelined by partners. This anecdotal evidence is supported by other research. For example, when Google investigated what makes teams successful, it found that the top dynamic of an effective team was psychological safety.[6]

Accordingly, to benefit from the power of performance analytics, partners need to create a psychologically safe environment for everyone involved in the process. It can also be helpful to avoid binary debates in favor of idea exploration and insight consensus.

Conclusion

For most firms, a rigorous assessment of the value equation will fall in favor of implementing technology as part of a partner performance management solution. Fit-for-purpose technology enhances the partner performance management process by driving efficiencies, improving effectiveness across talent and business domains, and enabling data-driven decision-making. Capturing the full value technology is a firm competency in itself. The success of any technology solution will also depend on an effective, well-managed implementation that solves pain points, builds trust and momentum, and keeps evolving with the firm.

References

1   Nick Jarrett-Kerr and Jonathan Middleburgh, "Edge International 2024 Survey on the Management of Partner Performance", www.edge.ai/2024/06/partner-performance-management-survey-results-2024/

2   Ray D'Cruz and Michael Roch, "Partner Contribution and Reward Survey Report: Current Trends in Partner Contribution and Compensation Management in Professional Services and Advisory Firms" (Performance Leader, 2018), p7, https://info.performanceleader.com/partner-contribution-reward-2018

3   www.gartner.com/en/information-technology/glossary/best-of-breed

4   Jonathan Ferrar and David Green, *Excellence in People Analytics: How to Use Workforce Data to Create Business Value* (Kogan Page, 2021), p4.

5   Michael Roch, Maria Georgakopoulou, Polina Pavlova, and Ray D'Cruz, "Evolving Performance in the Professions" (Performance Leader, 2016), https://info.performanceleader.com/evolving-performance-management-professions-2016.

6   Jonathan Ferrar and David Green, *Excellence in People Analytics: How to Use Workforce Data to Create Business Value* (Kogan Page, 2021), p283.

Chapter 20:
Views from the profession

By Nick Jarrett-Kerr and Jonathan Middleburgh, principals, Edge International

Some initial observations

Over the past few years, both of us have consulted widely on performance management across the world and have discussed the topic with many managing partners. These discussions often – though not always – take place in the context of partner remuneration / compensation, though Nick has examples of at least two firms whose main aim was to encourage partners to be more business-like in their behaviors and in particular to devote significant time and attention to business development. Jonathan has encountered several firms where the stated purpose was partly to rationalize remuneration, to figure out how to incentivize important "partner" behaviors.

Over the past few years, it has become increasingly clear to us that the approach to managing partner performance has – certainly in the case of the larger firms – homogenized to some extent. We think that there are several reasons why this is the case:

- The influence of US firms entering the London market in considerable numbers;
- Global firms expanding;
- Major networks of firms and alliances such as Lex Mundi setting up best practice protocols; and
- The larger and most respected UK firms having a significant or major influence in the United States.

Firms across the world – not least in the US – are still somewhat obsessed with financial metrics, although not to the exclusion of other criteria. It is hard to get away from the fact that law firms have increasingly developed into businesses (as opposed to traditional professional service practices) where the maximization of profit is at the center of most firms' core objectives. It is therefore no surprise that partners are judged primarily on their financial performance, wherever the firm may be in the world. The commercialization and corporatization of the law firm is certainly true of the bigger firms, but the small firms and medium-size firms have also increasingly become more commercially minded and this has happened within a relatively short timeframe in the context of the overall history of the law firm.

What has slightly surprised us is how few firms have written performance management standards. Key performance indicators (KPIs), targets, and other metrics are almost universal – often very blunt or crude, but nonetheless nearly universal. But in our experience, it is still the case that very few firms set out their expectations of partners with clarity and in a written form. Based on our experience of multiple firms, this does not seem to have changed much in the last five years. It is also perhaps unsurprising that the question of underperformance remains an issue for most firms – and that there are still many firms where partners are failing to meet standards.

In the process of putting together this book we created a survey that we put out as a collaboration between the consultancy of which we are both principals (Edge International) and the publisher of this book (Globe Law and Business). What follows are the headline results of that survey. We round off this chapter, and the book, with some brief closing observations from one-to-one conversations we have had with managing partners and other senior leaders (e.g., CEOs, senior partners) of some leading firms in their respective jurisdictions.

The 2024 Partner Performance Management Survey

Between April and May 2024, Edge International and Globe Law and Business reached out to a variety of law firms to find out how they were managing partner performance. We also reached out individually via our social media networks, in particular, LinkedIn. 100 firms responded. Around ten percent of firms that responded to the survey have more than 100 partners, 15 percent between 50 and 100 partners, and the majority (75 percent) have fewer than 50 partners. Sixty percent of respondents to the survey are the managing partners or chief executives of the firm, with around 30 percent equally split amongst other leadership roles in the firm.

The survey provides, in our view, an interesting snapshot into the state of the profession this year across the world. It is, however, important to note that the results are not as deeply empirical as other surveys referred to earlier in this book, particularly in chapter three (Dr Heidi K. Gardner's in-depth research on lateral hires), chapter five (Professor Bree Buchanan's review of the role of wellbeing in promoting performance), and chapter six (substance abuse in the legal profession by Jim Lawrence). We all know that indiscriminate use of statistics and quantitative data can often misrepresent the picture. In many cases, the survey provides a more hopeful view but could be skewed by the responders coming from firms where lateral hiring has been more than usually successful, and where the incidence of poor mental health, burnout, and substance abuse has been well hidden or less than average. Obviously, managing partners and responders to our survey cannot hope to know absolutely everything about what is going on in their firm and within the heads of their co-workers. As Paula Davies points out in chapter seven, "many legal leaders assume that engaged lawyers are happy and functioning well at work. That may not always be true because, for some, engagement and stress (and aspects of burnout) co-exist." This is echoed by Jim Lawrence in chapter six when he states (with regard to substance abuse), "statistically speaking, every large law firm likely has numerous employees currently needing help with addiction issues, but many of these employees are scared to seek help because of societal stigma and career concerns".

Does underperformance affect firms?

Underperformance continues to affect firms' profitability in a similar way that it did when Edge International conducted previous surveys in 2011 and 2018. The 2011 survey found that the bottom line of 70 percent of firms had suffered by up to ten percent, and by 2018, the proportion of firms thus affected was around 90 percent. The 2024 survey suggests that the average effect on profits remains high, as can be seen from Figure 1, which shows that over 40 percent of firms have experienced an adverse effect on profits of more than five percent.

Figure 1: The extent to which issues of partner underperformance have affected the bottom line in any of the last three financial years

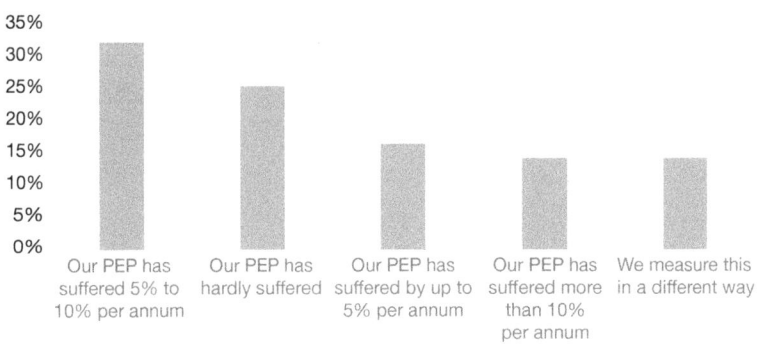

Nearly two-thirds of firms say that they are quite likely or very likely to be forced to take further action in respect of partner underperformance over the next two years. By contrast, a quarter feel that further action is not likely. These numbers are in stark contrast with the surveys in 2011 and 2018, where nearly all firms felt that further action was likely and only around five percent thought there would be no need for further action. As it seems probable that levels of underperformance have remained the same, one possible conclusion is that firms have become better at addressing partner performance management issues proactively.

Dealing with underperformers

We asked firms how they deal with, manage, and support underperformers. Figure 2 illustrates the typical ways in which firms support their underperformers. Three-quarters offer some form of coaching and many also offer some types of other assistance. One firm commented that the firm is extremely equitable so will utilize any means possible.

Figure 2: How firms support underperformers

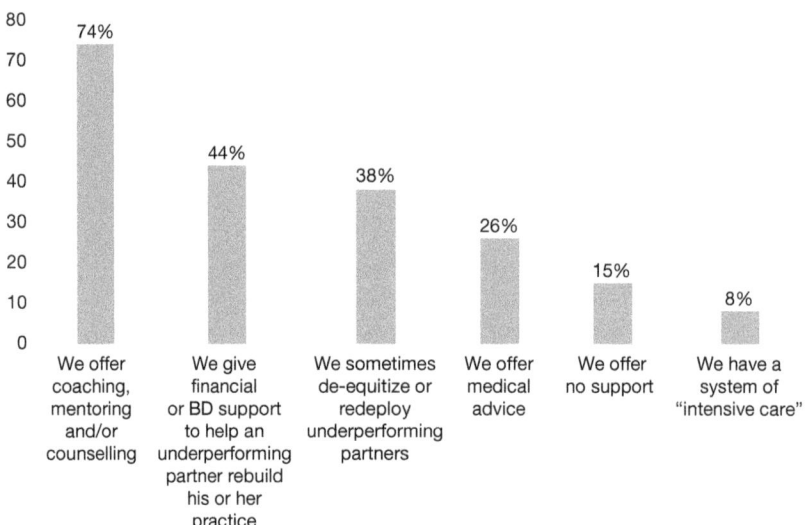

We asked over how long a period partners are typically given an opportunity to meet standards or to regenerate their practice. Unsurprisingly, there was a mixture of responses. Just over 40 percent of firms think that 12-24 months is about right and only 17 percent would allow longer than that. A quarter of firms think that the period will vary depending on the compelling nature of the partner's business plan for revival. Around 15 percent think that six to 12 months is a reasonable timeframe for a partner to turn it around.

Not all firms are willing to reveal what percentage of equity partners have left the firm over the past five years primarily as a result of underperformance issues. Of the 70 or so firms that answered, half said that none had left and 30 percent reported that a small number (up to five percent) had left in such circumstances. Only ten percent of responding firms admitted that as many as one in ten had left in circumstances of underperformance. The percentage of non-equity partners leaving primarily due to underperformance issues was somewhat higher, with more than half of firms reporting attrition of up to ten percent of non-equity partners.

In the context of departing partners, we were interested to know how the departure was ultimately effected. Figure 3 illustrates this, with 60 percent of respondents reporting voluntary departure as the most common method, with heavy negotiation necessary in a significant percentage of cases.

Figure 3: Mode of departure of equity partners leaving in the last five years

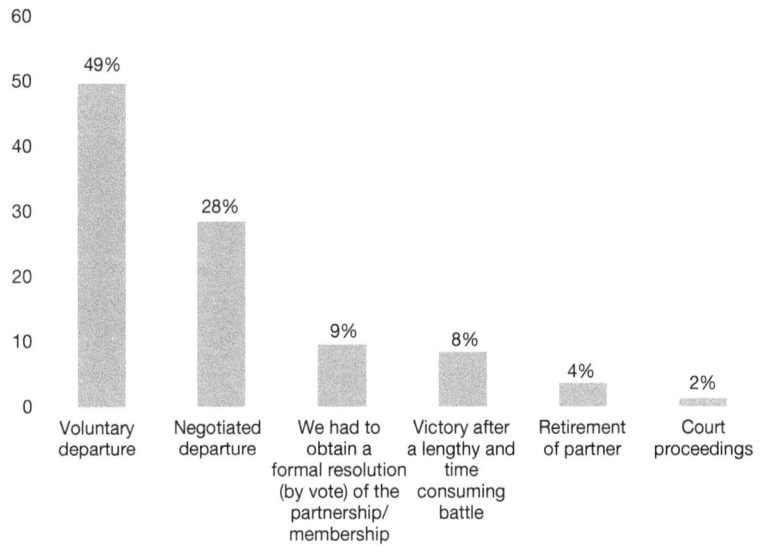

Lateral hires

We then asked about lateral hires, specifically those who joined the firm at least two years ago (see Figure 4). Forty-three percent of firms reported that more than half their lateral hires have largely met expectations, with a further 21 percent stating that all have met or exceeded expectations. Fifteen percent of firms report that more than half of their lateral hires have met more expectations than they have failed, which gives a general satisfaction rate of nearly 89 percent. However, a significant minority (23 percent of firms) report that more than half have failed to meet expectations. We interpret these responses as showing a slight improvement on our 2018 survey, which seemed to show a disappointment rate of 36 percent.

Figure 4: The attrition rates of lateral hires who joined between two and five years ago

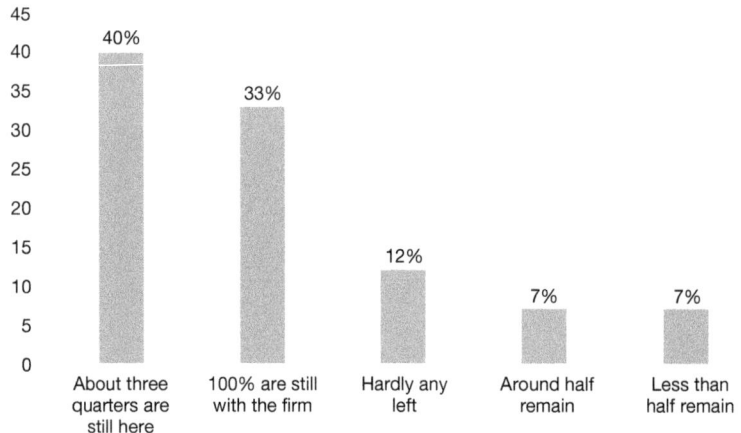

Stress and wellbeing

The survey asked what percentage of partners have suffered from severe stress, clinical depression, or another significant emotional / mental wellbeing issue that has led to departure from the firm (or long-term sickness) over the last five years. Whilst the majority of partners have suffered no such issues, there appears to be a significant percentage of partners that have experienced incidences of stress and mental health issues, as shown in Figure 5.

Figure 5: Stress and wellbeing issues leading to departure from the firm or long-term sickness

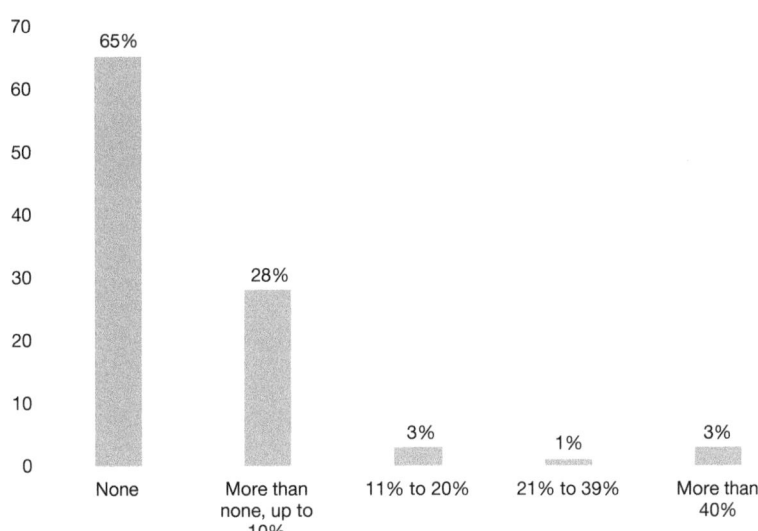

Alcohol and substance dependency

We asked to what extent partners have – within the last five years – experienced alcohol or drugs substance dependency or other types of dependency issues. We also asked if any other addictions (such as gambling) had been encountered. Figure 6 shows a low incidence of alcohol and drugs dependency or substance addiction / other issues. One respondent stated that he had observed some cases of "more than social use of alcohol as a coping mechanism" but that he was "hard pushed to say there is anyone dependent that is observable".

These figures seem on the low side compared to the data summarized by Bree Buchanan in chapter five. For example, one Australian survey that Bree references suggested that 35 percent of respondents were drinking at a hazardous level. It may simply be the case that senior leaders underreported the incidence of alcohol and substance dependency in this survey, which asked questions about a range of partner performance issues and was not a focused survey on the issue of wellbeing or substance abuse.

Figure 6: Dependency on, or addiction to, alcohol, drugs and other substances or issues

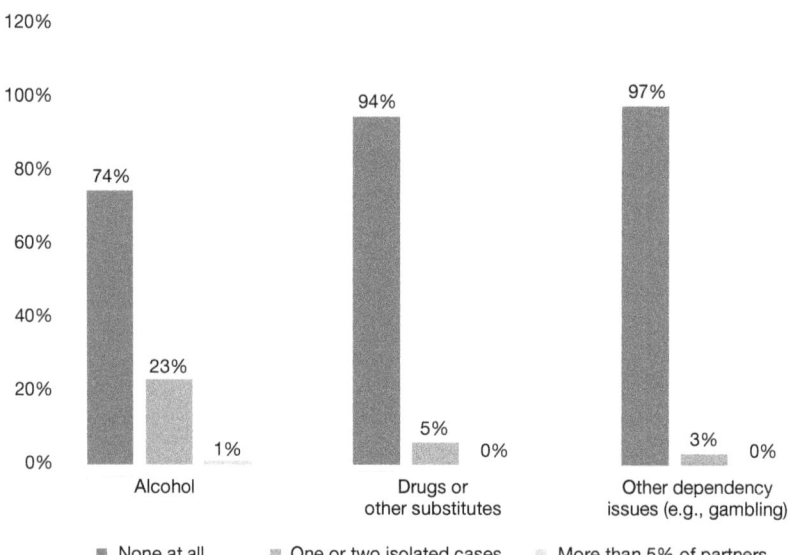

Conflicts between partners

A quarter of respondents have used external help over the past five years to try to resolve a conflict between partners. Four firms who did rely on external help said that coaching and mentoring and some level of mediation had been used. Another firm sought mediation regarding a laterally hired non-equity partner, and the matter had been resolved at that level. One firm reported that it had used management consultants to lead to agreed behavior codes, and another responded that it had obtained legal advice.

Thoughts from individuals

This is the last of 20 chapters that we have had the privilege to either write or review. We hope readers will have learnt as much as we have in the process of putting together this book. We have worked with and chatted to colleagues across the world – both fellow contributors to this book and other senior law firm leaders who we reached out to. As we pointed out at the start of this chapter, we in any event had a store of knowledge about how law firms go about dealing with partner performance, based off the many conversations we have had with senior law firm leaders on this subject in the course of consulting to law firms or speaking to prospective clients, or to active and/or past clients.

We thought that we would conclude this book by referencing two or three such conversations to illustrate the variety of approaches used by different law firms when it comes to managing partner performance. As it happens, the firms in question are geographically disparate – one in Australia, one in China, and one in India. We have deliberately chosen not to name all the firms, nor the senior leaders we talked to, because these are not formal case studies. We neither think it would be wise for readers to treat the examples either as illustrative of best practice or representative of the approach in their respective jurisdictions. We will recount the headlines of each of these conversations and round off with some final concluding remarks.

We spoke to Malcolm Shelton Agar, who over a period of more than 25 years was variously managing partner, managing director, chief operating officer, and chief executive officer of several firms in New Zealand, Australia, and Southeast Asia. We spoke to him about his extensive career in law firm management and his experiences with evolving performance management practices, particularly the challenges of balancing financial metrics with other aspects of partner performance.

In his early management career, Malcolm had very little financial data available to measure or benchmark partner performance. Metrics then became important, but created challenges in assessing partner contributions, even when a Balanced Scorecard approach was adopted. Malcolm mentioned that it was, in practice, difficult to score well overall if the partner scored poorly on the financial metrics, even though the financial criteria were not just based off personal billing but also took into account whether you were a responsible partner and all the other issues relevant to a team billing work product.

Malcolm's experience in Southeast Asia was in a smaller but highly profitable firm with a strong and tightly run leadership that largely adopted a patronage system of partner rewards. The whole ethos was to pay partners more than they could get from working in a competitive firm. In Southeast Asia, Malcolm said, there generally remains a culture of conflict avoidance, and poor performing partners were able to remain at the firm but were rewarded less than others.

Malcolm also spent time in a smaller Australian firm, which was able to operate on a true partnership basis. In that firm, every partner would fill out an annual business plan, which would then be peer reviewed by two partners, then approved by the board and published for all to see. These business plans would all have deliverable objectives by which the partners would be judged. They would be asked how they were doing against their objectives and whether they thought that they had achieved equity of contribution. Reviews became conversations about plans going forward. The system worked, according to the individual, because the firm was small with 30 partners in one building. His feeling was that such a system only really works when there is collegiality in the corridor and consensus – partners have to know each other.

Malcom Shelton Agar's conclusions were firstly that formal performance reviews can often prove to be unconstructive, and unhelpful. Setting objectives and reviewing those objectives works if the objectives can be tied into the achievement of equity contribution, though this can also be difficult in bigger firms where there seems to be very little concept of partners having any form of ownership or sovereignty, and the best most partners can do is to hope to influence things somewhat. They are not individually autonomous, let alone usually able to shape the direction of others except in very limited ways.

Malcolm's comments chimed in an interesting way with those of a senior leader in a top 20 firm in India. The individual in question had performed increasingly senior management roles in two previous firms and had thus experienced the performance management culture of three top 20 firms in the jurisdiction in question. The individual told us that there is great sensitivity around attrition in India and when partners leave a firm there is a lot of speculation as to why the partner is leaving and as to how the firm is doing financially. So firms tend to refrain from exiting underperforming partners and rather retain them and sideline them, rather than actively managing the underperformance in question. Where the particular partner is a really bad performer, actually providing bad advice or mismanaging transactions, he or she will be asked to leave – however this happens in very few cases. In most cases, the partner is kept on – often as a hedge against a higher performing partner leaving, as there is a lot of movement of partners between firms in the jurisdiction in question.

In the largest firms there is a similar reluctance to ask a partner to leave – rather, the partner will be "encouraged" to leave through messages delivered via performance appraisals, lower bonuses, and so on. Active performance management is rarer – the performance management system and allocation of bonus are the two principal levers used to "manage" suboptimal performance. The top 20-30 firms in India all have formal performance management systems below partner level with a formal "set piece" annual performance review. There are also informal sessions in these firms where a more senior partner will coach or provide feedback to the lawyer in question. Very few firms in the jurisdiction extend their performance management systems to partners – three or four of the more mature firms have introduced partner-level appraisal. But most partners do not like being appraised and in practice it can be a bit of a nightmare trying to get partners to fill out their self-appraisal form. The odd mature firm has 360 peer-to-peer partner appraisal, but this is very much the exception to the rule – most partners are not ready for peer-to-peer appraisal. Precisely because partners have options to go elsewhere, feedback given to partners tends to the anodyne and partners will vote with their feet and leave if the feedback is too piquant.

A third conversation was with a senior leader in a firm with several hundred partners in China. This individual told us that most law firms in China operate, in his experience, an eat-what-you-kill model. As in India, underperformance is not managed proactively and it is rare for a partner to be kicked out of a partnership. Partners in this individual's firm invariably start off as salaried partners and many do not make it into the equity – even lateral hires are brought in, typically, as salaried partners and have to prove themselves over the course of a couple of years before being brought into the equity. In the firm in question there is a hybrid lockstep system with some blocks on speed of progressing through the equity – it is rare for partners to go down in the points. While there is an assessment committee and ad hoc groups to assess each of the 500+ partners, the rump of the assessment is to do with money, i.e. how much the partner has billed, originations, profitability etc. As indicated, it is rare for an individual to go down in the points and generally there is a collectivist culture in China, so that the individual is treated sympathetically for the most part. Although there is an assessment committee, in practice it is the chair of the firm who has the final say when it comes to both assessment and remuneration.

These conversations are emblematic, as we see it, of the following key points.

First, most large firms around the world now have approaches to partner performance management that would not come as a shock to senior leaders in firms the other side of the world. The global legal community is, if not a village, certainly not a vast archipelago of scattered islands, with the far-flung islands utterly isolated from others. The larger law firms across the world are attuned to what is going on elsewhere, whether through membership of one of the networks or alliances, or through attendance at International Bar Association (IBA) meetings or through what they read or consume via social media (or via other sources of knowledge).

Second, many of the differences in approach seem to stem from factors such as the firm's size, its maturity, and the dominance of founding partners rather than its geography. Smaller and first-generation firms often embody an idiosyncratic approach that does not easily translate into replicable "best practice".

Third, it is difficult to maintain the culture and collegiality of true partnership in the bigger firms. We were once told by an equity member of a global firm that many of the features of his so-called "partnership" resembled a short-term employment contract with no statutory protection from unfair expulsion. Members of global firms often seem little more than employees for whom performance requirements remain strictly monitored and rigorously enforced.

Law firms must never forget, however, that whatever their size, they remain people businesses where one of the ingredients of their intellectual capital is the human capital that come into and walk out of the office environment (whether actually or remotely) each day and for whom productivity and profitability stem from their professionalism, know-how and care-why. They must never be treated as machines but as fallible humans who may need help and support when underperforming.

Final observations

Stepping back from these conversations and the 2024 survey, and reflecting on our recent experience of consulting to and speaking to multiple firms about performance management issues, we would add a couple of additional observations.

The role of technology in performance management is at present relatively limited. Ray D'Cruz's chapter on technology (chapter 19) outlines some of the technological solutions that are currently available. With the explosion of AI solutions, we find it hard to believe that the use of technology in performance management will not similarly explode over the next five to ten years. We are aware of several providers / start-ups trying to develop technology solutions in this space, including the use of AI / bots to coach senior lawyers. We anticipate that the future of performance management will be technology based – albeit there may be no substitute for one-to-one conversations with a human being when it comes to managing the performance of senior law firm leaders.

There is a linked point, partly about what technology can offer and partly about the opportunities that it will afford to those who fully understand its implications and limitations. We strongly suspect that technology will indeed continue to make lawyers obsolete in highly process-oriented, commoditized, fields of work. The conveyancing of property is an obvious example. Blockchain solutions might well, for example, rationalize the conveyancing process in a jurisdiction like the UK, which has a very cumbersome, highly inefficient, system.

For the foreseeable future, however, technology will not replace the highly experienced lawyer – the trusted adviser who has impeccable judgement and therefore the ear of the client; the technical maven whose expertise goes beyond technical knowledge and stretches to the crafting of highly innovative solutions that provide high-value for the client; the lawyer who combines both judgement, expertise, and a knowledge of how things work in practice, who is for the foreseeable future going to be highly valued by clients in "bet the farm" transactions and matters.

Technology will deal with the drudge work. The firms that will continue to thrive are those that develop increasingly rounded partners who combine all of the skills outlined above, as well as excellent interpersonal skills. These skills are not inherent – they require focused, sustained, and career-long learning and development and the firms that invest in their top talent will, in our view, reap the rewards financially. Those firms that treat partner performance management as a low priority activity will, correspondingly, in our view, flounder.

Our closing thought is this. During our professional lifetimes, the role of the law firm partner has been transformed beyond recognition. When Jonathan did a summer internship at Linklaters in 1987 it had (to the best of his recollection) around 50 or so partners. Twenty years earlier, an Act of Parliament (a provision of the Companies Act 1967) was required to allow professional partnerships to have more than 20 partners. Jonathan was told that this was because Linklaters wanted to make up a 21st partner and was unable to do so. In 2024, by contrast, Linklaters elected 27 new partners in that year alone. DLA Piper announced 63 new partner promotions. The role of the partner has evolved from – in the vast majority of firms at the start of our careers – high street specialist to (in the mid-sized to top firms) multifaceted professional, requiring a highly developed basket of skills – technical, commercial, client-related, and technological.

The evolution of the law firm partner is far from over, in our view. The development of partners and the management of their performance will only grow in importance. This book is a snapshot of some of the key issues around partner performance management in 2024. It would be a rash commentator who speculated what the landscape will look like in 2044.

About Globe Law and Business

Globe Law and Business was established in 2005. From the very beginning, we set out to create legal books that are sufficiently high level to be of real use to the experienced professional, yet still accessible and easy to navigate. Most of our authors are drawn from Magic Circle and other top commercial firms, both in the United Kingdom and internationally.

Our titles are carefully produced, with the utmost attention paid to editorial, design and production processes. We hope this results in high-quality publications that are easy to read and a pleasure to own.

In 2021, we were very pleased to announce the start of a new chapter for Globe Law and Business following the acquisition of law books under the imprint Ark Publishing. Our law firm management list is now significantly expanded with many well-known and loved Ark Publishing titles.

We are also pleased to announce the launch of our online content platform, Globe Law Online, which allows for easy access across firms. Details of all titles included can be found at www.globelawonline.com. Email glo@globelawandbusiness.com for further details and to arrange a free trial for you or your firm.

We'd very much like to hear from you with your thoughts and ideas for improving what we offer. Please do feel free to email me on sian@globelawandbusiness.com. Happy reading and thank you for your time.

Sian O'Neill
Managing director
Globe Law and Business
www.globelawandbusiness.com